EMOTIONAL FITNESS CONDITIONING

EMOTIONAL FITNESS
CONDITIONING

An Action Plan for
Lifelong Emotional Health

·

RONALD L. BERGMAN, PH.D.
with
ANITA WEIL BELL

A PERIGEE BOOK

A Perigee Book
Published by The Berkley Publishing Group
A member of Penguin Putnam Inc.
200 Madison Avenue
New York, NY 10016

Copyright © 1998 by Ronald Bergman, Ph.D., and Anita Weil Bell
Book design by Lisa Stokes
Cover design by Charles R. Björklund

First edition: September 1998

Published simultaneously in Canada.

The Penguin Putnam Inc. World Wide Web site address is
http://www.penguinputnam.com

Library of Congress Cataloging-in-Publication Data

Bergman, Ronald L.
    Emotional fitness conditioning : an action plan for lifelong emotional
    health / Ronald L. Bergman with Anita Weil Bell.—1st ed.
        p.   cm.
    Includes index.
    ISBN 0-399-52435-5 (tradepaper)
        1. Emotional maturity.   2. Self-help techniques.   I. Bell, Anita Weil.
    II. Title.
    BF710.B46   1998
    155.2'5—dc21   97-52655
                                                                              CIP

Printed in the United States of America

10   9   8   7   6   5   4   3   2   1

If you have any major medical or mental disorders, it is crucial to consult
with the appropriate physician or therapist prior to beginning the program.
You should also consult with your doctor periodically throughout the course
of your EFC Program. The EFC Program is not and should never be considered a substitute for appropriate medication for physical or mental illness,
nor is it a substitute for ongoing therapy when needed. The publisher and
authors assume no responsibility for any health, welfare, or subsequent
damage that might be incurred from use of these materials.

DR. RONALD BERGMAN'S NOTE:

All names, identifying characteristics, and other relevant details of the
anecdotal case material and/or patient journal entries mentioned in *Emotional Fitness Conditioning* have been modified for the express purpose of
preserving patient anonymity and confidentiality.

All the aforementioned case material is fundamentally based on real people I have seen in my practice. However, demographic details are changed
and examples are further layered with other multiple disguises, so that
anyone who believes he or she recognizes himself, herself, or anyone else
in this book will be in error. Some case examples are composites, also dis-
guised to protect privacy.

It's important to keep in mind that basic themes and issues exist for all
of us human beings. Therefore, similarities to real people are inevitable
and in that sense are entirely coincidental. That the themes exist for all of
us makes my work "do-able." That these themes manifest in an endlessly
interesting tapestry makes the work worth doing.

For my wife, Robbi, my life soul mate and the most emotionally fit person I know, and for my children, Brandon, Blake, and her husband, Mitch. They inspire and nourish me in my own struggle to become better today than I was yesterday and better tomorrow than I am today: the essence of Emotional Fitness Conditioning. And for A.T.S., who gave me more than I could ever put into words.

contents

ACKNOWLEDGMENTS   ix

INTRODUCTION   1

1
Emotional Fitness Conditioning—The
New Personal Growth Revolution   11

2
The Essential Elements of Emotional
Fitness Conditioning   29

3
Feelings Identification and Tolerance (FIT)   51

4
Empathy   73

5
Insight   97

6
Assertiveness   119

7
Starting Your Emotional Fitness Conditioning Program   141

8
Fitness Focused Meditation   171

9
Fitness Guided Visualization   193

10
The Emotional Fitness Journal   221

11
Exercise for Emotional Fitness   243

12
The Impact of Emotional Fitness Conditioning   269

APPENDIX:
EFC Self-Assessments and EFC Action Exercises   282

Emotional Fitness Conditioning Progress Chart   296

Resources   297

About the Authors   308

acknowledgments

THIS BOOK WOULD NOT HAVE HAPPENED WITHOUT THE VISION, SENSITIVITY, AND DEDICATION OF MY AGENT, Faith Hamlin. She believed and it helped me believe as well. For this and so much more, I thank her.

I want to express my profound appreciation to my collaborator, and now my friend, Anita Bell. Her attunement to my ideas was extraordinary. Her professionalism is consummate, her talents, energies, and devotion to task are remarkable. She gave a special clarity to my ideas and words that I sometimes did not see myself. I look forward to future collaborative efforts with her.

I wish to thank Penguin Putnam, the publishing giant, for their courage in taking a chance with a first-time author. I especially want to thank my editor, Sheila Curry, for her trust in the process and for providing myself and Anita with the emotional space to do our work.

Last, as I did in the acknowledgments section of my doctoral dissertation many years ago, I want to pat myself on the back: that time, for finishing my dissertation leading to the completion of my degree and the rewarding work of being a therapist; this time, for finally accomplishing my long-standing goal of writing and publishing a book.

Anita Bell wishes to thank her parents, Shirley and Gilbert Weil, who have always given her such a wealth of emotional support and love. And her husband, Jonathan Bell, for his incredible exuberance and love.

We hope that those of you who will be reading this book enjoy it and find in it as much personal meaning, growth, and Emotional Fitness as we did in the writing of it.

introduction

WOULD YOU LIKE TO EXPERIENCE MANY OF THE BEN-
EFITS OF PSYCHOTHERAPY WITHOUT THE COST? OR
maximize your progress if you are already in therapy? Perhaps you don't feel the need for professional help but are
interested in gaining self-knowledge and emotional
strength.

Emotional Fitness Conditioning (EFC), the new personal growth revolution, can help you achieve your goals.
With EFC, you can actually train yourself to become emotionally fit, just as you can exercise to become physically fit.
The EFC Program provides a practical plan for using four
simple Training Techniques to strengthen the Core Components of Emotional Fitness.

The Core Components of Emotional Fitness will enhance your awareness, self-esteem, and resilience. They will
empower you to establish and maintain healthy relationships and gain optimal satisfaction from your work. You'll
discover how to cultivate your creativity, intuition, and
spirituality.

Once you are familiar with the Core Components, you
will be ready to evaluate your level of Emotional Fitness,
and identify areas of weakness and strength. Then you can

take action to master emotional skills and raise your level of Emotional Fitness.

Understanding how the Core Components affect your emotional life is the basis of Emotional Fitness, but action is also necessary. Fitness is acquired through knowledge plus action in the emotional as well as the physical realm.

While self-knowledge and self-acceptance are worthy goals on their own, EFC will bring your growth to another level. The Training Techniques can actually help you turn away from self-destructive or self-defeating behavior. You'll find, as you progress in the Program, that you'll have more energy and fortitude to follow up on your awareness and move in new directions. The program works from both the inside (thoughts and feelings) and outside (behavior) to create positive change.

Emotional Fitness Conditioning goes beyond an intellectual discussion to offer a step-by-step plan for mastering emotional skills and resolving personal issues. It is your personal workout plan for achieving emotional health and freedom.

EMOTIONAL HEALTH

Do you ever feel controlled by your emotions? Do you sometimes feel helpless in the face of mood swings, anxiety, anger, resentment? Does the burden of the past and fear of the future prevent you from enjoying the present?

The Emotional Fitness Conditioning Program offers a plan for taking control of your emotions and learning to marshal them as your allies. This does not mean repressing valid emotions, even when they are uncomfortable or difficult. It means acknowledging, recognizing, and coping with difficult emotions so that you can improve the quality of your relationships and become more successful in love, work, play, and all the endeavors that matter in your life.

In the past, it often took many years of psychotherapy to work through issues, gain insight, and experience growth.

With EFC, insight and growth can begin to take place in a few months. The techniques of EFC work on unconscious, conscious, and interpersonal levels to create tangible results. The training also evokes physiological changes that promote physical and mental wellness.

Through the EFC Program, you are likely to experience dramatic changes in many aspects of your inner life, including your level of self-esteem, your ability to cope with stress, and your cognitive processes. You are also likely to see concrete behavioral changes in your outer life, including all levels of interpersonal relationships, your work, and perhaps even your physical health.

The Program will help you to alleviate anxiety, heal emotional pain from the past, facilitate communication, and nurture more satisfying relationships. You'll gain a greater capacity for coping with emotional difficulties and resilience for recovery from stressful life situations. Increased energy and better physical health are other bonuses you can expect. The EFC Program is truly an emotional "prescription" with only beneficial side effects.

This is a grounded Program, based on concepts that incorporate the most respected theories of psychology and clinical experience. The techniques are adaptations of time-tested, proven practices. This adaptable self-help program can be done on your own or used as an adjunct to therapy. It can be customized to address your personal issues and lifestyle.

EMOTIONAL FITNESS CONDITIONING IN PRACTICE

This book is designed to enable you easily and systematically to learn about and utilize Emotional Fitness Conditioning to create positive change in your life.

The first half of the book explores the Core Components of Emotional Fitness—the pillars of your emotional life. You will take simple quizzes called **Self-Assessments** to identify your personal strengths and struggles with these various Core Components. Once you start on the EFC Program, you can use these Self-Assessments to personalize your training.

You'll learn a fresh, concise language for discussing and understanding your emotions: a vocabulary you can share with your loved ones, friends, and colleagues. This language will shed light on the mysteries of your mind, clarify its dark corners, and allow you to take inventory of your emotional life. The **EFC Action Exercises** will help you understand your issues and focus your goals as they relate to each Core Component.

The stories of some of the people who have changed their lives through the EFC Program will illuminate the Core Components. While the stories are fundamentally based on real people I have seen in my practice, all names, identifying characteristics, and other relevant details have been modified to preserve patient anonymity and confidentiality. In some instances, examples are composites designed further to protect identity while still conveying relevant emotional themes.

Next, you'll learn how to use the four basic **Training Techniques** of EFC and start the **EFC Program**. An easy-to-follow schedule is given for a four-month Program, which you can extend and adapt to fit your needs.

The EFC Program is realistic and user-friendly, designed to accommodate a busy lifestyle. It requires commitment and consistency, but not a great deal of time. With a minimum investment of time—just three to four hours per week including exercise—you can realize a tremendous return.

EFC is not and never claims to be a cure-all for everyone and everything. But it is a very powerful and inclusive program for change. After years of seeing EFC enhance the lives of people of all ages and backgrounds, I have great confidence that this program will help you create a more satisfying, meaningful life. I welcome you to this opportunity for self-discovery, empowerment, and growth.

THE EVOLUTION OF EMOTIONAL FITNESS CONDITIONING

Developing the concepts and practice of Emotional Fitness Conditioning has proven to be a fascinating journey for me as a mental health care professional and an individual.

Twenty-five years ago, I was trained as a long-term, insight-oriented therapist and research psychologist. My training included research, psychodynamic, behavioral, and cognitive therapy.

Because of my background and training, I still believe that long-term "talk therapy" can be a highly effective approach for those who have sufficient time, money, and commitment. But as time constraints and financial resources become limited by a number of factors, a lengthy course of psychotherapy is impractical or impossible for many people.

As the 1990s progressed, I began to hear this type of question with greater frequency: "Dr. Bergman, is there anything else I can do to work on my issues? I feel like the therapy is helping, but I want to move it along by doing more on my own."

Many patients found talk therapy valuable, but they also wanted to know how to work independently to further their therapeutic goals. The fifty-minute hour—once, twice, or even three times a week—was useful, but sometimes it was not enough. And, in many cases, even one session a week was becoming too much of a financial burden.

THE MANAGED-CARE FACTOR

The issue of health insurance and health care for Americans is extremely complex, and I would not presume to know all the answers. Undoubtedly, there are valid economic principles behind the advent of HMOs. In some cases, I'm sure that managed care is the best alternative from a dollars-and-cents standpoint. But from a mental health perspective, managed care leaves much to be desired.

In 1997, it was noted in *Behavioral Health Management* that "the percent of the premium dollar that is devoted to behavioral health has continued to decline. Only a few years ago it was six to eight percent. It is now as low as two percent."

What this translates into for the average mental health consumer is limited reimbursement and less freedom of choice. Often, even in the case of serious mental illness, many insurance companies strictly limit the number of psychotherapy sessions for which a patient can receive reimbursement. Some plans offer partial reimbursement for thirty sessions a year, while others set the limit at ten or even four sessions. Many patients simply cannot afford to pay for therapy out-of-pocket.

This poses a serious dilemma for the behavioral health provider. Psychotherapy often requires an initial building of trust and relationship, followed by a gradual uncovering of complex emotional issues and personal history on the part of the patient, followed by working through the issues. Each patient has a different rate of disclosure, gaining insight, and overcoming resistance to change. With traditional psychotherapy it is enormously difficult, and in many cases impossible, to make significant progress without a substantial number of consecutive sessions.

Many people assume doctors complain about HMOs because they are motivated by greed. Let me admit that I do want and need to bring in a solid income, like everybody else. But I can honestly say money was not my motivation for becoming a psychologist. The impetus was that I wanted to make a positive impact on people's lives. It may sound trite, but it's true. I greatly benefited from my own experience with therapy and was motivated to help others by becoming a therapist.

The traditional model of therapy worked well for the first two decades of my practice. But as insurance coverage for many people shifted to managed care, I found that my ability to help patients was often restricted. The reimbursement limitations and economic realities forced many people to cut their course of therapy short, long before any significant progress could be achieved. The rhythm and flow of the therapeutic process was rudely interrupted. The established ways of working with patients were insufficient, given the curtailed time frame.

It became clear to me that I had to develop new ways of working. When a patient had a particularly difficult issue, I could always say, "We'll talk about it more next time." Now, there might not be a next time.

Clearly, people needed concrete ways to continue to pursue the goals of therapy on their own. They needed some structure for continuing the growth process when therapy was interrupted or limited.

COMPLEMENTARY MENTAL HEALTH CARE

Beyond financial concerns, there were other significant changes that prompted the development of Emotional Fitness Conditioning. Another major influence was the alternative health-care movement.

In the last decade, there has been a noticeable shift toward self-care, preventive steps, and an independent attitude toward health care. Alternative medicine has grown into a $27-billion-a-year industry. A 1995 Time/CNN study found that 47 percent of those surveyed had already sought help from an alternative-medicine provider and 84 percent of those people would go back again for alternative treatments.

Millions of people no longer completely depend upon their physicians to cure what ails them. They read up on health concerns, go to the health-food store for vitamins and herbal remedies, pick and choose among holistic practitioners. Many individuals consider their physicians to be partners in the health-care mosaic, rather than all-knowing, all-powerful "fixers."

The same principle applies to mental health. Many peo-

ple have come to realize that it is not always feasible or wise
to rely on a therapist as the sole conduit of emotional health.
They are seeking ways to develop emotional wellness independently. One of my reasons for developing the Emotional
Fitness Conditioning Program was to provide a type of "com-
plementary medicine" for the emotions.

THE TIME IS RIPE FOR THE NEW PERSONAL GROWTH REVOLUTION

If you are a baby boomer in age or in spirit, you are part
of the generation that has always resisted listening to authority and maintaining the status quo. Our generation has
constantly gravitated to questioning, seeking, and taking action to induce change. In the 1960s and early 70s this energy
focused on political and social transformation to a large degree. For the last twenty years, there has been more of an
emphasis on self-transformation.

The most obvious manifestation of this belief in the potential for change has been the physical fitness revolution.
Spurred on by fitness role models, many of us pumped,
jumped, and stepped ourselves into a frenzy for the past two
decades. The emphasis has been on the physical side of the
mind-body equation.

Many Americans may have been motivated to work out
by an unconscious desire to shore up a weakened sense of
self after the era of the Vietnam War and the disappointment that stemmed from the unfulfilled promises of the 60s.
Others may have been interested in staying in shape to
savor the sexual freedom of the 70s, or simply to look good.
Undoubtedly, the unceasing appetite of the baby-boomer
generation to remain youthful has also been a factor in the
upsurge of exercise.

Whatever the impetus, the physical fitness revolution
has had an upbeat influence on many people's lives. But it
is never enough for true fulfillment and lasting satisfaction.
No matter how fast we run or how much weight we lift, the

effects are finite. Ultimately, the body grows older and no one ever truly wins the race against age. Even when we do look and feel terrific, it can be a hollow triumph without a core.

Physical fitness is only one-half of the whole that creates a person with a fully realized life. The other piece of the puzzle is Emotional Fitness: the mind side of the mind-body whole.

Emotional Fitness is essential for enjoying the pleasures of the physical body and so much more. It is crucial for generating healthy relationships and productive work. It can actually grow and increase as we age. And it can be passed on as a meaningful legacy to the next generation.

As parents, aunts, uncles, teachers, neighbors, or employers, we can provide younger people with a language for understanding emotions and tools to build emotional skills. We can live our lives as role models of empathy, awareness, and emotional maturity. EFC has implications not only for us as individuals, but for the larger educational and social fabrics.

one

Emotional Fitness Conditioning—The New Personal Growth Revolution

B Y THE EARLY 90s, IT BECAME CRYSTAL CLEAR THAT THE TIME WAS RIPE FOR THE NEXT STEP IN PERSONAL growth—the **Emotional Fitness Revolution**. I realized that one reason people often focused on physical instead of emotional development was that the physical was more definable and measurable. In order to bring the quest for Emotional Fitness to a widespread audience, it had to be made tangible.

Physical fitness provided a model. There are three basic components of physical fitness: cardiovascular capacity, muscular strength, and flexibility. To achieve balanced physical fitness, it is necessary to develop these components through three basic types of activity: aerobic exercise for the cardiovascular system; strength training or weight-bearing exercise for muscular strength, and stretching for flexibility.

Of course, many exercise choices have benefits in more than one area. For example, yoga can increase muscle strength as well as flexibility. Running both improves cardiorespiratory capacity and strengthens certain muscle groups. Step aerobics and aerobic dance classes can work on all three areas.

I decided to use the physical fitness model to create an Emotional Fitness model. This was a two-step process. First, it was necessary to define Emotional Fitness and the qualities that comprise emotional health. Second, specific Training Techniques for strengthening these qualities needed to be established.

WHAT IS EMOTIONAL FITNESS?

Do you ever wonder why some people can handle stress and challenge better than others? Why certain people attract more love, admiration, respect, and friendship? Why some individuals have a greater capacity to appreciate life and bask in higher levels of self-esteem and self-acceptance?

These attributes are all hallmarks of Emotional Fitness. And while genetics, experience, fate, fortune, and other variables play a role, the qualities of Emotional Fitness can also be consciously cultivated through training.

As I sought to identify the qualities that comprise Emotional Fitness, I delved into the vast body of brilliant thought, research, and common sense that is available. I reviewed some of the classic religious and philosophical writings of the East and the West that explore the inner world of thinking and feeling. I also looked for answers in the writings of such luminaries of twentieth-century psychological thought as Sigmund Freud, B. F. Skinner, Albert Ellis, Carl Rogers, Fritz Perls, Alexander Low, and Heinz Kohut.

Then I began to review my patient histories, twenty years of notes on people of all ages and backgrounds who had trusted me with their most intimate thoughts, worries, and hopes. Certain themes began to emerge, and the pillars of Emotional Fitness took shape.

These universal qualities were distilled into the four Core Components of Emotional Fitness: **Feelings Identification and Tolerance (FIT), Empathy, Insight,** and **Assertiveness**.

I did not invent these Components. They are a distillation of decades of psychological thought and thousands of years of the collected wisdom of world cultures. That is why the Core Components are universal. You can clearly see them in others, and you can find and nurture them in yourself. Virtually all emotional issues can be categorized under one or more of these Core Components.

Feelings Identification and Tolerance (FIT) refers to the ability to label or identify your feelings specifically and accurately. It also involves the ability to withstand emotions and channel or express them productively. FIT encompasses delay of gratification, patience, self-control, frustration tolerance, impulse control, and stress tolerance—emotional skills that are crucial for a productive life.

Empathy is the ability accurately to identify and relate to the feeling state of another person with tolerance and understanding. Empathy involves identification with the entire range of human feelings, including joy and satisfaction, as well as sorrow, fear, and insecurity.

Insight pertains to understanding the psychological and emotional forces that produce your thoughts, feelings, and behaviors. It concerns learning to connect your past to the present and understanding the impact and legacy of your family of origin. Insight also includes the ability to look beneath the surface to the underlying reasons for your behavior and emotions.

Assertiveness begins with a clear view of your reasonable, legitimate rights—a balanced sense of entitlement. Healthy Assertiveness requires taking a well-defined stand in your attitude, communication, and behavior, based on your valid rights and needs.

DISCOVERING THE TRAINING TECHNIQUES THAT WORK

With the four Core Components in place, the next step in the birth of Emotional Fitness Conditioning was to discover how to develop these traits. While we're all born with certain predispositions, which are further shaped by our life experience, I firmly believe that we also have a tremendous capacity for growth. If I didn't have faith in the human po-

tential for change, I couldn't be a therapist! In fact, it is
through my experiences as a therapist that I know firsthand
of the enormous capacity we humans have for productive
growth and change.

After much thought, review of research, and analysis of
case studies, four Training Techniques evolved. I call them
**Fitness Focused Meditation, Fitness Guided Visual-
ization, the Emotional Fitness Journal, and Exercise
for Emotional Fitness**.

Since these are based on four techniques I had practiced
myself for many years, I knew experientially as well as clini-
cally that they produce powerful results. Not only do I believe in practicing what I preach, but I often use myself as
an experimental subject.

MEDITATION: THE POWER OF STILLNESS

As a graduate student in the 1960s, I was introduced to
the behavioral technique of systematic desensitization (SD),
used primarily in the treatment of phobias and anxiety. One
of the cornerstones of SD was the use of relaxation techniques to counter the physiologic effects of anxiety.

The SD techniques reminded me very much of the meditative practices I had learned while studying Eastern religions as an undergraduate philosophy student. It occurred
to me that perhaps meditation could be an important therapeutic tool.

I began to practice meditation myself and found it to be
very useful for reducing anxiety, focusing concentration, and
producing a deeper level of self-awareness. It was truly a
revelation for someone like me, known to be a bit hyperac-
tive at times, to experience the power of stillness and quiet.

As I began to "prescribe" meditation to my patients in
the 1970s, I found that everyone who stayed with the practice reported positive benefits. This was later borne out by
a great deal of research on the physical and psychological

effects of meditation, which we'll examine in detail in chapter 8.

VISUALIZATION: FROM THOUGHT TO REALITY

My own experience with visualization began with my exposure to meditation/relaxation. I found that directed visualizations enhanced and extended the meditation process and made it more personally meaningful. My training in hypnosis, which melds guided visualization with relaxation to create heightened suggestibility, further confirmed the effectiveness of imaging. Prior to creating the EFC Program, I taught visualization during patient sessions, workshops, and lectures for many years, with a great deal of positive feedback from participants.

In my own life, I've often used conscious visualization as a tool for imagining desired outcomes, and this practice has helped me turn my goals and dreams into solid realities. In fact, the EFC Program itself and this book are products of a long and successful series of visualizations.

JOURNALING: COMMUNICATING WITH THE INNER SELF

Since the days when I wrote to express my teenage angst, the written word as a form of self-expression has always come naturally to me. After my own introduction to therapy, I have found informal journal writing to be a terrific tool for fostering insight, as well as an emotional release. It has helped me work through many issues and find validation as well as new directions through a variety of life's impasses.

In my private practice, I have long recommended journal writing as a therapeutic tool and found it to be highly enriching for all types of individuals. People who tend to focus too heavily on verbalizing profit from the opportunity for quiet self-reflection. And those who have difficulty communicating about their emotions verbally find writing to be especially liberating.

For people who have a hard time opening up to a therapist, the journal is a way to "prime the pump," eventually paving the way to improved verbal communication. In addition, patients have often reported unexpected benefits from their journaling: an idea, an insight, or a creative solution spontaneously emerges.

EXERCISE: CONNECTING THE BODY AND MIND

Meditation, visualization, and journal writing all met the criteria I had established for Emotional Fitness Conditioning Training Techniques. I had experienced their benefits firsthand. My patients had confirmed their effectiveness. They were recognized tools of the modern therapeutic repertoire, supported by a respectable number of research studies. And their application ranged far and wide beyond the therapeutic setting.

For thousands of years these practices had been embraced by people of different cultures for wide-ranging emotional, spiritual, and intellectual benefits. Clearly, these were techniques with a wealth of potential for Emotional Fitness Conditioning.

Still, I felt there was one ingredient missing . . . another element that was needed to balance the EFC equation. Finally I realized that the missing link was the physical side of the mind/body whole: Exercise for Emotional Fitness.

When my son was born in 1981, I was almost thirty-six years old. Since my daughter was born ten years earlier, I knew it took a lot of stamina to keep up with little ones. And although I had always been somewhat athletic, I felt I needed more systematic physical activity to keep up my energy level for parenting.

Several of my friends had taken up jogging, and I thought this might be a logical way to prepare for running after a toddler. Jogging led to running, which ultimately led to racing in the Orange Bowl and New York City Marathons. I am devoted to running, and it has helped me be a better person, parent, husband, and therapist in many ways.

As I became aware of the potent emotional benefits of regular physical exercise, I began to recommend it to my patients. At first, this evoked surprise—why is a mental health professional worrying about physical fitness? But those who were open enough to try exercise found it gave a noticeable boost to their mental well-being.

BRINGING EFC TO MY PATIENTS

With the Core Components firmly delineated, and the Training Techniques established, it was time to introduce the EFC Program to my patients. I had been recommending the Training Techniques for many years, but now I was determined to present the program more systematically and see how well it worked.

The results were dramatic and encouraging. This is not to say that the EFC Program worked miracles for everyone—there were still plenty of people who resisted practicing the Training Techniques. But for those who took an active role and used the Training Techniques consistently, the progress was extraordinary. Their level of Emotional Fitness increased exponentially. And it was far more than self-knowledge they acquired.

Many people who fully participated in the EFC Program literally changed their lives—from the inside out. Knowledge of the Core Components of their emotional makeup, coupled with the conditioning effects of the Training Techniques, proved to be an incredible catalyst for growth.

CAROL'S STORY

Carol, a married special education teacher with two children in their late teens, was on permanent overload.

In her late forties, Carol was a petite woman with an appealing smile and intelligent brown eyes behind her glasses.

During the first eight years of her marriage, Carol had been a full-time homemaker and had established a pattern of taking care of all the household duties. When she went back to work, she started doing "double duty" and never asked for additional help around the house. Her greatest difficulty involved the Core Component of Assertiveness.

Carol's husband, Larry, who was immersed in running his own printing business, seemed to take her efforts and her presence for granted. They had settled into a routine that he appeared to find adequate but she found frustrating and draining. Still, she couldn't seem to find a way to change their relationship without starting a futile argument. Carol was well aware that her chronic headaches were a symptom of her psychological state, but this knowledge only added to her repressed anger.

Carol worked on developing Assertiveness by using her Emotional Fitness Journal to identify what she needed from her family and how she felt about her present role. She employed Fitness Guided Visualization to imagine scenes with her husband and children where she asked for their help with specific tasks. Another facet of her EFC Program was Exercise for Emotional Fitness. She elected to take a Body Conditioning class at the local Y and found that working with free weights gave her a sense of strength and empowerment.

After three months of practicing the EFC training techniques, Carol's headaches diminished to the point where she could stop taking medication. Over the next few months, she learned how to communicate with greater Empathy and made progress in marital counseling with Larry. She developed enough Assertiveness to give her children appropriate household responsibilities and stopped trying to do everything for everybody. With these changes in place, Carol had extra time and energy to study Spanish, a step toward broadening her teaching opportunities.

Brian was tall and lanky, with an attractive yet anxious appearance. He had a natural talent for drawing and liked to read, particularly books on philosophy and psychology. But he had not yet been able to channel any of his many interests into a career path.

His difficulties could be traced back to grade school, where his dyslexia had initially gone undiagnosed for many years. Struggling with this condition during his early school years, along with his father's critical attitude, had set Brian up for failure. At twenty-four, he was temporarily unemployed, living back at home with his parents, and mildly depressed.

When Brian took the Self-Assessment quizzes to identify his strengths and difficulties with the various Core Components, he found that his primary difficulty was with Feelings Identification and Tolerance (FIT). He worked on this Core Component by visualizing himself in various situations that would provoke anxiety, such as a job interview or asking a woman for a date. Through Journaling, he explored the source of the uncomfortable feelings these situations aroused and how his emotions influenced his actions.

Fitness Focused Meditation helped Brian learn to tolerate these uncomfortable feelings better and reduce his overall anxiety level. His Exercise for Emotional Fitness choice was to build up to running five miles every morning, right after meditating. He discovered that running alleviated his depression and began to boost his self-esteem.

One morning on his favorite jogging trail, Brian noticed a young woman walking her golden Lab. After "accidentally" running into her a few more times, he struck up a conversation, which led to a coffee date. They started dating frequently and developed a warm relationship. The woman told

Brian that she admired his ability to talk about his feelings openly, another skill he had acquired through the EFC Program.

After six months of EFC activity, Brian went back to college to finish his degree in commercial art. He also took on a part-time job, with the goal of saving up for his own apartment. Through the EFC Program, Brian had gained enough Emotional Fitness to start taking his place in the world.

MONICA'S STORY

Monica, age thirty-seven, was a striking, successful woman with a chic brunette bob and green eyes. After ten years at a large advertising agency, she had started her own firm and worked hard to build up a solid client base. Her business was thriving, but she had reached a point in her life where she was unfulfilled by work alone. Monica wanted to have a family and was frustrated by her single status. Her image of herself as being bright and confident was undermined by her inability to sustain a relationship with the right man.

Through her Emotional Fitness Journal and the Core Component Self-Assessments, Monica was able to identify a difficulty with Empathy as one of the major problems in her past relationships. She had a revelation that the competitive, fast-paced, no-nonsense style that worked so well in her career was a drawback in her romantic life.

Meditation helped Monica to become calmer, quieter, and more empathic in her interactions. She used visualization as a tool to develop her attunement with other people's feelings. Her Emotional Fitness Journal was a place where she could safely explore these themes.

After about three months of EFC training, Monica began to date Gregory, a freelance copywriter whom she had met through business several years ago. She had never considered him as a possibility before, since his looks and income didn't match her own. But now that Monica was more emotionally evolved, she was able to recognize and appreciate Gregory's intelligence, kindness, and loyalty.

In less than a year, Monica and Gregory had fallen in love and become engaged. She introduced Gregory to the EFC Program and hoped it would help them both navigate the challenges of marriage and, eventually, parenthood.

ROBERT'S STORY

Robert, age forty-two, was torn apart by his recent divorce. After years of tolerating his wife's mood swings and drinking binges, he could not comprehend how she could leave him for another man.

The stress took a toll on Robert's health and aggravated his suffering from chronic gastrointestinal problems. His work as a heating/cooling systems engineer was stable, but not particularly satisfying or engaging. He felt as if he had nothing going for him except his two school-age children. Robert adored his kids, but he was often too depressed and physically unwell to interact with them fully during their weekend visits.

Robert used the techniques of Emotional Fitness Conditioning as an adjunct to psychotherapy. While he needed to work on all the Core Components, Insight was a special concern. It was imperative that he gain awareness of how his childhood caretaking role with his mentally ill mother influenced his adult relationships.

By writing in his Emotional Fitness Journal, Robert learned how to connect his past with his present. He used visualization to practice asserting his legitimate rights and stop feeling like a victim. An exercise regime of fitness walking increased his stamina and reduced his stress level.

After practicing Fitness Focused Meditation for several months, Robert became interested in natural health and started reading books on this subject. He adopted a healthier diet and outlook, which alleviated his gastrointestinal ailments. Robert also began to take steps to disengage from the enabling role with his ex-wife. His weekends with his children became less of a burden and more of a joy, as his emotional and physical fitness grew.

EFC IS FOR EVERYONE

Carol, Brian, Monica, and Robert are just four examples of the many people whose lives have been enriched by EFC. These people range in age from teenagers to senior citizens. They encompass diverse races, religions, and socioeconomic backgrounds. EFC resonates with people who are traditional, progressive, artistic, down-to-earth, cheerful, pessimistic, worried, and well—a wide range of temperaments, predispositions, and life circumstances. The flexibility of the EFC Program makes it applicable across the spectrum.

USING EFC IN CONJUNCTION WITH THERAPY

For many people, the EFC Program can be used on its own as a self-help program.

However, it is strongly advised that if any of the following conditions apply, you should undertake Emotional Fitness Conditioning only under the supervision of a mental health professional or physician. These conditions include but are not limited to:

—*Severe depression; suicidal thoughts*
—*Serious or chronic physical illness*
—*Taking medication for emotional problems*
—*Patterns of severe physical, mental, or sexual abuse*
—*A diagnosis of obsessive-compulsive disorder*
—*Severe anxiety/panic disorder*
—*Any diagnosed major mental illness, such as schizophrenia or bipolar affective disorder (manic-depression)*

—*Drug or alcohol addiction or extreme behavioral
addiction, such as sex addiction*
—*An eating disorder such as bulimia or anorexia*
—*Post-traumatic stress disorder*

Remember, these conditions certainly do not preclude participation in the EFC Program and you should not be discouraged. Many of my clients have used EFC Training Techniques in conjunction with psychotherapy and/or psychoactive medications and made remarkable progress.

However, if you have any of the above conditions or other unusual circumstances, it is crucial to consult with the appropriate physician or therapist prior to beginning the program. You should also continue to consult with your doctor periodically throughout the course of your EFC Program. The EFC Program is not and should never be considered a substitute for appropriate medication for physical or mental illness, nor is it a substitute for ongoing therapy when needed.

If you are coping with current, acute stresses, I also suggest you consider using the EFC Program in connection with counseling or therapy. These stresses might include divorce or death of a loved one, an abusive relationship or the legacy of childhood abuse, serious difficulties with children or parents, illness in the family, addiction or eating disorder, financial or career-related hardship, extreme anxiety, or mood swings.

I have often seen the EFC Training Techniques help people through crises, illnesses, and emotional traumas. But it is also essential to seek out a mental health professional or peer support group when you are coping with extreme difficulties.

EFC IS PROACTIVE AND PREVENTIVE

While EFC can be helpful in times of emotional crisis and difficulty, it can also be considered preventive mental health care. You can benefit from it at any time, including when you're feeling emotionally strong and well.

No one should have to endure a heart attack before starting a cardiovascular exercise program, or suffer from lower back pain before stretching, right? The best time to start self-care and prevention is before you get ill. The strong, well-nourished, balanced body is less likely to develop illness or injury, and better able to recover. The same principle applies to Emotional Fitness.

If you are not facing any special challenges at this juncture in your life, it is an ideal time to start the Program. In fact, if you start the Program when you don't have extra stress, you have a window of opportunity to fortify your emotional resilience. Then you'll be in better position emotionally to face whatever comes your way. The EFC Program certainly can't prevent the inevitable sorrows and problems of life, but it can put you in a much stronger position to weather any difficulties that arise and manage them better.

The emphasis here is on wellness, not illness. Yes, the EFC Program can be a way to heal emotional pain. But it can also be a way to bring more emotional joy, awareness, and expansion into your life. It is an open-ended, evolutionary process.

In my own practice, I resist the trend of "medicalizing" therapy. This trend emphasizes the diagnostic labeling of patients with conditions that need to be treated and cured. In my view, this puts a negative slant on the entire therapeutic process.

In the new world of Emotional Fitness, there is nothing "wrong" with you that needs to be made "right." Personal growth is a process of education and training, not treatment for a specific condition or resolving one particular issue.

WHAT YOU CAN EXPECT

EFC is not a magic bullet that is guaranteed to produce happiness. But it does have a major impact on the four areas that are key facets of the subjective state we call "happiness": self-esteem, relationships, work and leisure time satisfaction, and physical health.

Self-esteem is a successful outcome of productive strengthening of the Core Components: one of the end products of Emotional Fitness, in a sense. The basic ingredients of self-esteem are overall self-image, body image, and ego ideal. All three of these elements are nourished through the Training Techniques. Self-defeating behavior is diminished while self-enhancing behavior expands.

In the relationship arena, EFC often leads to long-lasting improvements and changes in patterns of behavior. Participants in the EFC program have reported results ranging from a sharp reduction in petty arguments to the healing of major marital rifts. EFC can also elevate your interest in sex, as well as improve sexual responsiveness.

In the area of job satisfaction and performance, the development of the Core Components can produce many measurable results. Enhanced creativity, greater productivity, better delegating skills and co-worker relationships, and more confidence in the workplace are frequently noted.

On the physical side, the benefits of the EFC Program are highly visible and rewarding. Feelings Identification and Tolerance supports your awareness of the connection between the mind and body. Insight and Empathy reduce energy-draining emotions, while Assertiveness builds your physical confidence. EFC Training Techniques have the positive "side effects" of relaxing your body, reducing the physical toll of stress, and strengthening muscles and bones along with the emotions. Leisure-time activities tend to become more rewarding, and you'll be motivated to enjoy the fruits of your labors and take time to "smell the roses."

How long will it take before you experience tangible results and positive changes in the way you think, feel, communicate, and act? The answer is that it could take anywhere from a few weeks, to a few months, or perhaps somewhat longer. A great deal depends on where you are starting from, where you want to go, and how open you are to change.

Since you're reading this book, it's likely that you believe in the potential for change, at least on an intellectual level. But you may have resistance to change on a subconscious level. Most of us humans do, to some extent. It's the law of inertia, a natural impulse to stay in one place, where it feels safe and familiar.

It can be difficult to become more tuned in to Feelings Identification and Tolerance, especially if you have a strong system of denial built up. It can be painful to open yourself up to feel and act with Empathy. It can be frightening to look at how your family of origin has affected your emotional life and to cultivate Insight. It can be intimidating to challenge the status quo in your relationships and demand your legitimate rights through Assertiveness.

I want you to know that I understand that it's not always easy to start and stay with the EFC Program. But I know you can do it!

As with any worthwhile endeavor, the EFC Program requires an initial act of will and a commitment to something in which you believe. In this case, all you need to believe in is yourself, and your capacity to learn, grow, and achieve Emotional Fitness. The rest will unfold through the EFC process itself.

EFC ACTION EXERCISE: IS EMOTIONAL FITNESS CONDITIONING FOR YOU?

To find out if the Emotional Fitness Conditioning is a viable program for you, ask yourself these questions:

1. Have you ever been interested in gaining the insights and benefits of psychotherapy?
2. If you are in therapy now, do you feel the desire to further your progress by taking action outside the sessions?

3. Do you ever wish you had more knowledge of how your emotions affect your life?
4. Are you seeking a better understanding of how your past affects your present?
5. Would you like to be able to manage your emotions more productively?
6. Could your relationships benefit from greater awareness of your emotional makeup and those of the people who matter in your life?
7. Would your relationships be enhanced if you could communicate with more Empathy, Insight, and healthy Assertiveness?
8. Would you like to teach your children or other young people how to manage their emotions more productively, and build a foundation of Emotional Fitness?
9. Do you acknowledge that the state of your physical body influences your mental state?
10. Do you believe that knowledge plus action can result in positive change?

The key to this questionnaire is simple. If you have answered even one of these questions with a "yes," then the Emotional Fitness Conditioning Program is for you!

two

The Essential Elements of Emotional Fitness Conditioning

E MOTIONAL FITNESS IS NO LONGER A MYSTERY. THROUGH THE EFC PROGRAM, YOU WILL BECOME familiar with the Core Components of Emotional Fitness and how they affect your life. Then you will learn to how to use the Training Tools to strengthen these components in yourself.

EFC has a simple structure to encourage crystal-clear understanding. There are four Core Components of Emotional Fitness, and there are four Training Techniques. These work together synergistically to raise your level of Emotional Fitness.

CORE COMPONENT #1: FEELINGS IDENTIFICATION AND TOLERANCE (FIT)

Feelings Identification and Tolerance is a fundamental goal of every form of psychotherapy. In the language of psychology, it is usually referred to as "affect" identification and tolerance. Affect means feelings, identification refers to labeling or specifying, and tolerance is the ability to withstand emotions and channel or express them productively. In the EFC Program, I have replaced the term *Affect* with *Feelings* because it is easier to relate to and remember.

FIT encompasses delay of gratification, patience, self-con-

trol, frustration tolerance, impulse control, and stress tolerance—skills that are crucial for a productive adult life. The
results of limited FIT can range from violent behavior to addiction or depression. More commonly, a symptom of weakness in
this area is procrastination—the avoidance or delay of a task
that is not perceived as immediately gratifying or pleasurable.
We avoid the task that is perceived as unpleasant because we
are not comfortable with the emotions it arouses. But, as you'll
come to realize, this avoidance only exacerbates the discomfort.

From infancy on, life is filled with conflicts between
what is instantly pleasurable, comfortable, or easy and what
needs to be done for a variety of worthwhile reasons. One
important outcome of FIT is the ability to set aside an immediate pleasure to achieve a future gain. But this alone is not
enough for complete emotional fitness.

What makes a person emotionally fit in a wider sense is
the capacity to *recognize and experience* adverse feelings,
then proceed to tolerate and express them productively,
rather than suppressing the emotions or expressing them in
a destructive manner.

Maryann, an administrative assistant and divorced
mother of two young children, was generally perceived as
being quite emotionally mature. She always took care of her
family and handled her job diligently. But she sometimes
erupted in bursts of anger at the children, a symptom of the
repressed rage she felt at being trapped in an endless "double shift" as a single working mother.

When she became involved in the EFC Program, Maryann's Emotional Fitness Journal gave her an outlet for expressing her angry feelings on paper. Fitness Focused
Meditation also helped her to feel calmer and more in control.
As her Exercise for Emotional Fitness, she took up tennis
again, a sport she had loved as a teenager. Playing tennis gave
her a terrific release of tension and outlet for her anger. These
EFC activities, along with her heightened Feelings Identification and Tolerance, gave Maryann sufficient emotional resources to tolerate her feelings without exploding in anger at

her kids. Later, Maryann started going to a single parents' support group, where she found validation for her emotions and learned coping strategies from her peers.

From the first call of the alarm clock to flossing before bedtime, most lives are filled with situations that require varying degrees of self-discipline, impulse control, and delay of gratification. Take a minute to think about how you handle these challenges in your own life. How do you manage the uncomfortable feelings that are unavoidable? Do you have any healthy mechanism for expressing unpleasant feelings and channeling them productively? Do you often have to rely on denial, repression, or outbursts of emotion to get through the day?

If you have ever been in therapy, you know that the therapeutic process encourages you to talk about your emotions so you can begin to take steps to express them productively, assert your legitimate rights, and make appropriate changes. The techniques of EFC work in a similar fashion. Meditation and journaling shed light on repressed feelings and provide a forum for self-analysis. Visualization and physical exercise build fortitude for tolerating those feelings and proceeding with more adaptive responses and courage, instead of avoidance or volatility.

SELF-ASSESSMENT FOR FEELINGS IDENTIFICATION AND TOLERANCE (FIT)

Following is a basic Self-Assessment for Feelings Identification and Tolerance. The purpose of this Assessment and the others that follow is to start you thinking about how the Core Components affect your personality, your relationships, and other facets of your life.

At this point, you might want to find a special notebook or diary to use as your Emotional Fitness Journal. The Self-Assessments can be the starting point of your Journal and be used to set goals and chart your progress as you move through the EFC Program.

Answer the questions "True" or "False" to the best of

your ability. Of course, you will have to generalize in some cases and choose the answer that reflects your most likely response. Try to be honest and answer instinctively; don't "sugarcoat" your responses or select the one that you intellectually believe to be correct.

There are no right or wrong answers in the Basic Self-Assessments, no grades or judgments. The Assessments are a tool to help you evaluate your current level of Emotional Fitness and understand how the Core Components relate to your own life.

SELF-ASSESSMENT FOR FEELINGS IDENTIFICATION AND TOLERANCE (FIT)
Respond to each item with either "True" or "False."

1. I tend to be guilty of procrastination or avoidance too often.
2. I often find myself reacting strongly to a given situation without really knowing why.
3. I'm generally viewed as someone who is impatient or intolerant.
4. It's usually not good to feel things too intensely.
5. I'm the kind of person who likes to be in control most of the time.
6. Strong feelings usually make me uncomfortable.
7. It's usually better to make decisions with your head, not your heart.
8. The axiom "Persistence pays" is often a strategy for failure.
9. It's usually safer to keep feelings in check and toned down.
10. I've been known to have a problem with my temper.

Two or more "True" answers indicate a need to work on Feelings Identification and Tolerance. The higher the number of "True" answers, the greater the need to work on this particular Core Component.

CORE COMPONENT #2: EMPATHY

Empathy is the ability to identify accurately and relate to the feeling state of another person with tolerance and understanding. Empathy involves identification with the entire range of feelings, including joy and satisfaction—as opposed to sympathy, which relates more narrowly to feelings such as sorrow or fear.

Empathy is one of the most admired human qualities in every area of human interaction. If you think of the people you love and admire, it is likely that many of them exhibit unusual Empathy. From timeless religious figures and celebrities to friends and colleagues, people who impart Empathy often have a special role in our lives.

In the realm of close relationships, Empathy is a key to harmony and longevity. *Empathy not only connects you to other people; it empowers you and the people with whom you are connecting.*

If you show Empathy on a daily basis through affirmation and encouragement, emotional closeness will grow. And if you have sufficient Emotional Fitness to be able to maintain Empathy during conflict and disagreements, relationships will flourish and resolution of conflicts will come sooner with less disruption. Ideas that might ordinarily be perceived as negative or critical will be heard in a less defensive way. The ability to express Empathy during arguments is fundamental to a healthy relationship.

Almost everyone, on every level, is more responsive when you use Empathy. This emotional skill is as important in the workplace as it is in the family. Consider how you react to criticism. If a boss or teacher says to you "I know you worked really hard on this report and the effort really shows, but I think with one more draft it could be even better," it is certainly more motivating in the long run than "This report doesn't work; fix it."

Empathy is also a major element of healthy parent-child

relationships. Eric, a corporate lawyer, thought of himself as an involved parent and couldn't understand why he had alienated his teenage son, Jason. He insisted that all his scrutiny and attempts to guide his son were for the boy's own good.

Not surprisingly, Jason reacted to his critical, overly involved parent by being even more rebellious than most teenagers. First he had his nose pierced, then he got a tattoo of his favorite rock band's logo. At school, Jason was very bright and couldn't help getting good grades, but he refused to participate in any of the extracurricular activities that would help him gain admission to his father's alma mater, an Ivy League college.

Eric tried family counseling, but Jason quit after the first session and refused to go back. However, Eric was receptive to the idea of taking action through the EFC Program. As he thought about his own past, Eric realized his own father had been hypercritical. Instead of rebelling, Eric had spent his life in an attempt to please his father, yet he never felt as if he had done quite well enough.

Through journaling and visualization, Eric relived his own feelings as a teenager, striving to please his overly critical father. This naturally gave rise to feelings of Empathy toward his son. He began to see that Jason was using his outrageous appearance to mask his deep insecurity. Since Jason felt he could never live up to his father's high standards, he wasn't even going to try.

Gradually, Eric began to look at his son as a human being deserving of Empathy, instead of as an adversary who had to be defeated. He realized that the argumentative, relentless stance that worked well in his court battles had no place in his home. Through Fitness Focused Meditation, he was able to learn to modulate his response to his son—to "mellow out" and back off to some extent. He found that the more he empathized with the boy's struggles to find his own identity in life and the less he tried to control, the more likely Jason was to make the right decisions on his own.

As you explore this Core Component in chapter 4, you'll learn that the development of Empathy begins in early infancy. By using Emotional Fitness Conditioning, you no longer have to be a prisoner of your past. Whatever level of Empathy you learned from your parents and whatever your starting point, you can develop this precious quality through the EFC Program.

SELF-ASSESSMENT FOR EMPATHY
Respond to each item with either "True" or "False"

1. If I feel something strongly, and believe it deeply, it probably means it's true.
2. Given an opportunity, most people would take advantage of you if you let them.
3. I'm not very interested in what makes people tick.
4. A lot of people would like you to feel sorry for them.
5. Emotionally speaking, children are just "mini-adults."
6. Relationships tend to go better when each person works to have his or her own needs met.
7. Talking about my problems with others has rarely done me much good.
8. Listening to other people's troubles is too upsetting.
9. I think my needs are somewhat different from those of most people I know.
10. I envy other people's success.

Two or more "True" answers indicate a need to develop greater Empathy. The more "True" answers, the greater the need to work on this particular Core Component.

CORE COMPONENT #3: INSIGHT

The Core Component of Insight refers to the quality generally called "psychological mindedness" in therapeutic circles. It pertains to understanding the psychological and emotional forces that produce thoughts, feelings, and behaviors. In one important aspect, psychological mindedness involves learning to connect your present to your past, by acknowledging the potent legacy of your family of origin.

Insight also includes the ability to look beneath the surface of behavior into its underlying reasons and meaning—a classic goal of traditional psychotherapy. Freud stated that the goal of psychoanalysis was "to make the unconscious conscious." Emotional Fitness Conditioning produces a similar result, either with or without the guidance of a therapist.

With EFC, you will gain an awareness of your Emotional Template—the model of life that becomes internalized through early relationships. EFC offers a fruitful and relatively uncomplicated way to learn about your Emotional Template and how it influences your thought, feeling, and behavior patterns. As training advances, EFC can go beyond understanding to actual transformation of your Emotional Template.

There is another important function that Insight training will serve in your life. Insight bestows an enlarged capacity to understand others as well as yourself. Your heightened Insight will help you understand other people's Emotional Templates and some of the reasons for their behavior. In many instances, this will allow you to act with greater Empathy or Assertiveness, where appropriate, and communicate with more success.

Viveca, by her mid-thirties, had suffered through a series of unhappy relationships with men who were creative and intelligent, but emotionally unstable. One of these three men became addicted to cocaine, another left Viveca abruptly without explanation, and the third put her through years of heart-wrenching scenes until she was drained.

Through EFC Insight training, Viveca was able to recognize how her Emotional Template was directing her adult relationships. Her mother had been a narcissistic woman who used Viveca as a pawn in power struggles with her husband. During the years of her parents' embattled marriage and the ensuing divorce, Viveca had became embroiled in her mother's psychodramas and tried to fulfill her parent's unrelenting demands for attention and comfort. As Viveca's Emotional Template was being formed, pleasing her mother was a primary yet ultimately unreachable goal.

Through EFC Insight journaling and psychotherapy, Viveca realized that she equated love with need. She had a compulsion to try to make everything "right" for her boyfriends, as she never seemed to be able to do for her mother.

With her newly honed Insight, Viveca was prepared to seek out a more balanced relationship with a man who could give as well as take. She became involved with a slightly older man whose first wife had succumbed to prolonged illness. This man had highly developed Empathy skills and Insight, which Viveca found a refreshing change from the self-absorbed creative types she had been involved with before.

SELF-ASSESSMENT FOR INSIGHT

Respond to each item with either "True" or "False" to the best of your ability.

1. My childhood was close to being perfect.
2. My past can't be too important as far as my life goes now.
3. I'm pretty much aware of everything going on in my life.
4. Children are so resilient that they can bounce back from adversity without much long-term impact.
5. I'm nothing like either of my parents.
6. Heredity is a much stronger influence on you than environment.
7. What happens to you in your life is largely a matter of luck, either bad or good.
8. If I'm not aware of something about myself, it can't be affecting me very much.

9. I really don't believe I have too many personal flaws.
10. My personality now is nothing like it was when I was a child.

Two or more "True" answers indicate a need to work on Insight. The higher the number of "True" answers, the greater the need to work on this Core Component.

Note: If you have been in therapy, and/or have already developed an unusual degree of Insight, it's possible that you'll have no "True" responses on this Assessment. But whatever your starting point, you can always benefit from deeper understanding of your Emotional Template and greater Insight!

CORE COMPONENT #4: ASSERTIVENESS

Assertiveness begins with a clear view of the reasonable, legitimate rights of oneself and others—a balanced sense of entitlement. Assertiveness requires taking a well-defined stand in attitudes and behaviors, based on valid rights.

Many people have a tendency to confuse Assertiveness with aggressiveness. Through your EFC training, you will learn to differentiate between the two and find a healthy, realistic level of Assertiveness for yourself.

Difficulties with Assertiveness can produce two extreme personality types: the narcissistically entitled individual and the co-dependent. Many of us are familiar with the classic use of the term *co-dependent*, in reference to a person whose partner has a drinking, drug, or behavioral addiction. But in EFC terminology, you will also learn to recognize more subtle forms of co-dependency. And these tendencies, if you find them in yourself, can be redirected as you develop healthy Assertiveness.

Jennifer, a thirty-two-year-old project manager, went to seminars on career development and was consciously assertive in her career. But she had difficulty with a colleague who was inappropriately sexual in the office, commenting on her appearance, telling lewd jokes, and sometimes touching her in an overfriendly manner. Jennifer realized that his behavior could be labeled sexual harassment, yet she was conflicted about bringing it to the attention of higher management.

Jennifer used the EFC techniques to develop her Assertiveness and change her style of interacting with this colleague. She wrote in her journal about the situation and how she might set firmer boundaries to discourage the harassment. Through Fitness Guided Visualization, she rehearsed telling him firmly she didn't want to hear any more jokes or comments about her appearance. She imagined making it clear both through body language and in words that she would not tolerate any touching.

After a month of practicing the Training Techniques, Jennifer was prepared to exhibit more Assertiveness in the office. Her colleague was surprised at her change in attitude, but he quickly got the message. It increased Jennifer's confidence overall that she was able to translate her EFC goals into action and see concrete results.

SELF-ASSESSMENT FOR ASSERTIVENESS
Respond to each item with either "True" or "False".

1. If I'm angry, I'll usually keep my mouth shut.
2. I often find myself unsure of what my real needs are.
3. In life, it's the aggressive people who tend to get what they want.
4. My belief is that speaking your mind will get you in trouble.
5. Going out on a limb for what you believe in will unnecessarily complicate your life.
6. I view those who are always asking for what they want as pushy and demanding.
7. If getting what I want hurts someone else's feelings, then it's probably not worth it.

8. I'm rarely sure that I'm right.
9. It's hard for me to trust my feelings because they are always changing.
10. In relationships, whoever has the power makes the rules.

Two or more "True" answers indicate a need to develop Assertiveness skills. The more "True" answers, the greater the need to work on this Core Component.

THE WHOLE IS GREATER THAN THE PARTS

While there are four individual Core Components of Emotional Fitness, it is paramount to understand that they work together to create a state of emotional health. The Core Components support and depend upon one another, just as our different physical systems act in concert to keep our bodies healthy.

This is how the different elements work together to create the whole of Emotional Fitness:

1. Feelings Identification and Tolerance lets you recognize and label your feelings. This emotional skill also helps you tolerate feelings that may be anxiety producing, uncomfortable, or difficult in some way, setting the stage for healthier expression.
2. Empathy teaches you to recognize and understand the feeling states of other people, which are likely to be a major factor in your own emotional life and relationships.
3. Insight brings awareness of how your early upbringing, family history, and past experiences affect your emotions. Insight also orients you to recognize the often subtle psychological forces that motivate all of us.
4. Assertiveness lets you assert your legitimate rights and needs, supporting your emotional wellness with action.

Let's imagine, for example, that you feel highly anxious when driving on busy highways. FIT will allow you to identify the anxiety without berating yourself, yet tolerate these feelings and proceed to drive on the highway when necessary. Empathy will help you view other drivers as being generally cooperative and law-abiding, instead of speeding maniacs deliberately trying to cut you off at the pass. Insight might bring the realization that your father instilled in you a sense of fear and incompetence when he taught you how to drive, by acting nervous and critical. Assertiveness will give you a sense of competence in all areas of your life and more faith in your ability to take on challenges, including highway driving.

As another example, let's assume that you, like me, are reluctant to learn new technology, such as an advanced computer program. FIT will help you recognize that technology often arouses feelings of inadequacy and fear of failure. Through EFC training you will develop sufficient Feelings Tolerance to plunge in and learn a new skill despite the fear. Empathy will tell you that many other people share this techno-anxiety. Insight will remind you that learning a new computer program reminds you of struggling with mathematics as a child. Assertiveness will assist you in feeling entitled to sufficient time and training to learn the program thoroughly.

These are just a few everyday examples of how the Core Components can work together to help you through the difficulties of daily life. In chapters 3 through 6, you'll learn much more about marshaling these emotional skills to address your deepest issues, enhance your relationships, and achieve your goals.

REPETITION AND RHYTHM

While understanding the Core Components initiates the process of building Emotional Fitness, it is only a beginning. Your foundation of intellectual knowledge must be followed by consistent action for transformation to unfold. Your mind produces thought and your body produces energy. When they work together, the synergy creates change. The four Training Techniques of EFC are selected to maximize this force.

One of the reasons that the EFC Program has proven to be so effective is that the Training Techniques draw upon our innate need for repetitive, rhythmic activities. Think back to when you were a child, and you loved to play the same games over and over again, or have a favorite book read to you repeatedly. Then reflect on the activities that give you the greatest pleasure and sense of peace now. Can you identify a repetitive or rhythmic quality in these favorite pastimes?

Everything about our bodies is rhythmic and repetitive: our heartbeats, our breath, the way our nervous systems operate. Similarly, nature itself has a highly repetitive quality, with patterns continuing day after day, season after season. Rhythmic activities have an intrinsic capacity to tap into our inner selves, by bringing us in touch with both our body rhythms and the rhythms of nature around us.

You close your eyes and focus on your breath in meditation. You sit down every day to write in your special journal. You lie down and start your visualization practice with the same evocative imagery. You walk, run, swim, or engage in other rhythmic forms of exercise. All these Training Techniques stimulate a positive conditioning effect through repetition.

As you practice the Training Techniques over a period of time, the activities can even take on the soothing quality of a personal ritual. You may find yourself sitting in the same place and position to meditate. You might prepare for visualization by turning off the lights, putting on the same comfortable outfit, and lying down in a safe, familiar spot. Journal writing can be turned into a nourishing ritual, if you write with a special pen and notebook at a certain time of the day or evening. Exercise can take on a ritual feel as you systematically put on your sneakers or swimsuit, do your warm-up and embark on your regime.

This is not to suggest that there is anything cultlike or quasi-religious about the EFC Program and Training Techniques. EFC is a self-help program based on sound psychological principles. The ritualistic quality of the Training Techniques is not intended to have religious overtones, although it can have spiritual qualities. Rather, it taps into our universal need to take time out from the mundane world, to rhythmically nurture our deeper selves.

THE EMOTIONAL FITNESS REINFORCEMENT LOOP

The power of the Training techniques also derives from the Emotional Fitness Reinforcement Loop, which involves a similar training process that has often been noted in physical fitness. This means that the more you do an activity on a regularly scheduled basis, the more competently you will be able to perform it and the easier it becomes. Then you start to experience the various benefits of the activity and are inspired to continue.

First you practice the Training Techniques, which satisfy the basic human urge for rhythmic activity. After a month or two, your power and concentration increase and you can perform the Training Techniques with greater intensity. However, it still takes a basic act of will and self-control to practice on a regular basis.

Before too long, you begin to notice the benefits of the Training Techniques and enjoy an upsurge in your Emotional Fitness level. On a physiological level, endorphins and other neurotransmitters evoke pleasurable feelings. On the psychological level, you gain a sense of ego mastery, competence, and goal attainment. Soon, the Training Techniques start producing their own rewards, and you find yourself looking forward to your EFC activities. The Emotional Fitness Reinforcement Loop has been activated.

For example, you might start practicing Fitness Focused

Meditation for twenty minutes, three times a week, because you are determined to see if this Program works. For the first week or two, your mind jumps around and you are distracted and unable to achieve the meditative state; however, the rhythmic quality of the deep breathing is pleasant enough to induce you to continue. By the third week, you are more comfortable with the ebb and flow of your thoughts and you can achieve deep relaxation.

By the sixth week, you are able to go deeper into the meditative state. The experience itself is highly pleasurable, and you also find you have steadier energy, sharper concentration, and less anxiety throughout the day. The Emotional Fitness Reinforcement Loop has been activated and fuels your commitment to continue meditating. Meanwhile, the practice strengthens your Core Components, triggering further substantive growth in your inner life.

Once you get started, the EFC Program is self-perpetuating. All you have to do is take the first few steps, and the rest follows naturally.

TRAINING TECHNIQUE #1: FITNESS FOCUSED MEDITATION

Meditation is a tool that can be used by everyone, from spiritual-seekers to skeptics. For thousands of years, in hundreds of diverse cultures, people have used meditation for spiritual enhancement. In the last two decades researchers have begun to study its health benefits as part of the burgeoning mind/body science of psychoneuroimmunology (PNI). The evidence confirms what practitioners have always realized: meditation is a profound tool for self-transformation.

On the physical side, leading researchers such as Dr. Dean Ornish, Dr. Bernie Siegal, and Dr. Herbert Benson have documented the role of meditation in managing heart disease, hypertension, and many other diseases.

On the mental health side, research has confirmed that

meditation can reduce depression and anxiety. Another intriguing study on personality changes resulting from meditation reported increased self-reliance and self-confidence, less nervousness and neuroticism.

The EFC program offers a way for you to channel the power of this practice to achieve Emotional Fitness and pursue your personal goals. From an EFC standpoint, meditation works on various levels to energize Feelings Identification and Tolerance (FIT), Empathy, Insight, and Assertiveness. The rhythmic quality of meditation allows you to nurture the Core Components by tapping directly into your right-brain function, the seat of intuition and creative problem-solving ability.

The EFC Program provides a basic meditation exercise focused on stillness and breath, which you can practice at home, on your own, for ten to twenty minutes, three times a week. In this practice, you'll add specific affirmations, or positive statements regarding your EFC Core Components and goals, before and after you meditate.

Repeating these statements when you are in a highly suggestive and receptive state affirms them on a deeper emotional level. The alpha-theta brain waves produced during the meditative state act to reinforce these potent messages and prime your subconscious to work on the Core Components of Emotional Fitness.

TRAINING TECHNIQUE #2: FITNESS GUIDED VISUALIZATION

Visualization involves evoking specific mental images to achieve a desired goal, which could be anything from relaxation to specific problem-solving to a sports victory. It is an extension of the natural mental process in which an image, event, or outcome is pictured in your "mind's eye."

The capacity to visualize positive outcomes is a classic tool of athletes, performers, and successful people engaged in a wide variety of endeavors. It is one of the quintessential "secrets of success" and a natural trait of optimists. On the other side of the coin, negative visualization can induce or aggravate anxiety, fear, negativism, paranoia, and depression.

PNI researchers are documenting the power of visualization or imagery in preventing and healing disease—a phenomenon that has been instinctively understood for thousands of years. Numerous studies confirm that physiological changes in oxygen consumption, blood pressure, pulse, and respiration can occur during visualization. In addition, many therapists are now including this technique as part of a "multi-modal" treatment for conditions such as depression, anxiety, and obsessive-compulsive disorder.

In EFC training, learning to gain awareness and control over the visualization process is vital to expanding your Core Components. Fitness Guided Visualization works by evoking and rehearsing images and scenes that relate to Core Component concerns. It allows you to customize your EFC program to address specific issues in your life.

As part of the EFC training, you will learn how to practice Fitness Guided Visualization using various sample "scripts," which you can fill in with details that pertain to your own life. Throughout the EFC Program, the goal is to practice Fitness Guided Visualization at least three times a week, for fifteen to twenty minutes per session, rotating and refining the scripts to address the four Core Components of Emotional Fitness.

TRAINING TECHNIQUE #3: THE EMOTIONAL FITNESS JOURNAL

Putting thoughts on paper has always been a natural impulse of people seeking self-knowledge. Journal writing is a universal form of self-therapy and exploration—from young people who find comfort confiding in their diaries, to great philosophers and authors who explore complex ideas in their journals. Journaling is also widely encouraged in many types of psychotherapy, as well as through self-help modalities and support groups.

In EFC training, the Emotional Fitness Journal is a tool for consolidating the more intuitive gains of visualization and meditation, and intensifying the training effect. The goal is to write for fifteen to twenty minutes, three times a week or more. If you want to write longer entries or more frequently, it can only help, but you don't have to feel pressured to compose long treatises.

In fact, there is no need to try to be clever, insightful, or find solutions in your journal writing. The process naturally stimulates problem-solving ability, connects the past to the present, and nourishes the Core Components. You'll be amazed at what emerges when you let the words flow from your mind to your pen (or computer keyboard) without inhibitions.

The thrust of the Emotional Fitness Journal is to provide a forum for self-dialogue about issues, struggles, and solutions that arise in your daily life connected with the Core Components. In a sense, the journal is a type of talk therapy conducted with one's self. It is also a valuable resource if you are seeing a professional therapist.

The EFC Program will provide you with sample entries and questions that you might want to explore in your Emotional Fitness Journal. But these are only suggestions—you can follow your instincts and express your ideas in whatever format works for you.

TRAINING TECHNIQUE #4: PHYSICAL EXERCISE FOR EMOTIONAL FITNESS

If you've ever been involved in a form of exercise that you truly enjoy, you know firsthand the amazing effects it can have on your psyche as well as your body. It's no surprise that researchers are now busy studying the measurable impact exercise exerts on mental health, as well as physical well-being.

Studies have found that aerobic exercise can be an effective symptomatic treatment for some people with moderate depression and those who are prone to anxiety. Clinical evidence also suggests that aerobic exercise can improve memory, verbal fluency and creative problem-solving ability. Research has also shown its value in diminishing acute stress reactions.

There are many reasons for this phenomenon. Exercise boosts oxygen delivery to the brain. It also stimulates the release of "feel-good" neurotransmitters, such as endorphin, leading to the well-known experience of "runner's high."

From an EFC standpoint, exercise creates more emotional energy, stamina, and resilience. Strenuous workouts instill feelings of mastery and confidence that build your self-esteem and Assertiveness. When you recognize discomfort yet finish a difficult workout, Feelings Identification and Tolerance skills are strengthened. The rhythmic nature of exercise and oxygen uptake can begin spontaneously to expand Insight via a meditative-influenced action.

When you begin the EFC Program, you'll design a balanced exercise routine for yourself that may include aerobic activity, strength training, and stretching. A minimum of thirty minutes of exercise three times a week is recommended. Of course, you'll want to check with your physician before embarking on a new exercise routine.

Once you've been exercising regularly for a few weeks, you can begin to enrich the experience and link it directly to the EFC program by adding visualization. Affirmations and imagery concerning the Core Components can be incorporated into your workout sessions to maximize progress.

THE EMOTIONAL FITNESS CONDITIONING PROGRAM

The EFC Program gives you a systematic workout plan for building emotional wellness by developing the Core Components through the Training Techniques. Basically, the Program consists of the following activities:

ACTIVITY	FREQUENCY	DURATION
Fitness Focused Meditation	3 times a week	10-20 minutes per session
Fitness Guided Visualization	3 times a week	15-20 minutes per session
Emotional Fitness Journal	3 times a week	15-20 minutes per session
Physical Exercise for EFC	3 times a week	At least 20 minutes per session

This entire program requires only three to four hours per week, or the equivalent of an hour every other day—a modest investment of time for a major return! If this amount of time sounds like a lot, don't worry. Chapter 7 will provide many practical suggestions on how you can work the Program into your busy schedule.

There are two Training Tracks for the four-month EFC Program:

The Basic Track

For the first two months (or longer, if desired), you can use the Training Techniques to strengthen all four Core Components. The Basic Track will familiarize you with the EFC methods, begin the conditioning process, and help you establish specific goals and build momentum.

The basic schedule is to direct EFC activities toward developing FIT for the first week, Empathy for the second week, Insight for the third week, and Assertiveness for the fourth week. This sequence is repeated during the second month of the Program.

For the third and fourth months (and, it is hoped, long afterwards) you can either elect to continue with the Basic

Track for increased familiarity and comfort, or shift to the Customized Track.

The Customized Track

This track allows you to focus on developing one or more specific Core Components. The selection of this Core Component can be based on needs brought to light by the Self-Assessments, by therapy, or other means. The Customized Track provides a deeper, more personalized EFC experience and the freedom to adapt the program to your individual needs and goals.

three

Feelings Identification and Tolerance (FIT)

I F YOU READ WORKS OF PSYCHOLOGY, ATTEND LEC-
TURES, OR TALK WITH A MENTAL HEALTH PROFES-
sional, you're likely to hear frequent references to "Affect
Identification and Tolerance." In this context, "affect" means
feelings and "identification" denotes the ability to identify
accurately what you are feeling. Tolerance refers to the capacity to experience and withstand all types of emotions and
continue to behave productively.

In the language of EFC, the simpler term *feelings* re-
places *affect*. The first Core Component is called Feelings
Identification and Tolerance and is referred to in the EFC
Program by the acronym FIT. This also happens to have an
important double meaning, by linking Feelings Identification and Tolerance directly to Emotional Fitness.

All the Core Components of Emotional Fitness ultimately rely upon and have their roots in FIT. The personal
growth process begins with the ability to recognize, specify,
and understand the full range of your feelings without judgment or denial. It is also essential to be able to tolerate these
feelings and continue to function in a healthy and mature
manner. Patience, delay of gratification, frustration tolerance, self-discipline, and impulse control are other manifes-

tations of Feelings Tolerance, and fundamental skills for an emotionally fit life.

Feelings Identification and Tolerance, like the other Core Components, starts to develop in early infancy. Feelings begin as diffuse physical sensations based on primal needs such as hunger, thirst, the urge to eliminate, and the desire to stay warm and safe. Preverbal feelings relate to bodily impressions of pleasure and pain in their most basic forms.

When it comes to pleasure and pain, human beings have more in common with a one-celled organism such an amoeba than we would probably like to believe. The human organism has primitive survival mechanisms hardwired into the brain, just as the amoeba does. These mechanisms are directly linked to bodily feelings of comfort, pleasure, nourishment, discomfort, pain, and danger.

If you put some water containing amoebae on a slide, then add a tiny bit of sugar to the water, you can observe under a microscope that the amoebae will react by moving toward the sugar source. If you add a drop of diluted hydrochloric acid, the amoebae will react by closing themselves in and moving away from the acid. It's a very basic illustration of the innate drive of all organisms, no matter how simple or complex, to move toward pleasure and nourishment and away from pain and danger.

As soon as infants emerge from the womb (and even in utero), they have a strong inclination toward pleasurable feelings and away from discomfort. Babies react to stimuli and their bodily needs with both movement and sound. Parents or caregivers respond to body language and vocalization (crying, cooing, gurgling, etc.) and come to know what the babies are feeling. Empathy, instinct, and experience also help adults understand the needs of preverbal infants.

This basic interplay sets the stage for the development of Feelings Identification and Tolerance.

The skill with which the caregivers perceive and respond begins to tell the developing children what can be expected from other humans and the surrounding environment.

Parenting requires a tricky balancing act of indulgence and discipline, closeness and separation, protection and letting go. No one in the world can be a perfect parent. Inevitably, almost all of us grow up with some degree of difficulty in the area of Feelings Identification and Tolerance.

If the caregivers respond well and consistently, children develop an underlying feeling that the environment is a place where their legitimate needs are likely to be met. They learn that frustration will be tolerable and that the world of other humans and feelings is generally pleasant and safe.

However, even the most caring parents cannot always read children's needs accurately and respond appropriately. A certain amount of pain, discomfort, and frustration is inevitable.

As children progress into the toddler stage, Feelings Tolerance begins to unfold through the many lessons of growing up. In toilet training they learn to withstand the discomfort of "holding it in" until they can reach the potty. In play interactions, they learn to tolerate the frustration of sharing with siblings and other children. These are the baby steps of FIT, as self-control, delay of gratification, and other tasks of life lead to the socialized child.

As children develop language, they soak up cues from caregivers about how to express feelings. They may learn sufficient vocabularies for expressing feelings and be encouraged to do so freely. Or, by example and/or instruction, they may be taught that it is not safe, acceptable, or lovable to express feelings. The nuances of how the parents respond to negative as well as happy expressions of feeling profoundly influence the development of Feelings Identification styles.

Children with unresponsive or critical and harsh care-givers may find their feelings to be threatening and difficult to tolerate. Overly indulgent, hyperattentive parents can also sometimes raise children with low emotional pain toler-ance. Children with caregivers who are inconsistent can grow up to be uncertain about the safety and productivity of expressing feelings and reaching out to have their needs met. Yet even the most well-meaning, protective parents can raise children who have difficulty expressing negative or un-pleasant feelings.

The good news is that the FIT patterns ingrained in you as a child are not intractable. Yes, you will have basic tend-encies, strengths, and weaknesses. But if you view Feelings Identification and Tolerance as a tangible skill, you can ac-quire it through the Training Techniques of Emotional Fit-ness Conditioning.

RITA'S STORY

By age thirty-two, Rita, a photo editor, had given up on dating and the hope of finding a life partner. She had suf-fered from too many disappointing relationships and was afraid to "put herself out there" anymore. She felt she couldn't bear one more man who didn't call back when he said he would, or mysteriously lost interest after a few dates, or turned out to have another girlfriend.

While it was true that Rita had broken a few hearts her-self, she didn't pay much attention to this part of her per-sonal history. What she couldn't forget and couldn't withstand was the threat of one more rejection.

Although she didn't realize it until she started the EFC Program, one of the roots of Rita's problem was that she had diluted skills in the area of Feelings Identification and Tol-erance (FIT). She was unable to tolerate the insecure feel-ings aroused during the process of starting a new relationship.

In my private practice, I see this type of situation all too often. And it is not only women who find it hard to tolerate the delicate feelings involved in the "dating game." Many men are deeply afraid of exposing themselves to possible rejection and disappointment. And while women usually have friends with whom they share these feelings, men are often ashamed of their vulnerability and have no outlet for expressing their emotions. They may develop negative expectations about dating or find it so uncomfortable that they withdraw from it altogether.

The EFC Program provided Rita with a way to cope with the stress and difficult emotions aroused by looking for love. Fitness Focused Meditation and regular aerobic exercise helped her to feel calmer and more in control. Fitness Guided Visualization gave her an opportunity to envision the type of relationship and response she wanted from a man.

In her Emotional Fitness Journal, Rita also used the technique of Dual Viewpoint writing to imagine a social situation from both her side and a male counterpart's perspective. This useful technique—which involves writing from another person's imagined viewpoint as well as one's own—helped Rita to realize that uncertainty and self-doubt were inevitable on both sides of the dating situation. It eased her resentment toward men and led to enhanced feelings of Empathy. She gained sufficient strength in the area of Feelings Identification and Tolerance to withstand the anxiety of dating and decided that the discomfort was manageable and worth the effort.

IDENTIFICATION

From the onset of psychotherapy, theory and clinical evidence have shown that talking about emotions opens the door to healing and growth. In the rather repressed society of Freud's day, the very idea of speaking freely about intimate emotions was somewhat radical. Now, with the widespread advent of talk shows, self-help books, therapy, and peer-support groups, we tend to think that most people are open about their feelings. But this is far from true.

Many people have strong defenses against recognizing and discussing their deepest feelings. They may preoccupy themselves with distractions so that they are too busy to contemplate their emotions. These distractions may be socially acceptable preoccupations, such as work, hobbies, TV, sports, etc. However, when feelings are too painful to confront, many people self-medicate with drugs or alcohol to avoid or alter their emotional states.

It is a natural response to shy away from identifying feelings that you perceive as painful, embarrassing, dangerous, or destructive. But you will find that the longer the emotions remain unnamed and ignored, the more power they will gain.

Disowning your feelings separates you from your true self. And the longer you deny strong feelings, the more stubbornly they stick with you. The price of this repression can be as subtle as a vague sense of dissatisfaction, or as blatant as an anxiety attack or an episode of depression.

In Emotional Fitness Conditioning, your first goal is to learn to identify your feelings honestly, without editing. As you gain experience in this practice, you will find that naming your feelings actually disarms them. Once they are exposed to the light of day, you gain control. The Training Techniques will help you tolerate your feelings and channel them into a productive force.

The famous quote "We have nothing to fear but fear itself" helped a nation through the darkest days of World War II. This truth can also be applied to the emotional life.

As you progress in the EFC Program, you'll learn that it's okay to feel anxious, resentful, angry, or whatever, as long as you can tolerate your feelings, express them in worthwhile ways, and move on with Emotional Fitness. You will have an enhanced ability to identify your feelings objectively without judging them as "good" or "bad." Much of the guilt and low self-esteem associated with negative feelings will be dissipated. You'll realize that feelings are only feelings—they can't harm you if you choose to act with Empathy and appropriate Assertiveness. You may also find that you have a greater ability to recognize and appreciate your positive emotions.

EFC ACTION EXERCISE: FEELINGS IDENTIFICATION AND TOLERANCE

1. In your Emotional Fitness Journal, list as many different words as you can for your feelings (up to thirty). Divide them into two columns, for positive and negative feelings.
2. Pick out the most prevalent negative feeling. Write down three ways this emotion impacts on your actions or life.
3. Next, write down a scenario where you develop the Emotional Fitness to prevent this negative emotion from impacting on your life. What can you do to channel the negative emotion more productively, or move through the feeling to the desired action?

You will find that the power of a negative emotion diminishes once you accurately identify it and gain confidence in your ability to tolerate it.

TOLERANCE

While the uninitiated may think that psychotherapy involves little more than an endless stream of talk, in fact, learning to tolerate as well as identify feelings has always been a goal. From Freudian psychoanalysis to modern behavior therapy based on the ideas of B. F. Skinner, the value of learning to manage uncomfortable feelings has consistently been emphasized. This is also a primary goal of EFC training.

Freud stated that in the treatment of phobias, for example, the patient would have to move beyond Insight and be able to face his greatest fear in actuality before the treatment could be considered successful. The behaviorists addressed this issue more directly with the technique of desensitization. This method was designed to help patients manage anxiety and resulting avoidance by using relaxation techniques to replace anxious feelings with a sense of calm.

Alexander Low, a prominent postwar psychiatrist, is known for his influential work in this area of affect tolerance. As the founder of the worldwide Recovery self-help movement, he stressed the importance of facing uncomfortable and unpleasant emotions with courage, through a process he called "training the will." Emotional Fitness Conditioning works directly to strengthen your ability to tolerate difficult feelings and grow through the effort, replacing avoidance with the courage to act when action is required.

DELAY OF GRATIFICATION

One of the hallmarks of emotional maturity is the ability to delay gratification. This is a basic social survival skill that parents try to impart to their children from the time they are toddlers. From the very first "no-no's" to the onset of adulthood, the pull between immediate pleasure and the future gain continues as we mature.

For example, my sixteen-year-old son had an important exam in the morning. But his favorite sports team was playing on TV the same night he had to study for the test. He faced a classic human dilemma, assuming, of course, that studying while the game was blasting on TV was not a viable option.

Clearly, the immediate pleasure was watching the game on TV. The future gain was the prospect of doing well on the exam, and, ultimately, keeping up his grades for college. In this case, I was proud to see that my son had sufficient FIT skills to tolerate the frustration of missing the game and delay his gratification in favor of the long-range result.

For well-functioning individuals, delay of gratification is required throughout the day. No stable relationship or goal attainment can be achieved without this emotional skill.

Many of the people who achieve difficult goals in life have an unusually strong capacity to delay immediate gratification. The budding Olympic champion spends countless hours striving toward his goal, instead of indulging in the playful pastimes of other children. The aspiring ballerina forgoes ice cream to stay slim and endures bleeding toes when she dances *en pointe*. The successful entrepreneur invests every penny she has, takes on the burden of a huge loan, and works twelve hours a day to build a business.

What nearly all achievers have in common is an inordinate talent for delaying immediate gratification, withstanding uncomfortable feelings, and demonstrating persistence. These abilities are inherent qualities of the Core Component of FIT which you can augment through the EFC Program, without the necessity of the total devotion of an Olympic athlete.

SELF-CONTROL

In order to maintain self-discipline, delay gratification, and endure unpleasant feelings, you need a sufficient reservoir of self-control. In the spirit of Emotional Fitness, self-control is not about rigidity or stoicism. Instead, it is about being in control in the most positive sense. This entails recognizing and experiencing a wide range of feelings without resorting to impulsive or destructive behavior.

Individuals who have difficulty with impulse control have a tendency toward alcohol or substance abuse, promiscuity, behavioral addictions, and/or venting anger at other people. What they are actually "acting out" is their inability to cope with feelings such as anger, anxiety, boredom, and frustration.

Many people with impulse control problems believe that identifying their feelings is potentially dangerous. They may not want to open a Pandora's Box of emotion for fear that expressing feelings will make them vulnerable in a hostile world. And they also tend to lack sufficient Emotional Fitness to withstand the negative feelings that accumulate. The combination of being afraid to express feelings along with a diminished ability to tolerate them is too much to bear.

Traits of the so-called "addictive personality" include anxiety, restlessness, insecurity, and a tendency always to reach outside the self to find satisfaction and inner soothing. These are all symptoms of unease with feelings and the emotional life. Lacking the ability to tolerate feelings, there is a strong lure to alter them with substance abuse or other addictive behavior.

Roger, a twenty-eight-year-old computer programmer, had been smoking marijuana every night since he was fourteen years old. As a teenager, Roger had never confronted his turmoil and anger, which was exacerbated by a problematic relationship with his stepfather. Instead, Roger developed the habit of getting high to tranquilize himself and disconnect from his emotions.

As an adult, Roger managed to relegate his smoking to the evening hours and was functional and moderately successful in his work. He refused to acknowledge that he had a substance-abuse problem and had no intention of quitting.

It wasn't until Roger took a job at a government agency where he was subject to random drug testing that he was forced to confront his addiction. With the threat of drug testing hanging over his head, Roger was able to stop smoking marijuana "cold turkey." But he found that his sobriety brought a flood of repressed feelings to the surface. He had trouble controlling his temper with his wife and felt a constant undercurrent of uneasiness and anxiety.

Through counseling and the EFC Program, Roger came to realize that his real task was not only giving up his marijuana use but also learning to understand and tolerate his emotions. He needed to identify the reasons for his anxiety and anger, and build the stamina to withstand the occasional discomfort of living substance-free.

It took Roger several months before he was willing to try practicing Fitness Focused Meditation or Fitness Guided Visualization. In the meantime, he found that writing in his Emotional Fitness Journal was cathartic. He also took up bike riding as his Exercise for Emotional Fitness. With these EFC training tools, Roger was able to control his anger without turning to marijuana for relief.

Even for those of us who don't have any illegal or socially unacceptable habits, self-control can be a problem, linked to a deficit of FIT. Although we might know what is healthy and right, it can be awfully hard to follow our own good advice. This is the "neurotic paradox": the inability to do what we know is best for ourselves. The neurotic paradox results in the situation where you know what is good for you but can't seem to do it; therefore, you continue to behave in self-defeating ways.

Food is often involved in these struggles because it has both chemical mood-altering properties and emotional significance. For example, perhaps you like to eat sweets after lunch. Sweets remind you of being rewarded when you were "good" as a child. In addition, the dessert brings a temporary lift to your blood sugar level.

Then you learn that the sugar rush is followed by a crash, exacerbating mid-afternoon fatigue, which makes it difficult to concentrate at work. Also, your favorite cookies are eighty calories each, and your pants are getting a little too tight. However, when you don't have sweets after lunch, you feel deprived on both emotional and physical levels. A typical neurotic paradox results.

Feelings Identification and Tolerance can help in two ways with this quandary. FIT lets you accurately identify the feelings aroused by cookie deprivation and understand their origin. And it gives you the ability to withstand the discomfort of not munching your favorite sweet and delay gratification. You can enjoy a sense of satisfaction stemming from your emotional strength, instead of needing the immediate reward. You can still have cookies when you choose, but you're free to select that option without compulsion.

PROCRASTINATION

Procrastination is one of the most common symptoms of difficulty in the area of Feelings Identification and Tolerance. Procrastination occurs when you put off doing something that is perceived as unpleasant, unrewarding, or emotionally painful. This may be a tiresome chore, such as tedious paperwork or housecleaning. It can also be a task that you may consider to be rewarding yet requiring an intensive effort, such as sitting down at your computer to work on a writing project or planting spring bulbs in your garden.

The procrastination arises when the proposed action arouses feelings of physical or mental discomfort. This can be as simple as aching knees from kneeling in the garden or as complicated as feelings of inadequacy when facing a blank computer screen. Whenever you use your physical or mental muscles in a new or challenging way, it typically involves some level of discomfort.

If you perform arm curls with a pencil instead of a ten-pound barbell, you're not likely to develop big, bold biceps. If you take a leisurely stroll, it doesn't do as much for your heart as a brisk walk up a steep hill. To some extent, the phrase "No pain, no gain" applies to every worthwhile endeavor in life.

There must be a challenge to the muscle to stimulate its growth. Without that challenge, there is no potential for any significant progress, growth, or accomplishment. We all know this as adults, but we resist it on an unconscious level, to varying degrees.

This is where Emotional Fitness Conditioning comes into play. It gives you the emotional strength to tolerate the unpleasant feelings long enough to allow adaptation and growth to occur. The Training Techniques work individually and in concert to expand your reservoir of FIT, so you can respond positively to challenges. This resource can be very useful in both the personal and professional realms.

Leslie, a public relations director for an art museum, enjoyed writing press releases and didn't mind organizational tasks. But she always felt nervous making follow-up phone calls to the media to promote coverage of her museum. When reporters and editors said they were too busy to talk or rejected her story ideas, she found it stressful and demoralizing.

This aspect of her job was crucial, since without follow-up calls the media people would never notice her material in the unending blitz of information they received. Yet Leslie often procrastinated about doing the follow-up calls and missed potential placements.

Through her EFC training, Leslie learned to identify and tolerate the uncomfortable feelings that the follow-up call work evoked. She started off every morning with a Fitness Focused Meditation that included the customized affirmation "I am confident when I call people. My feelings of discomfort are manageable." She created a Fitness Guided Visualization that began with evoking the sensory impressions of lying on a beach, totally relaxed. Then she carried those relaxed sensations into a visualization of making her follow-up calls.

Through EFC training, Leslie also learned to use her physicality to gain greater confidence. She discovered that when she went to a Step class during her lunch hour, she came back to the office feeling optimistic and confident. If she made her follow-up calls at that time of the day, she projected enthusiasm and energy that elicited a positive response. After four months of EFC Training, Leslie was able to double her media placements for the museum and secure her position in the process.

**EFC ACTION EXERCISE: UNDERSTANDING
PROCRASTINATION**

1. In your Emotional Fitness Journal, write down three goals
   or tasks that you never seem to accomplish due to
   procrastination.
2. Next to each activity, write down the emotions that arise
   when you think about doing it. Don't settle for the surface
   reasons, such as "not enough time," or "don't have the
   right tools." Delve deeper and try to pinpoint the emotions
   that are standing in your way.
3. Evaluate these emotions. Are they based on something
   that happened in your past? On some belief system? On
   some reality?
4. If you could tolerate these feelings, is there anything else
   that would keep you from working toward accomplishing
   your goal or completing your task?

*As you develop greater FIT skills, you will learn to toler-
ate difficult emotions and carry on with energy and
conviction.*

FIT AND DEPRESSION

Despite the fact that we live in a "true confessions" society, many people have no one with whom they can safely,
honestly discuss their emotions. They may be ashamed of
their feelings and angry at themselves for harboring negative feelings. When this anger turns inward, it can often result in depression.

Depression is often described as a feeling of emotional
emptiness and hopelessness. Depressed people may be so
overwhelmed by painful emotions that they block them off,
creating a type of self-anesthesia. The walled-off feelings induce a weight of blocked energy and inertia.

Emotional Fitness Conditioning training, particularly in the area of FIT, can help to release trapped feelings, allowing depression to lift. In addition, the Training Techniques can have a direct effect on mood on many levels.

The Emotional Fitness Program alone is not a cure for depression, which can have multiple causes, including biological as well as situational factors. Anyone suffering from this complex condition should work with a doctor to determine the best treatment. However, EFC Training Techniques can be very useful as adjunct therapy for depression, particularly if special attention is paid to increasing FIT skills.

FIT AND PHYSICAL ILLNESS

Limitations in the area of Feeling Identification and Tolerance can also be a contributing factor to physical illness. Researchers in the field of psychoneuroimmunology (PNI) are finding evidence that negative emotions and chronic stress can lower immunity, leading to a greater susceptibility to many types of ailments.

When faced with stress, the body readies itself for "fight or flight," a reaction elucidated by the Nobel Prize–winning researcher Dr. Hans Selye in his work on the stress-response syndrome. The fight-or-flight response causes heartbeat to increase and blood pressure to rise. Blood flow to the digestive organs is constricted, and blood sugar level rises. Muscles tense up for movement or protective action.

This "stress response" was a useful survival mechanism in the days when people literally needed to stand and fight or turn and flee in response to a threat. In modern society, however, there are few acceptable ways to respond physically to stress. If your boss pressures you with a deadline, you can't suddenly dash through the woods to work off your increased heart rate. If the IRS sends a distressing notice, you can't club someone over the head with a tree branch to utilize clenched muscles. Also, it is well known that even perceived or imagined stresses can produce increased heart rate and tensed muscles because the body may still react as if the stresses are real.

When the biochemical and muscular effects have no outlet, their effects continue to act on the body for a prolonged period, placing stress and strain on the bodily systems. The outcome can be a back pain or headache, high blood pressure and increased risk of heart attack, or a greater vulnerability to any type of illness.

The power of EFC is that it provides you with fitness-oriented outlets for dealing with painful or unpleasant feelings, including stress. The Training Techniques offer constructive ways to express, channel, and process the upsetting feelings. This limits and diminishes the harmful influence that stress can exert on your physical and mental health.

FITNESS FOCUSED MEDITATION AND FIT

Fitness Focused Meditation will help you nurture your ability to identify intuitively and understand your feelings. This Training Technique will also help you tolerate difficult emotions, such as anxiety, anger, impatience, and frustration. It will allow you to withstand stress better, enhancing your sense of well-being. When you practice meditation regularly, you'll enjoy a higher degree of control over your feelings and be able to manage them more productively.

As a starting point, the act of meditation itself provides good practice in the skill of persisting through uncomfortable feelings. When you begin to meditate, it's not unusual to feel fidgety, uneasy, or just plain bored. If you continue to breathe and focus until you've completed your twenty-minute session, you're already increasing your FIT stamina.

Once you take it a step further and frame your meditation sessions with affirmations, you can maximize the benefits. Targeted suggestions on developing your FIT skills can be planted into your subconscious, where they take root and flourish. You might make a general suggestion, such as: "It is safe for me to identify and acknowledge my feelings." Or you can affirm your ability to tolerate a specific emotion, for example: "When I feel anxious I breathe in a slow, calm way. This makes me feel safe and in control."

You may find that as you develop your FIT ability through meditation, you experience a positive side effect of better physical health. Studies conducted by Dr. Herbert Benson, who brought meditation to a mass audience with his landmark work *The Relaxation Response*, have indicated that meditation can help patients with muscle pain, headache, insomnia, and many other conditions.

Meditation has also been utilized by the researcher/cardiologist Dr. Dean Ornish as part of his holistic program for recovering heart disease patients. Dr. Ornish's lifestyle intervention program has drawn a great deal of attention for controlling or even reversing coronary artery disease conditions in participants. A crucial element in recovery is learning to manage stress more effectively, which is directly related to Feelings Tolerance.

In the psychological field, meditation is increasingly being used as part of a multimodal treatment to help patients cope with panic/anxiety attacks and obsessive compulsive disorder. Patients in these programs are learning to enhance their ability to tolerate extremely uncomfortable feelings through regular meditation practice.

FIT AND FITNESS GUIDED VISUALIZATION

A number of research studies indicate that guided imagery, or visualization, has a profound effect on mind/body health. This effect may be partially due to the opportunity to visualize desirable outcomes and express positive feelings during visualization sessions.

A study conducted at the UCLA Neuropsychiatric Institute indicated that imagery produces positive changes in immune functioning. Researchers believe that this result was related to the opportunity for expressing feelings, as well as the specific imagery on immune function. Visualization has also been a mainstay in cognitive, behavioral, and other types of therapy for a variety of emotional conditions.

You'll find that Fitness Guided Visualization is a potent healing tool when dealing with emotional as well as physical pain. It will increase your aptitude for tolerating all types of feelings and provide a sense of mastery that boosts self-esteem.

Rhonda, a forty-two-year-old divorced mother, had serious problems with anger management regarding her ex-husband, John. Since they had joint custody of their two young children, Rhonda had to see John every weekend. Sometimes she couldn't control her anger and exploded at John in a bitter tirade when he came to pick up the kids. Then she spent the rest of the weekend feeling guilty for exposing her children to this trauma.

As part of her EFC Program, Rhonda created a series of visualizations about managing her anger. To bring herself into a receptive state, she would practice five to ten minutes of deep, meditative breathing. Then she would focus on one of her Fitness Guided Visualizations:

It's Friday at 6 and I'm getting the kids ready for their weekend with their father. I can hear their excited chatter and footsteps running around. Now I hear the doorbell ring.

I feel that anger in my stomach that I always feel when I'm going to see John. I stop for a few minutes before going downstairs, sit on the bed and close my eyes. I inhale deeply into my abdomen. I breathe out slowly, exhaling the anger. In and out. In and out. In and out. That feels better.

I come downstairs with the kids' overnight bags. I say hello to John and even smile. I ask what they're going to do this weekend and he tells me about some outdoor plans. He seems surprised that I respond pleasantly and don't make any cutting remarks. I feel better about it, too.

The kids seem relieved that there's not going to be a scene this time. They're excited to see him. Whatever happened between us, I have to admit that John tries to be a good father and the kids love him. That unknots the anger a little when I think about it.

When they all leave, I feel relieved and pleased with myself. I know my anger at John is still there, but I kept it under control and that feels good. I deserve a treat.

I get into a nice hot bath scented with herbal bath oil. I breathe in and out, just letting my muscles melt into the warm water. The deep breathing is relaxing. I feel relaxed and warm and good.

Rhonda found that doing this type of visualization on the evening before John's weekend visit helped set the tone for a more civil meeting with him. If she still felt the anger welling up when he arrived, she would excuse herself for a minute and go into the other room. She would close her eyes, breathe deeply, and spend a few minutes evoking the relaxing feeling of the visualization. Then she could return in a calmer frame of mind and control any unfair outbursts. She felt good that their children were able to start the weekend with their father without any upsetting scenes.

FIT AND THE EMOTIONAL FITNESS JOURNAL

Journaling is a form of self-therapy, with many of the same healing qualities as talk therapy. Like therapy, the act of writing helps you uncover the emotions underlying your thoughts, moods, and actions. Naming these feelings can free you from their negative power. You gain a sense of control over your emotions once they have been identified and revealed.

How often in your busy life do you set aside some time to identify your feelings? Journaling provides a special time for the worthwhile, but often neglected, habit of self-reflection.

It offers you a safe haven for exploring your feelings, without any judgment.

The only rule when you write about Feelings Identification and Tolerance in your journal is "No Censorship Allowed." Your Emotional Fitness Journal should be kept in a private place, so that you can identify your feelings without any fear. This is your private channel for self-expression.

In my work, I spend much of the day helping other people learn to identify and tolerate their feelings. But I don't have much time to explore my own emotions, which sometimes get overlooked, even with my psychological background. Journaling gives me a precious place to uncover my own feelings and nourish my FIT aptitude.

Here is an example from one of my own Emotional Fitness Journal entries, written some years ago:

> *I took my wife and children to a play and then dinner yesterday. I felt very irritable before we went out but relaxed more during the evening. By the time we got home, I felt a great sense of relief.*
>
> *This all felt extremely familiar to me in a vague way. As I think about this now, being very honest about it, it all felt like a great sense of responsibility, like a burden, taking the family out to do something different, wondering if they would enjoy it, if it would be worth the cost. It made me feel weak and uncertain. I hate feeling like that.*
>
> *It's like trying to learn a new skill. You feel so unsure of yourself. That's something like I feel. It's occurring to me that I probably have avoided all kinds of new experiences because of my intolerance for feeling unsure of myself, and even weak because of it.*
>
> *Even as I write this now, I'm starting to feel better and stronger. It seems like I need to continue to work at labeling my own sense of uncertainty and believe it's O.K. to feel that way sometimes. I feel hopeful that if I identify these feelings honestly and accept them, I can start doing different things without an underlying sense of anxiety*

beforehand. Somehow, just writing this, I feel freer and stronger.

FIT AND EXERCISE FOR EMOTIONAL FITNESS

Exercise for Emotional Fitness has a twofold effect on FIT. First, it dramatically increases your ability to tolerate difficult feelings, such as anxiety, stress, anger, and mild depression. Second, it can actually induce feelings of well-being, due to increased oxygen flow and the action of endorphins and other neurotransmitters.

As with meditation, the process of staying with an exercise plan is in itself a lesson in Feelings Tolerance. As you continue to work through the initial difficulty of your exercise regime, you'll gain faith in your ability to triumph over emotional challenges as well as physical hurdles. Your Feelings Tolerance level will experience an upsurge.

Exercise has a tremendous capacity to help people tolerate even extremely painful feeling states, such as depression. A study conducted by Dr. John Greist and his associates at the University of Wisconsin had depressed psychiatric outpatients participate in a walking/running program. Patients who ran consistently showed a rapid and remarkable degree and rate of improvement. Several other studies, along with anecdotal evidence, indicate that aerobic exercise can exert an antidepressant effect.

Another facet of mental health in which exercise has a well-documented effect is stress reduction. Exercise provides a much-needed outlet for some of the physical responses to stress. The rhythmic nature of exercise works in concert with your heartbeat and nervous system, while the movement releases muscle tension.

Exercise is both a natural tranquilizer and a stimulant—with the best properties of both. It has an immediate effect on your capacity to manage and tolerate the full range of feelings that are part of an emotionally fit existence.

EFC ACTION EXERCISE: SETTING YOUR FIT GOALS

1. In your Emotional Fitness Journal, list your three top goals in life at this time. These could be related to your personal or your professional life.
2. How does your present capacity to identify and tolerate feelings help or hinder your present progress toward these goals?
3. How would an enhanced capacity for FIT help you achieve these goals?

As you practice the Training Techniques, you'll find that enhanced Emotional Fitness can give you the persistence to attain your most significant goals.

four

Empathy

THE SECOND CORE COMPONENT OF EMOTIONAL FIT-
NESS IS EMPATHY: THE ABILITY TO IDENTIFY, UNDER-
stand, and be respectful of the feelings of another person.
Empathy is essential for achieving healthy human interaction, from the home to the workplace to the world at
large. Without Empathy, there would be no community,
no family, and no chance for survival. Empathy is the saving grace of human society as a whole, as well as intimate relationships.

Empathy is often misunderstood and confused with
sympathy or compassion, which are also admirable qualities, but more limited. Sympathy and compassion involve
sharing in other people's sorrow or suffering, and trying
to alleviate them if possible. Empathy is the ability to
identify with *the entire range of emotions*: joy, triumph,
satisfaction, and confidence, as well as anger, fear, and
sadness.

Empathy is open-minded and nonjudgmental, acknowledging all the nuances of the emotional spectrum. It entails
going beyond the obvious emotion that is being expressed
and taking time to consider the deeper meaning.

The empathic person is also adept at picking up nonverbal signals: tone of voice, nonverbal sounds, body language,

and facial expressions. Communication researchers estimate that 90 percent or more of an emotional message is expressed through nonverbal means. Empathy helps you pick up these signals, which can be even more significant than words.

Empathy, through both verbal and nonverbal means, has a far-reaching impact. By developing greater Empathy through Emotional Fitness Conditioning, you can impart this quality to everyone in your sphere and start a ripple effect. When you treat people with Empathy, the sense of being understood puts them in a stronger position to show Empathy to someone else. So whether you act on an individual, local, or global level, you are making the world at large a better place with your enriched empathic ability.

EMPATHY IS NONJUDGMENTAL

Empathy implies a nonjudgmental attitude, one of understanding and tolerance. Empathy does not, however, mean that you endorse or condone unacceptable behavior in others. The Core emotional skill of Empathy allows you to understand and possibly disagree, without judging.

The empathic attitude is achieved by considering the psychological/emotional frame of reference of the other person. For example:

—*A clerk in a store has an unresponsive or unpleasant attitude when you ask for help. Instead of rushing to the manager to complain, you realize that the clerk is probably underpaid and overtired.*
—*You are eager to talk with your husband as soon as he arrives home from work, but he wants to turn on the television news first. Instead of taking this*

as a personal rejection, you acknowledge that he
needs a half-hour "breather" to unwind before he
is ready to interact.
—Your assistant doesn't finish typing a report before an important meeting. Rather than intimidating him with a reprimand, you realize that
he has trouble setting priorities and needs more
direction.

More and more employers, managers, and business
consultants are acknowledging the importance of Empathy in the workplace. The method of "ruling by fear" results in far less long-term productivity than managing
with Empathy. Empathy is key to teamwork, loyalty, and
motivation. From the everyday treatment of employees, to
benefits such as health insurance, child-care leave, and
"flextime," the corporate manifestations of Empathy are
all around us.

As the workforce becomes increasingly diverse, many
companies are also aware of the need for sensitivity training
to minimize conflict among people of different genders,
races, and nationalities. Diversity initiatives and sensitivity
training are linked to Empathy, as it strives to foster understanding among people of different backgrounds.

Ideally, Empathy is not selective, but in reality it often
tends to be. It is often somewhat easier for people to empathize with others of "their own kind." It does not require out-
standing Emotional Fitness to show Empathy to someone
with whom you have a lot in common. EFC Training will
help you to expand this skill. You can learn to have more
empathy both with people like yourself and with those who
are perceived as different.

Most of us find it hardest to empathize with people who
commit acts that we consider immoral. When faced with
that type of challenge, it is crucial to keep in mind that Em-

pathy does not necessarily entail forgiveness or acceptance. Empathy involves understanding how or why other people's emotional makeup leads to their behavior, whether you approve of it or not.

I had an unforgettable lesson in Empathy when, early in my career, I worked with individuals referred to me through the Department of Parole and Probation, who had been found guilty of violent crimes. It took quite an act of will—and some guidance from a mentor—for me to learn how to sustain an empathic attitude with people who were lacking in Empathy or even a basic moral sense themselves. Yet without empathic communication, I would have been unable to be helpful to these patients.

To fulfill my responsibilities as a therapist, I needed to stop defining these men by their crimes. Instead, I learned to look at their essentially human qualities first and then consider the societal, environmental, and familial forces that shaped them. In this way, I could relate to these individuals without condoning their crimes, and hope to make headway during their therapy sessions.

EMPATHY AND THE HEALING ARTS

If you have ever been in therapy, you know that Empathy is at the root of the therapeutic process. The projection of genuine Empathy and empathic communication by the therapist makes you feel cared about, as well as understood, and this experience helps you treat others with similar Empathy.

Carl Rogers, one of the most influential psychologists of the twentieth century, was the founder of "client-centered therapy" and a guiding light of the Human Potential Movement. Rogers believed that Empathy is the most important ingredient in therapeutic relationships, and, by implication, in all other human relationships.

Rogers stated that, in essence, the core of the therapeutic endeavor was to attempt to understand exactly what the other person is communicating. He considered it essential for a therapist to project Empathy, unconditional positive regard, and warmth. Through this example of the therapist, the patient could learn the art of sensitive communication and apply it to other relationships in his or her life.

More recently, Heinz Kohut, the Chicago-based psychoanalyst and founder of modern self-psychology, also stressed the impact of Empathy. He wrote that for people to become truly whole, they must feel that their point of view is understood with sensitivity and without judgment. Only then will they be able to grow themselves and be able to transmit this empathic understanding to others.

For both Rogers and Kohut, the centrality of Empathy in their therapeutic endeavors implies that empathy is central in all relationships. Kohut goes on to say that Empathy does not have to be a natural endowment; individuals can develop and strengthen this quality to make all their relationships more satisfying.

It is not only mental health professionals who utilize Empathy as a healing tool. The quintessential family doctor who knows and cares about her patients co-mingles Empathy with reassurance and authority. The nurse who makes a hospital stay more tolerable has strong Empathy skills. A talented massage therapist or personal trainer who knows how to tune in to his clients' bodies, find the tension, and work it out is employing Empathy.

And you certainly don't have to be a health-care professional to harness the healing power of Empathy. You can be a parent who kisses a child's scraped elbow to "make it all better," or be a friend to someone who is battling a serious illness. Numerous research studies have found that people with supportive friends and families have much higher rates of recovery from various kinds of serious illness. The healing power of Empathy cannot be overstated.

EFC ACTION EXERCISE: CULTIVATING EMPATHY

1. In your Emotional Fitness journal, list three qualities or behaviors that you would like other people to show to you more often (for example, patience, affection, or acknowledgment of achievements).
2. Pick three important people in your life. Write down how you can offer each one of these people more of the qualities/behaviors you want others to show to you.

Empathy has positive repercussions. It often flows back to you, in one form or another.

EMPATHY, SOCIETY, AND MODERN CULTURE

Throughout human civilization, Empathy has been one of the most universally admired traits, inspiring many of the world's major religious movements. The healing, empathic nature of Jesus is a major theme in Christianity. The Buddha also epitomizes the empathic spirit. Judaism has always taught Empathy as a fundamental duty of the devout.

The Golden Rule is the distilled essence of Empathy in action: "Do unto others as you would have them do unto you." The Ten Commandments also pertain to treating others with due respect and Empathy. This Core Component transcends personal Emotional Fitness to have a major spiritual and societal influence.

From a societal standpoint, without Empathy, there would be no community. From the first cavemen who shared their food with the weaker members of the tribe, to the modern man who gives his seat on a crowded train to an elderly woman, Empathy is what makes our civilizations civilized.

Once you start thinking about Empathy in this light, you will see countless examples of how it is the thread that holds the fabric of society intact. Without Empathy, we would never be able to maintain a generally lawful society. There would be no marriage, family, government, or community life. There would be no schools, hospitals, or neighborhoods. Empathy is not a sign of weakness in a society; it is a measure of strength and a necessary ingredient for a civilization's survival.

In fact, even higher forms of animal life can display quite a bit of Empathy, both toward members of their own species and toward humans. Dolphins have been known to push drowning people toward the shore. Chimpanzees have been seen helping each other reach for water and putting their arms around the shoulder of a friend hurt in a fight. Dogs may be "man's best friend" because of their instinctive ability to show Empathy for a person who is sad or unwell, and also to acknowledge happy moods with a playful response.

Empathy inspires attraction on a wide range of levels, including mass appeal. Popular talk show hosts and television reporters emit Empathy via electronic media. Superstar singers and actors attempt to project Empathy in their performances. The world's most popular performers are generally those with whom we make an empathic connection because they seem to express our very thoughts and feelings for us.

A well-known research study of over seven thousand subjects conducted by Harvard research psychologist Robert Rosenthal found that individuals who had a strong ability to read other people's feelings through nonverbal cues tended to be more popular, outgoing, and well adjusted. This study confirms what any astute observer of human behavior will notice.

Most of us prefer work associates who help us through roadblocks, empathize with pressures, and applaud our successes. Our favorite friends and relatives are the ones who share in our moments of joy, sorrow, and hope. We fall in love with people who project Empathy and treasure this quality in our partners.

EMPATHY ENHANCES INTIMACY

Preston, age twenty-eight, considered himself to be an attractive man and had worked hard to obtain an MBA and a secure position in the banking industry. He knew he was considered a "good catch," and a lot of women expressed interest in him. But he wasn't hunting for a trophy wife; he was looking for an intelligent, caring woman who wanted to raise children, someone who made him feel cherished and secure. He wanted a woman who did not remind him of his socialite mother, whom he resented for shunting him off to boarding school so he wouldn't interrupt her busy schedule.

Preston had dated dozens of women over the years. But the women he was most attracted to inevitably broke up with him. Since the women were always vague about their reasons, Preston worried that perhaps he was an inadequate lover. Although he kept playing the field, he became insecure about his sexual performance.

Preston finally fell in love with Susan, a bright, cheerful physical therapist who was warm and nurturing. Everything seemed to click and he started fantasizing about a future with her, including children and a house in the country. He was devastated when Susan told him she didn't think their relationship was going anywhere. This time, Preston pressed Susan for the reason for the breakup. Susan said that she thought he needed to see a therapist and work out some of his own issues before he was ready for a lasting relationship.

When Preston became involved in EFC training, his Self-Assessments indicated that he had the greatest difficulty in the Core Component of Empathy. He began to work on this skill by writing about some of his past relationships in his Emotional Fitness Journal. Analyzing these relationships, Preston realized that he hardly knew anything about the women he dated—their hopes, conflicts, or personal history. He had spent the majority of his time with women talking about himself, enjoying their attention, just as his mother had basked in the glow of her social whirl while ignoring him. So, although he was actually quite insecure, he tried to present himself as powerful and confident. What was missing from the perfect picture he tried to paint was Empathy.

During Fitness Focused Meditations, Preston directed his subconscious to develop and exhibit greater Empathy. In his Fitness Guided Visualizations, he imagined being with Susan and encouraging her to talk about herself. He used Dual Viewpoint Journaling to write about their relationship from both their points of view.

Preston was quite nervous about contacting Susan again and risking rejection. In order to prepare himself, he worked on building his Feelings Identification and Tolerance through EFC Training Techniques. When he felt ready, he got in touch with Susan and she accepted a dinner invitation.

When Preston told Susan about his EFC experience, she was touched that he had made the effort to work on his emotional issues and was willing to let down his facade and become more open and vulnerable. But instead of dwelling on his own struggles, Preston encouraged Susan to talk about her own inner life. Reassured by his interest, Susan was willing to become involved with Preston again, this time on a less superficial level.

When their intimate relationship resumed, Preston used his empathic skills in the bedroom. He paid more attention to the nuances of Susan's responses during lovemaking and encouraged her to express honestly what she wanted. By focusing on her feelings, he became more confident that he was a satisfying lover. He learned to approach her sexuality with greater sensitivity and, in the process, bring them both deeper pleasure. When Preston presented Susan with a beautiful engagement ring, he felt confident that she would say "yes," and she did.

EMPATHY IN MARRIAGE AND OTHER INTIMATE
RELATIONSHIPS

In a sense, marriage is a lifelong exercise in Empathy. Once the initial physical excitement has faded, Empathy can continue to grow for a lifetime and bind a couple together with love. Without Empathy, a marriage cannot be truly fulfilling and is unlikely to last forever.

(When I mention "marriage" here and throughout the book, please be aware that the same information applies to any long-term, intimate, living-together relationship. Whether you're gay or straight, legally married or not, the dynamics of marriage are present in all types of lasting love partnerships.)

People are always searching for the "secret" of a long and happy marriage. As someone who has worked with hundreds of couples, I can tell you that Empathy is the key. If you are lucky enough to be a partner in a happy marriage, you're probably aware that Empathy is a treasured characteristic in a spouse.

One of the primary goals of marital therapy is to help couples learn to experience Empathy for their partners and communicate with Empathy. This skill is essential both for healing marital rifts and for changing unhealthy relationship patterns. When people begin to seriously practice EFC Training Techniques to enhance their empathic abilities, they can see dramatic results.

Allan, a prominent lawyer, came to counseling after his wife, Jeannette, threatened to divorce him. He was mortified at the thought of having the outside world see him as a failure in marriage and at the prospect of dismantling their home, family, and investments. He also wanted to avoid divorce because he genuinely loved his wife, although to hear her tell the story he gave little indication of his affection.

Jeannette complained that she couldn't stand Allan's constant criticism any longer. The clothes she selected weren't quite right; her cooking was critiqued, her parenting style was devalued, and even her ideas for home decor were ridiculed. Years of being unable to meet his perfectionistic standards had worn her down so that she felt utterly inadequate. Her husband, in turn, pointed to her insecurity as proof that she was childish and incompetent.

Through Emotional Fitness Conditioning, Allan came to acknowledge that he desperately needed to show his wife more Empathy if he wanted to save their marriage. His compulsion to win every argument worked in his profession, but it was detrimental in his marriage. His criticism was alienating her, making her feel chronically angry, and creating an atmosphere filled with tension.

To elicit more Empathy for his wife's situation, Allan was encouraged to write about his experience as a young law associate, when he was constantly belittled by one of the senior partners. This led to an awareness of how he was emulating his demanding father, a respected but much feared member of the judiciary. Allan used Fitness Focused Visualization to imagine how his wife felt when he was harsh and critical to her. He also combined meditation with his daily jogging routine, and as he ran he affirmed that he would treat his wife with greater Empathy.

Through these Training Techniques, he was gradually able to strengthen his Empathy skills and change his behavior toward Jeannette. He would catch himself before criticizing her and think about how it would feel. He was less judgmental about her taste and decisions. The small steps began to add up, and Jeannette felt encouraged that their marriage could be saved with further work in this direction.

EMPATHY AND THE "CHORE WARS"

The expression of feelings, attitudes, and ideas that would ordinarily be perceived as negative or critical sounds much less defensive when it is transmitted with Empathy. This is a basic tenet of couples counseling and many useful books on relationships and communication. It applies whenever you are negotiating with your partner, whether the issue is earthshaking or mundane.

Two-career couples can build up tremendous friction over the basic "3 Cs": cooking, cleaning, and child care. A national Roper poll found that half of all wives resented their husbands for not doing more housework. And many men, having grown up with mothers who didn't have outside jobs, still consider homemaking to be "women's work" on some level. Even when they do help out, they may feel demeaned and resentful. Clearly, both sides need to show more Empathy during domestic skirmishes, which can escalate into major battles and cause chronic dissatisfaction.

During twenty years of marriage, Doreen, a factory worker and mother of three teenage children, had established an unhealthy pattern of relating to her husband, Jack, an electrician. She took care of all the cooking, cleaning, and child care as if these chores were her sole responsibility. Then, when her frustration became intolerable, she would become so upset that she would erupt in an angry outburst and direct a litany of complaints against Jack. He reacted defensively to these explosions and whatever Doreen was trying to say got lost in the upheaval.

Doreen didn't believe in divorce, but she was beginning to find her marriage intolerable. She and Jack only argued over what she considered to be minor issues, but the disagreements were constant and unrelenting. She could barely control the undercurrent of annoyance and resentment that was reaching a boiling point.

Doreen had suggested marital therapy intermittently for years, but Jack always refused, saying that he didn't need a "shrink." Doreen courageously decided to start the process of change on her own.

As Doreen discovered the Core Components of Emotional Fitness, it became apparent that both she and Jack needed to display more Empathy in their relationship. Empathy training exercises, particularly Fitness Guided Visualization, helped Doreen strengthen this skill so that she could use it in her negotiations with Jack.

First, Doreen initiated a discussion with Empathy instead of accusation. She said that she knew Jack was under a lot of pressure with his business and it was hard for him to find extra time and energy for work around the house. But, like him, she also had to cope with a full-time job and would really appreciate more help with the chores.

By acknowledging Jack's pressures and deemphasizing blame, Doreen positioned them as a team instead of adversaries. She found that with this approach, Jack was much more responsive to her needs. She was pleasantly surprised when he offered to take over doing the laundry on weekends.

Doreen also learned the difference between true Empathy and projecting her own values or ideas onto her husband. As their dialogue continued, she learned that Jack didn't really care if she put dinner on the table every night or kept the kitchen floor spotless—those were her values, inherited from her mother. Jack was far more interested in being freed of the guilt and resentment that Doreen projected. He was quite willing to stop for takeout food or cook pasta a few nights a week, and take other steps to lighten her load, if it meant easing the tension between them.

Whatever the issues are between you and your spouse, the first step is to learn to communicate with sensitivity and respect for your partner's feelings. This is the only way to be heard and break through the anger, emotional distance, and power struggles.

EFC ACTION EXERCISE: EMPATHY BEGINS AT HOME

1. In your Emotional Fitness Journal, write down the name of a family member with whom you need to exhibit more empathy.

2. Write down the two or three behaviors or characteristics of these individuals that bother you most.

3. Imagine how you would approach a discussion about these behaviors with Empathy. Phrase your opening line in the most positive, supportive way you can. Continue writing what you might say to get the other person to understand your point of view.

4. How do you imagine he or she would feel about this approach and respond to it?

As you learn to communicate with greater Empathy, you'll find you get a markedly better response and break through many stumbling blocks in your personal relationships.

EMPATHY AND PARENTING

Parenting requires a boundless expression of Empathy. It starts the minute the baby is born and continues for a lifetime. From the helpless infant who needs a diaper changed to the rebellious teenager whose moods have to be handled with patience, parenting requires enormous Empathy. If you are a parent, cultivating this quality in your emotional makeup will make your job infinitely more manageable. Developing Empathy is one of the most important gifts you can give yourself and your children.

While parenting requires more Empathy than almost any other task in life, it also naturally inspires this trait. Most parents find an incredible wealth of Empathy within themselves when they have children, which is one of the most rewarding aspects of being a parent.

Parenting also gives us an opportunity to empathize with feelings of joy and happiness in others. The experience of empathizing with our children's pleasures and triumphs is one of the most thrilling aspects of being a parent. The mother who has fun watching her child play with a new toy or the father who gets a lift from watching his child's dance recital are both manifesting Empathy with their children's interests and efforts.

Empathy often flows most easily when children are young and innocent. Almost all parents can find it within their hearts to empathize with a crying baby or a young child who needs consolation. It is hardwired into our brains to empathize with the young—otherwise the human species couldn't survive.

Empathy becomes more of a struggle when our children become defiant toddlers or later start seething with teenage angst. The adolescent process of individuation that leads to young adulthood is frequently accompanied by some level of rebellion. During this process, teenagers often go out of their way to deflect our Empathy. They need to establish their own identities and claim their emotions as their own. In their self-absorbed state, many teenagers insist that adults can't possibly understand their emotions and cut off our attempt at Empathy. If you're coping with a rebellious teenager, the EFC Training Techniques can be a much-needed source of support.

When you are dealing with children of any age, one of the biggest challenges is to empathize with what they are actually feeling, instead of projecting your own frame of reference onto them. I clearly recall a summer night about seventeen years ago, when my nine-year-old daughter suddenly asked me: "How do people breathe?" Without reflecting on her emotional state and being preoccupied with what I was doing at the moment, I mumbled something about the mechanism of the lungs and diaphragm.

Soon after, I mentioned my daughter's question to my wife, who immediately opened up a dialogue with our daughter and discovered that she was feeling anxious about an argument she had had with a friend at day camp. The anxiety had induced a mild episode of hyperventilation, causing our daughter to become anxious about her breathing. She felt much better when we explained how she could relax and slow her breathing down to a normal level. We also led her into a discussion about her upset feelings regarding the situation with her friend.

Meanwhile, I learned another lesson about taking the time to listen with Empathy in everyday life, not just with patients. And once again I had a chance to admire my wife's innately empathic nature, for which I've always loved her.

THE EVOLUTION OF EMPATHY

Empathy is essential for effective communication. From Sunday School to the self-help bookshelf, we are deluged with reminders of the importance of Empathy. Yet it is still hard for us to consistently communicate with Empathy, especially when we are angry, afraid, or defensive. Even when we are well aware that Empathy produces the best outcomes in all types of relationships, it is often difficult to sustain an empathic attitude. We may know what is right but simply not have the Emotional Fitness to follow through on our knowledge.

Why is Empathy so hard to maintain, even when we understand it intellectually? The difficulty usually stems from our familial relationships and childhood experiences.

Empathy begins at a very young age and is shaped by our earliest interactions. Developmental psychologists have observed that infants exhibit Empathy just a few months after birth, by reacting to the crying of other babies. Between the ages of one and three, they may imitate the actions of someone else who shows distress, a behavior called "motor mimicry." As young children begin to develop their own separate identity, motor mimicry fades and the level of empathic response begins to vary greatly among different youngsters.

When a parent acknowledges a child's full range of emotions with Empathy, this capacity is nourished in the emerging personality. These opportunities for Empathy occur during dozens of small interactions throughout the day, not just when a child cries or needs help. For example, "baby talk" is a natural empathic response that matches the young child's voice and evokes attunement. The better understood a child feels in all the nuances of emotion, the greater his or her capacity will be for developing strong Empathy skills.

When a parent underreacts to emotions, the child can begin to avoid expressing the feelings that are not reciprocated. The child might learn to avoid expressing anxious feelings, or curiosity, or affection. Not only will the range of emotion be constricted, but Empathy abilities are also likely to be limited later in life.

Lack of parental Empathy during the formative years can result in extreme personality disorders, even criminality. Studies of violent criminals have indicated that many were raised in orphanages or foster homes, or in dysfunctional families where little Empathy was transmitted to them as children. Many antisocial and criminal personalities are formed through emotional neglect, in homes where Empathy is neither given nor taught.

In some cases of intense emotional and/or physical abuse the child can have a paradoxical reaction. Some abused youngsters become highly attuned to the shifting emotions of other people as a survival mechanism that enables them to sense feelings that might explode into violence. If this develops into an exaggerated or obsessive level of Empathy, it can cause great difficulty later in life, particularly in the area of relationships.

Empathy, and the other Core Components of Emotional Fitness, needs to be balanced and modulated. If we walked around in a state of total Empathy, we would be overwhelmed by other people's emotions and find it impossible to function. We need to balance Empathy with Assertiveness and realistic attention to our own feelings.

Some empathic individuals become so focused on empathizing with others that they neglect their own emotional needs. Or they utilize Empathy as a means of distraction from their uncomfortable thoughts and feelings. These imbalances can be an imitation of parental behaviors or a compensation for Empathy that was not received in enough quality or quantity in childhood.

Most of us were raised by parents or caregivers who were somewhere in the middle of the spectrum of Empathy—neither perfectly in tune with our feelings nor totally neglectful. The degree of Empathy we received probably fluctuated from situation to situation, from day to day. It is not easy for caregivers to maintain a high level of Empathy while dealing with their own worries and busy lives.

If you had highly empathic parents, you have a head start in this area. But if you did not, the past does not need to limit your future. Whatever degree of Empathy you were given as a child, and are able to give as an adult, it is not set in stone. By participating in the Emotional Fitness Conditioning Program, you can take control and consciously cultivate this skill. The techniques of EFC work on unconscious, intellectual, and physical levels to help you cultivate Empathy and achieve more mutually satisfying relationships in every area of life.

FITNESS FOCUSED MEDITATION AND EMPATHY

Fitness Focused Meditation nurtures Empathy through multilevel pathways. It induces greater attunement to yourself and others, teaches patience, and heightens sensitivity and tolerance. The practice lowers your level of tension, frustration, and anxiety, which makes it easier to maintain an empathic outlook. And it helps you connect with your right-brain and higher consciousness, where the potential for Empathy exists in abundance for all of us.

In the Eastern traditions of yogic and spiritual meditation, a primary aim is to produce a sense of "oneness" with all the other organisms on the planet. As enlightenment unfolds, the meditator's separateness dissolves into a profound illumination of the world as a whole, with every person, animal, plant, and cell part of an integrated entity. In the yogic model, this experience provides inspiration for awakening Empathy and taking action to help others.

Now, this may sound a little too lofty if you're a beginning meditator. Don't worry, there is no pressure to become entirely enlightened like a Buddhist monk who has been meditating six hours a day for a decade. All you need to do is sit down for twenty minutes, three times a week, and focus your thoughts on your breathing, or key word, as you will learn to do in chapter 8. Empathy will gradually begin to evolve from the practice itself, and you'll be encouraged to continue.

In Fitness Focused Meditation, we help the natural process along by adding affirmations to encourage Empathy. The deep breathing and alpha brain waves produced during meditation induce these suggestions to be imprinted deeply into both your conscious and unconscious mind.

Regardless of your spiritual inclinations, meditation will help you reduce stress and gain equilibrium when coping with the demands of your daily life. When you feel better about yourself, calmer and more confident, it is certainly easier to be empathic with others.

FITNESS GUIDED VISUALIZATION AND EMPATHY

Visualization allows you to personalize your EFC training to develop Empathy for specific people in your life. You imagine a particular person with whom you want to establish a more empathic connection. Then you seat yourself in a quiet, comfortable place and begin a few minutes of basic breathing to set the mood.

First you visualize the person in great detail. Next you imagine yourself in a detailed interaction with that person. You see yourself responding with deeper understanding and sensitivity than usual. You visualize the person's appreciative response and acknowledge the sense of pride you feel in your enhanced ability to empathize. You can also use a visualization to explore the other person's viewpoint and Emotional Template.

For example, one woman in the EFC Program wanted

to have more Empathy in her dealings with an exasperating elderly relative. This aunt refused to change her diet even though she had diabetes, took her insulin sporadically, and insisted that there was nothing anyone can do about their health: it was all fate.

As part of a Fitness Guided Visualization, the woman imagined this scenario:

> *I see myself sitting with my aunt in her apartment. We're sitting at the table and I can see the familiar details of the apartment. Cooking smells are in the air. I can see my aunt's face in front of me, so wrinkled, so old, but her blue eyes are still pretty. Someday I'll look like that.*
>
> *I ask my aunt why she feels that it's not worth bothering to try to take care of her health. She tells me she was always too busy taking care of her children and husband. She's twisting her wedding ring. Her hands are swollen with arthritis. I pat her hand and she smiles.*
>
> *I come to understand that her concept of being a good wife and mother meant worrying about her family, not herself. I ask her about her husband and she talks about how she adored him until the end. Her blue eyes get a faraway look.*
>
> *I think that perhaps my aunt has had a low level of depression since her husband died. What she really needs is more involvement in life, instead of focus on her illness.*
>
> *I shift to an image of taking her out to lunch, exactly where we will go and what we will eat. I spend a few minutes visualizing being in my favorite restaurant with her, watching her enjoy a nice meal. Then I visualize bringing her over to see my kids . . . she loves children. I see myself giving her more reasons to want to take care of herself and live a longer life.*

This visualization fostered Empathy—true understanding of the other person's feeling state—instead of the customary sympathy or pity that we give to the elderly or ill. It helped her to understand what type of help her aunt really needed, and to take appropriate action.

You can direct your Fitness Guided Visualization to center on your mate, child, relative, close friend, co-worker, or any other person in your life. You write the script, direct it, and co-star with the person who needs your Empathy.

After a time, life will start to imitate art. You will find yourself acting upon the empathic behavior and attitudes you visualize. You will be able to project more genuine Empathy and enjoy the self-esteem and peace of mind that this emotional skill bestows.

THE EMOTIONAL FITNESS JOURNAL AND EMPATHY

Writing in your Emotional Fitness Journal provides a venue for exploring your feelings about significant people in your world. You can vent anger, resentment, and disappointment in your journal. You can also take time to reflect on what you appreciate about other people. All these variations give rise to Empathy and greater understanding of others as well as yourself.

Anger and resentment block channels of Empathy. Journal writing offers a safe haven for expressing rage, pain, and other feelings that may be too damaging to verbalize. You have a chance to unearth repressed emotions and give them recognition—a therapeutic and cleansing process. Like psychotherapy, journaling can help to dissipate negative emotions through the sheer process of expression.

As you advance in your Emotional Fitness Conditioning, you can also use the journal to write about another person's viewpoint to deepen your Empathic understanding. One woman in the EFC Program had an ongoing argument with her spouse about calling to tell her when he was coming home from work late. Through her journal, she strengthened her Empathy skills by using Dual Viewpoint journaling technique. This simply means writing from your own point of view and the imagined or perceived viewpoint of the other person involved in the situation. Here is an example:

My viewpoint: *First, I feel mad, because calling is such a little thing and it means so much to me. And I guess it's a control issue, too. It makes me feel as if I have no control over our lives together. I feel like a teenage girl, waiting for that boy who doesn't call me for a date. I feel rejected, abandoned.*

I resent that my husband doesn't have regular work hours. My father was home for dinner at 6:30 every single night when I was a kid. Sure, I understand, my husband has a different type of career, with different hours, but it still makes me feel insecure. And if he's really late and doesn't call, I start imagining the worst: a car accident or a mugging. I don't know whether to be sad or mad.

My husband's viewpoint: *The reason I'm usually late is because I'm in the middle of a job or a meeting. I can't stop and call my wife; it would be unprofessional and make me look like a sap. I don't like feeling controlled. I don't want my wife to act like my mother and try to control me.*

I always come through for my wife and she should trust me. After ten years, she should know that I'll always come home when I can. She worries too much about little things. She's got to learn to relax and not worry so much.

Dual Viewpoint journal exercises can illuminate your own feelings about an interpersonal issue and broaden your perception of the other person's emotions. While you can never fully know what another person is feeling or thinking, it enhances Empathy when you make an effort to see issues from another person's perspective.

PHYSICAL EXERCISE FOR EMOTIONAL FITNESS AND EMPATHY

It's hard to be a font of patience, understanding, and Empathy when you're wound up or exhausted. When you are operating at peak power, you have more to give. And when you have an outlet for relieving stress, you can be more flexible and tolerant. Exercise for Emotional Fitness is instrumental in creating a mind-set that is conducive to Empathy. In addition, staying with a regular exercise regime gives you practice in patience and working through discomfort, valuable tools for maintaining relationships.

An intriguing aspect of Exercise for Emotional Fitness and Empathy involves spirituality. Many people find that their innate spirituality is stimulated by certain forms of exercise, such as walking, running, dancing, and yoga. This may be due in part to the rhythmic nature of exercise and the conduit it provides to our higher consciousness.

The release of endorphins and other physiological changes can also create a feeling of expansiveness toward others and help you act with Empathy. The thrust of exercise for Empathy is that when you feel energetic and balanced yourself, it is so much easier to project Empathy toward others.

EFC ACTION EXERCISE: SETTING YOUR EMPATHY GOALS

1. In your Emotional Fitness Journal list your two or three most important relationships, leaving space between each name for additional writing.
2. Next to each person's name, write down ways in which you could show him or her greater Empathy.
3. If you could act with greater Empathy, how would it affect each of these relationships?

As EFC training increases your ability to act with Empathy, you'll find that you also receive more of what you need from the people in your life.

---

five

Insight

T HE THIRD CORE COMPONENT OF EMOTIONAL FITNESS IS INSIGHT, OR PSYCHOLOGICAL MINDEDNESS. THIS pivotal skill involves understanding the psychological and emotional forces that produce your thoughts, feelings, and behaviors. It also encompasses the art of learning to understand better the connections between your past and your present.

Insight brings you to the next level of Emotional Fitness, by giving you the ability to look beneath the surface and understand why you feel and act the way you do. Very often, this leads back to your family of origin and the shape of your Emotional Template. Your Emotional Template is your internalized model of life, the way you unconsciously perceive, organize, and act on your experiences.

While your Emotional Template is molded at a young age, it remains open to new input and modification. Through Emotional Fitness Conditioning, you can actually reshape elements of your Emotional Template, creating more productive patterns of thought and behavior. With EFC Training, Insight generates potential for renewal and growth.

Insight training will allow you to see yourself with greater clarity and objectivity, especially regarding those areas that are not particularly flattering or easy to acknowledge. As you broaden your Insight, you'll gain self-acceptance and greater Empathy for yourself. Self-acceptance paves the way for improved self-esteem. Once you comprehend the psychological underpinnings of your emotions and actions, you'll find it easier to forgive yourself and move beyond self-reproach and guilt toward a more loving acceptance of yourself.

The self-acceptance that is inspired by Insight does not mean passively staying the same. In fact, shedding your self-directed anger will cause more energy to be available for making desirable changes in your life. An additional benefit is a reduction in anxiety or depressive moods.

Insight will help you recognize the psychological motivation of other people, as well as yourself. As you become more psychologically minded, you can often discern the reasons for other people's thoughts, words, moods, and actions. This sets the stage for better communication and enhanced Empathy in your interactions. What begins as an effort toward self-growth can expand to positively affect many other people in your world.

PSYCHOLOGICAL MINDEDNESS AS A THERAPEUTIC GOAL

The clichéd image of therapy is the patient lying on the leather couch for ten years, talking endlessly about his parents while the therapist says, "How do you feel about that?" In reality, long-term analysis is rarely practiced anymore, due to time and money constraints. Many courses of therapy now more briefly focus on handling crises, finding solutions, resolving conflicts in relationships, and other practical matters. Yet no matter how action oriented or short-term therapy might be, Insight or psychological mindedness is still a primary goal. You can never figure out where you are going without some understanding of where you have been or why.

Insight-oriented therapy originally emerged from the Freudian tradition, with its emphasis on clients' understanding of their unconscious motivations as a key to resolving emotional problems. The famous "Freudian slip" was an early effort to bring psychological mindedness to life for the average person. Freudian slips are those behaviors, slips of the tongue, etc., that reveal an unconscious motivation at work. A common example is the person who is talking about a spouse but unwittingly substitutes the word "mother" for "wife" or "father" for "husband."

A primary goal of the Freudian approach, which later evolved into psychodynamic or depth psychology, is to guide the patient past rote and reactive behavior toward awareness, conscious intention, and educated reflection. In modern cognitive and behavioral therapy, however, the emphasis is on helping clients learn how to manage difficult emotions and adjust unhealthy behavior.

To paraphrase Lawrence Wolberg, author of the classic textbook *The Technique of Psychotherapy*, in describing the insight or psychodynamic approach to therapy: If you treat the whole person, then the symptoms disappear and the individual gets better. Whereas the behavioral and cognitive approaches are described as: If you treat the symptoms or destructive thought patterns directly, then the whole person will benefit.

Interestingly, Wolberg goes on to suggest that despite theoretical differences, both psychodynamic and behavioral therapies attempt to instill self-understanding and awareness of the underlying forces at work in the emotional life. While the various schools of therapy use different language in describing this process, Insight is always a crucial part of the therapeutic endeavor.

For example, suppose a person was terrified of flying on planes, but was required to do so to get ahead in his career. A psychodynamic approach might be to explore the client's past. Perhaps a memory might surface of being trapped as a child in a hospital bed, restrained before minor surgery. The client would come to understand that fear of flying is related to fear of entrapment, pain, and loss of control.

The behavioral approach would help the client learn relaxation techniques to cope with anxious feelings related to his fear of flying and the related sense of confinement. The cognitive approach would have him examine his thoughts about feeling trapped and how his internal dialogue inflames the panic. In many modern psychotherapeutic practices, including my own, an eclectic approach is used, drawing from a variety of helpful therapeutic traditions.

The EFC Program is also deliberately eclectic, in order to incorporate the most useful techniques and benefits from many schools of therapy. The EFC Program distills the most fruitful essence of these different approaches, while the Training Techniques facilitate self-guided therapeutic discoveries.

As you do your EFC work in the area of Insight, you'll learn to look below the surface of your thoughts, feelings, and behavior. Any areas that are cloudy or murky will start to clear so that you can see right down to the bottom.

SURFACE TO DEPTH EXPLANATIONS

Genuine Emotional Fitness requires the ability to move from surface to depth explanations through Insight. This means learning to go beneath the surface of our thoughts, feelings, and behaviors to the deeper motivations and emotional fuel generating them. To gain a clear comprehension of why you feel and act the way you do, you need to know how your past affects your present, and what forces are still influencing your current life.

Let's look at the commonplace problem of having trouble getting out of bed in the morning. Perhaps when the alarm clock rings, you instinctively hit the Snooze button. Then you have to rush to get to work on time, or you have less time to do all the things you want to do that day. One possible surface explanation would be that you simply like to sleep. Another surface reason would be that you aren't getting enough sleep and you're still tired.

However, if you begin to look for the depth-oriented reason, you might realize that the alarm buzz reminds you of being awakened by your mother during your very stressful junior high school years. For you, those years evoke intense feelings of pressure and tension, just as your work does now. When you take it a step further, you realize that work has unpleasant parallels with school, with supervisors (teachers), cliquish classmates (co-workers), and nerve-wracking tests (job performance evaluations).

Once you've made this connection, you can construct an EFC action plan addressing the unwanted behavior of staying in bed. This could include affirming and visualizing yourself as being a competent adult now, strong and secure, and perfectly capable of handling your job. Or it could require a deeper look at the realities of your current employment situation, including the various options that might be available.

In many situations, merely making the connection between your present behavior/feelings and the past can give you the impetus to change. Once you understand the depth reasons for behaviors and emotions, they often begin to lose their hold on you.

Jim, a forty-eight-year-old store manager, had such difficulty getting up on time that he was constantly late to work, putting his job in jeopardy. He had already tried a variety of mechanisms to ensure that he got out of bed promptly, but even the loudest alarm clock placed across the room didn't help. He would get up, shut the alarm off, and go back to bed without being roused from his somnolent state. The situation became so acute that Jim went for a full physical checkup to see if some medical condition was causing his oversleeping, but a battery of diagnostic tests did not detect any organic reason.

In Jim's case, it took EFC Training Techniques to move from the surface to depth explanation. Journaling in particular helped him to recognize that his sleepiness involved a paralyzing sense of weakness and vulnerability. This stemmed from his childhood with a mother who was prone to periods of depression, when she would stay in bed much of the day, her door closed to keep the children out.

Jim mustered all the techniques of EFC Training to learn to tolerate these feelings without resorting to the destructive pattern of oversleeping. Initially emphasizing a focus on FIT skills, he developed the emotional strength to force himself to sit up in bed as soon as the alarm went off. Then he would do a few head and shoulder exercises to shake off the sleep, followed by a Fitness Focused Meditation. Through journaling and Fitness Guided Visualization, he was able to process some of the painful legacy of his depressed mother. An Exercise for Emotional Fitness workout routine at the local gym raised his overall energy level.

While Jim's sense of vulnerability remained with him to some degree, he was able to take control of the feelings and function with greater Emotional Fitness. Jim's tandem effort with Insight and FIT training demonstrates the synergy between the various Core Components. This led to an upward spiral of self-esteem and faith in himself. He was able to get out of bed promptly in the morning, feeling capable of facing his day.

EFC ACTION EXERCISE: SURFACE TO DEPTH EXPLANATIONS

1. List the one behavior pattern in your life you would most like to change.
2. List the surface reasons why you think you behave this way.
3. Write a paragraph on how this behavior started. How old were you? Did you learn it from someone or imitate someone who did it? When do you tend to behave this way now?
4. Free-associate about what might be the depth explanation,

or possible psychological reasons why you continue to manifest this unwanted behavior.

Taking the time to look into your past will often give you the Insight you need to break out of destructive patterns in the present.

THE ORIGINS OF INSIGHT

The precursors of the emotional skill of Insight begin in the early months of life. Infants and young children have limited cognitive abilities and are incapable of understanding the psychological and emotional forces that guide their behavior. But in their own way, at their own level, children have a primitive form of Insight at a very early age. This emerges from their understanding of their world and the people in it, and particularly their own role in the unfolding drama of life.

Initially, the infant sees and feels the environment around her, including caregivers, as part of herself. Gradually, it begins to dawn on the infant that she is separate from the environment. This is the precursor of Insight and an important element of overall cognitive development. At this early stage, the infant's awareness is largely limited to primitive sensory and motor experiences.

Soon the preverbal infant becomes more keenly aware of her surroundings and the people in them. Out of the interplay between the infant and parents or primary caregiver, she begins to form mental images regarding cause-and-effect connections. This primitive understanding begins with a connection between events that relate to the pleasure versus pain experience. Crying brings the comfort of a warm breast or bottle to suckle. Putting a finger in her mouth leads to a feeling of pleasure. Later, this process extends to objects in the immediate environment. Touching a mobile in a certain way might cause the pieces to tinkle with a musical sound.

The fundamental emotional task of an infant is to form a secure attachment to his mother or another caretaking adult. This is crucial for survival itself. The baby gradually learns to gain his parent's attention through smiling, eye contact, crying, and other actions. In these first stirrings of Insight, the infant discovers what responses his actions elicit. At the same time, parents transmit a model of understanding through their own responses to the child.

Another crucial challenge the infant faces is learning to tolerate separations from the primary caregiver. Dr. Anni Bergman, a developmental psychologist and child psychoanalytic researcher who studied the emotional life of children from birth to age three, found that this process is actually "negotiated" between the child and adult during their ongoing interactions. The child is an active partner and initiator in this process, rather than playing the helpless role that had been previously assumed by infant researchers.

For example, the two-year-old whose mother leaves for work might hold onto her leg and entreat her to stay by crying. She, in turn, soothes, pats, and reassures him. He responds to this reassurance and calms down, accepting her going to work and completing the negotiation process. The particulars of how these interactions continuously play out shape the foundation of the Emotional Template.

As the child matures and becomes increasingly verbal, he develops a growing ability to think symbolically or metaphorically. This cognitive process culminates around the age of twelve, by which time most children can express themselves in abstract terms and understand their emotional experience to some degree. By this age, the child who has had healthy developmental conditions will attain a certain level of Insight or understanding of events and their psychological connections, consistent with her age and emotional and intellectual abilities.

Many factors affect the degree of Insight that a child

achieves. Certainly, innate levels of intelligence and cognitive ability are a force in this process. The evolution of Insight is also furthered by the child's involvement in a continually interacting family system with mutual and reciprocal influences. Other crucial contributions to the development of Insight are made through exposure to wider social milieus, including formal education. Wherever opportunities exist for emotional learning, there is potential for nurturing Insight. However, the most profound opportunities exist within the crucible of the family.

When a child is exposed to parents and teachers who provide sound psychological explanations and responses to his emotional and behavioral experience, he is more likely to have an expanded capacity for Insight. Imagine three sets of grade school–age siblings who are constantly bickering. The mother of the first set says, "Stop that arguing or you're going to see the back of my hand." The next mother says, "Keep quiet, you two, or you're going straight to your rooms and no TV." The third mother says, "Kids, you don't have to argue to get my attention. I love you both and I have time for both of you," and she also helps the siblings resolve their conflict with each other. It's not difficult to guess which of these children is likely to demonstrate a stronger sense of Insight.

If a child is upset or ill, a variety of responses might be appropriate, depending on the age and circumstances. Simply trying to "make it all better" can be fine. With older, more verbal children, it might be appropriate to nurture Insight by looking for the underlying reasons for the problem. While both responses are loving and natural, the investigatory approach, at least on occasion, will tend to nurture keener Insight in the growing child.

Another way in which parents can potentially instill Psychological Mindedness is by the judicial use of explanations that appeal to what I call "intergenerational continuity." This means, for example, suggesting to a child that he acts or feels a certain way because his parents or grandparents did. This guides a child to think, "I am who I am because of where I came from," leading to a simple form of Insight. These explanations are especially valuable for children when they put a positive and encouraging spin on behavior and are expressed with Empathy.

For example, a parent might tell her child, "When I was your age, I liked to read by myself more than play kickball outside, too." The child then feels that her natural preference is acceptable because it is similar to her parent's, even if it makes her different from some of her peers.

However, intergenerational continuity can be a double-edged sword, with either supportive or detrimental potential. If it is misused in an angry and critical sense, it can discourage insightful thinking and lower a child's self-esteem. The parent who says "You're impossibly stubborn, just like your father" is limiting the child's ability to understand and modify his attitude.

Even when referring to intergenerational continuity is well-meaning, it can sometimes inadvertently be undermining. A little girl who is serious and shy might initially feel comforted when her mother tells her that she was the same way. The difficulty would be that the child might develop the belief that all the girls in her family have these qualities and this assumption becomes entrenched in her self-perception.

These limiting parental attitudes are often distilled into a "personal mythology" that is a crucial component of our Emotional Template. The personal mythology is an element of our Emotional Template that strongly influences the way we meet the challenges of life and define ourselves. We grow up with certain learned notions, generated in our family environment, about what we are and are not, what we can and cannot achieve. These can become personal mythologies, or internalized fictional ideas, with negative and self-limiting aspects. When we label and stereotype ourselves in inhibiting ways, we may create certain biases or prejudices against ourselves that restrict our lives.

One of the most insidious personal mythologies that parents sometimes instill is the theme of inadequacy, the message that the child doesn't "have what it takes" to perform certain functions or roles in life. This attitude can be generated by well-intentioned yet overprotective and anxious parents who hinder development of the child's own problem-solving skills. It can stem from hypercritical parents who rarely give praise or encouragement, or perfectionistic parents who are never quite satisfied. Or it can come from parents who themselves feel inadequate and uncertain.

The EFC Program will help you identify the root source of the limiting aspects of your personal mythology and expand your understanding of your Emotional Template and Insight level. Then, as you become more emotionally fit, you can begin to throw off the restraints of any restrictive personal myths. By gaining Insight into the origins of these myths, you can liberate yourself from any elements that may be working against you.

EFC ACTION EXERCISE: UNDERSTANDING YOUR PERSONAL MYTHOLOGY

1. In your Emotional Fitness Journal, write down three major elements of your personal mythology—the way you view, define, and limit yourself—that you feel may restrict you from achieving your goals.
2. How and when did the elements of this mythology begin to emerge? Did someone tell you that you were a certain way?
3. Write about special times in your current life when you feel limited by these personal myths and how you might modify these myths to make them more supportive.

As you enlarge your capacity for Insight, you will be able to discard the limiting elements of your personal mythology.

YOUR EMOTIONAL TEMPLATE

If you use a computer word-processing program, you may be familiar with templates or formats for certain tasks. For example, many programs have a template for a fax transmission, with spaces for the name and numbers of the addressee, your name, the number of pages, and a note. The template is set so that when you hit the tab button, your cursor moves from space to space automatically to fill in the data. You can modify the template, but it can be tricky and you need a solid acquaintance with the program.

Similarly, the human mind has what I call an Emotional Template. This is an established and patterned way of looking at your world, organizing and filtering your experiences, and reacting with characteristic thoughts, feelings, and behaviors.

The Emotional Template is already formatted and in place in the adult personality, and some believe it is intractable. However, from my personal and professional experience, I know that *the Emotional Template is not set in stone*. It is a mold that can be altered by life events of major impact, as well as psychotherapy, Emotional Fitness Conditioning, and other profound learning experiences. As you become familiar with the raw material, it becomes more malleable.

Your Emotional Template is formed in early childhood, from a combination of your genetic predisposition, inherent traits, and your early familial relationships. From birth, you began to soak up information about your parents, siblings, caregivers, and anyone else who came into your little world. You watched and digested how they reacted and how they treated you and one another. All this information was formatted onto your Emotional Template at an early age. Beneath the level of conscious awareness, these early observations about the world of relationships were incorporated into your emotional filter and became expectations and latent patterns of relating.

During the early years of life, human beings are completely dependent and vulnerable. For a helpless child whose very life depends on caregivers, every interpersonal relationship has a profound impact. The shape of these primary relationships molds the Emotional Template that will stay with us into adulthood. And all this occurs before we have advanced cognitive ability.

In the past, development psychologists surmised that the human personality was formed by the age of six. Based on studies of the last two decades, the statistic has been revised downward. Now the general consensus is that the human personality takes shape by the age of three. This is not to say that you are not deeply influenced by events that take place later in life. But the basic imprint, the Emotional Template, is already in place before you are even aware of it.

Actually, elements of your personality and Emotional Template are formatted even before you are born. The human body contains about 100,000 genes, of which 50 to 70,000 are involved in brain functions. With numbers like these, there can be no doubt that genetics play a major role in basic emotional makeup. However, many developmental experts believe that genes only create a probability for particular traits, rather than a guaranteed result. Genes interact with the environment and may need to be activated by experiences after birth. High levels of trauma and stress are possible triggers that may switch on latent genes involved in fearfulness, shyness, and some mental illnesses.

The "nature versus nurture" debate has generally settled into a truce. Most developmental experts agree that the personality is derived from a genetic blueprint that is altered and affected by upbringing and experience, especially early relationships. Some researchers estimate that 50 percent of a child's personality is derived from genetics and 50 percent by experience/environment. Others estimate that up to 90 percent of a child's personality traits are shaped by "nurture."

EFC acknowledges that genetics, environment, upbringing, and experience all mold the Emotional Template, to varying degrees in different people. There is no way ever to define the precise balance, and there is no need to do so. As much as developmental research can tell us, there will always be a certain degree of unknown variance in what shapes the personality and emotional life.

While understanding your upbringing is always useful, it's not necessary to figure out every nuance of what made you what you are today. It is sufficient to be aware of the basic shape of your Emotional Template and learn how to make it more flexible and primed for growth. Then you can use EFC Training Techniques to access and reshape any areas of your Emotional Template that may be sabotaging or holding you back.

INSIGHT AND RELATIONSHIPS

Joannie, a twenty-nine-year-old sales representative, had a long-standing pattern of relationships with men that lacked a genuine sense of intimacy beyond the physical. She was selective in her choices and not especially promiscuous. But once she did choose to become involved with a man she would "perform" in bed, feigning orgasms and focusing on her partner's satisfaction. She never let any of her boyfriends get to know her emotionally, believing that they would "run for cover" if she revealed her true feelings, insecurities, and hopes.

Joannie believed that her needs were of no real interest to men and they only wanted servicing. Not surprisingly, she failed to bond with her boyfriends and the relationships fizzled out, leaving her even more cynical and empty than before.

As her thirtieth birthday approached, Joannie became increasingly dissatisfied with her shallow affairs. Her sister, the one person with whom she was totally honest, encouraged her to seek counseling, which led to EFC training.

Through EFC journaling, Joannie came to realize that her current relationship pattern had, in a sense, started with her father, a busy physician. This was not as a result of outright abuse, but of benign neglect. As the youngest of four children, Joannie had always felt she had to perform to get her father's attention. As a little girl, performing meant getting him to pay attention to an essay that had won an award at school, or trying to become a good skier so he would be proud of her on the slopes. Yet despite all her attempts to elicit her father's love and attention, he was drained by the demands of his job and had little left to give at home.

It took several months of EFC work for Joannie to see the overall texture of her adult relational pattern and its connection to the past. Yet gradually Joannie came to see that she didn't need to win a man's love by performing in bed or servicing him. It was safe and desirable to reveal her true self as a complex, intelligent woman. Using the EFC Training Technique of Fitness Guided Visualization, Joannie changed her mind-set. She created a vision of being loved for herself and was prepared to seek that in reality.

Insight is instrumental in both establishing and maintaining healthy, lasting relationships. When you understand your motivations and the depth reasons for being drawn to certain people, you have greater potential to make emotionally fit choices.

Individuals who are lacking in the Core Component of Psychological Mindedness are often attracted to mates who re-create the circumstances of their childhood, especially the unresolved areas. A sober person who had an alcoholic parent might be drawn to a drinker. An individual whose parents were critical and perfectionistic might find himself unhappily married to someone with these traits. In psychoanalysis, this is known as "repetition compulsion"—the drive to repeat aspects of past difficulties over and over again. Without Insight, we can be doomed to repeating the mistakes of previous generations.

"Love is blind" and "love is a mystery" are fine phrases for pop songs. But in the real world, if you want a relationship that has growth potential and longevity, it's wise to apply psychological mindedness, along with responding to your heart, before you get too deeply involved. Emotional Fitness Conditioning will give you Insight into the underlying reasons why you might be attracted to certain people and help you avoid mistakes.

Insight training will also bring a deeper perspective to the relationships in which you are already involved. You will be endowed with clearer Insight into your own feelings and responses regarding the relationships. And as a fringe benefit, you will have a sharpened ability to understand the other people in your life.

It is probably true that no one can ever definitively know what another person is thinking and feeling. However, if you are close to someone, you can cultivate a large degree of Insight into his or her Emotional Template, feelings, and behavior. Insight training, combined with the practice of Empathy, can dramatically enlarge your capacity to relate and communicate. And once you understand the depth reasons for someone's behavior, there is greater potential to forgive, empathize, and help that person learn and evolve.

INSIGHT AND BEHAVIOR CHANGE

Almost everyone has had an epiphany, a moment of revelation resulting in a breakthrough. Suddenly we know *why* and then we know *how*. This burst of Insight can give us the courage to change undesirable behaviors, from annoying habits to serious addictions.

In peer support groups such as Alcoholics Anonymous, members transmit their Insights to newcomers to help them understand the process of addiction and the road to sobriety. Alcoholics and substance abusers often self-medicate to avoid the truth of painful feelings. The development of psychological mindedness can bring these truths to the surface, a prospect that can be intimidating. But by hearing others reveal their stories in a supportive atmosphere, they begin to get comfortable with introspection and self-expression, and learn that Insight can be safe and healing. This provides a buffer for emotional upset and a way to cope without turning to substance abuse.

In Emotional Fitness Conditioning, Insight can empower you to modify unwanted thought patterns and behaviors on many levels. It can free you from the trap of the neurotic paradox—the situation where you know what is good for you but can't seem to do it and you continue to behave in the same self-defeating ways. The first step is self-knowledge, followed by Empathy for yourself and forgiveness. Once you perceive the underlying reasons for your thoughts and actions, you'll find it much easier to forgive yourself for being flawed and human. With Insight Training Techniques, you'll learn to give yourself permission to be imperfect, inconsistent, and insecure.

However, self-acceptance does not imply that you throw up your hands and say, "That's the way I am and now I know why and that's it." EFC is about action and change, about realizing your true potential through the Training Techniques.

Along with viewing your liabilities with greater clarity, Insight will also bring your strengths into clearer view. In my practice, this process has been reinforced through my experience working with many retirees in South Florida. Often older people feel their struggles are insurmountable, believing that new ways of handling their difficulties would be impossible to learn. This attitude exacerbates feelings of hopelessness and depression.

One of the ways in which I work with senior citizens is by helping them identify the adaptive resources and capacities that have carried them through a long life. I encourage them to remember the strength, wisdom, and persistence they've shown through years of hard work, raising children, and dealing with adversity, along with other achievements. The goal is to rekindle appreciation of their basic human qualities, which many of us take for granted. Then they can feel energized and ready to commit to the EFC Training Techniques to promote change.

FITNESS FOCUSED MEDITATION AND INSIGHT

Insight is about making emotional and psychological connections. Meditation is also about connections—between the mind and body, the conscious and unconscious, and right-and left-brain functioning. Meditation expands awareness of the link between physiological functions, such as breathing, and your feelings and moods.

As you tune into your mind/body interface, you'll begin to make surface to depth explanations automatically. For example, you might realize that you have a pain in your neck because you feel burdened by your responsibilities. And a session of Fitness Focused Meditation, followed by Exercise for Emotional Fitness, will alleviate the pain. Or you might become mindful of how your breathing pattern affects your level of anxiety, and you start to practice deep breathing in stressful situations.

Meditation also provides relief from the repetitive and distressing thoughts that often occupy our minds. In a room full of shouting voices, soft-spoken wisdom can go unheard. In a brain full of the busy thoughts, Insights have little chance to be heard. As you meditate and silence the everyday thoughts, profound Insights often emerge, and you will have an opportunity to hear the subtle frequencies of your softer, wiser self.

INSIGHT AND FITNESS GUIDED VISUALIZATION

Visualization expands the meditative process via the deliberate use of imagination and mental images. With Fitness Guided Visualization, you can journey into your personal mythology and explore the origins of your Emotional Template. You can guide your visualizations into the specific areas of your life you seek to explore, better understand, and change.

A young woman who was pregnant with her first child had conflicted feelings about motherhood, as many women do. She and her husband wanted to have children, but she was afraid that she wasn't competent and energetic enough to be a good mother. In her personal mythology, she was intelligent but disorganized, with a low energy level. This image was reinforced by her own mother, a physically fragile and dependent woman.

By using a series of crafted Fitness Guided Visualizations to implant a positive image of herself as a parent, this mother-to-be prepared herself emotionally. She did not try to fit all the details of ensuing motherhood into one massive visualization. Instead, she created specific scenarios that dealt with one aspect of parenting and practiced each visualization for several weeks, until it was firmly established in her psyche. Here is an example of one of her visualizations:

I am sleeping and the baby wakes me up with crying. The cries are loud and piercing. I feel heavy and warm in bed, like I don't want to move. But I know I have the strength to take care of my baby. I take a deep breath, stretch my arms overhead, and get up.

I go into the little nursery. I turn on the light and pick up my baby. She is so warm and sweet. She smells so good. I love her so much it's like a physical warmth that goes through my whole body. I feel so proud that I gave birth to such a beautiful little baby.

I sit down in the rocking chair with her on my lap. She feels dry; she doesn't need a diaper change. I kiss her little cheek. It's so soft and warm. I pat her and rock back and forth. The rhythm is so soothing to us both. She stops crying.

I feel so overwhelmed with joy at our connection. Just my touch has the power to make her calm. I never felt so powerful before. Everything else I've ever done seems so insignificant compared to being a mother. I feel so accomplished, so complete. I could go on holding her, patting her, rocking her, holding her forever.

INSIGHT AND THE EMOTIONAL FITNESS JOURNAL

The Emotional Fitness Journal is often the most direct and dramatic tool for encouraging Insight. Journaling serves as a surrogate form of talk therapy, providing a forum for safe expression and exploration of your past and its effect on your present life.

In the course of the EFC Program, you will be given writing exercises that are designed to help you see the shape of your Emotional Template, understand your family of origin, and define your personal mythologies. These exercises will methodically guide you in exploring the interaction between your early life and your current state of Emotional Fitness.

You will also have the option of free-associating—writing about whatever is on your mind and seeing where it takes you. In this type of journal writing, connective links and Insight often emerge in spontaneous and unexpected ways.

Maria, a thirty-five-year-old homemaker, wanted to gain Insight into her fear of abandonment. While she had been happily married for seven years, she couldn't shake the fear that her husband would suddenly walk out. And she couldn't identify where this fear came from, since she was not a child of divorce and had no obvious history of abandonment.

Here are excerpts from a series of free-associative journal entries she wrote about her fear of abandonment:

1. I don't understand why I am so afraid that my husband will just suddenly up and leave me. I've heard about this happening and seen it on TV shows, of course, but I don't really know anyone whose husband walked out. And my parents are still married. My father never abandoned us. This insecurity makes me mad at myself. It makes me feel weak and neurotic.

2. I did have a boyfriend in high school who broke up with me out of the blue, after we had been going steady for over a year. And I thought we were really in love. Now I realize it was just puppy love, or teenage lust, but at the time, it really shocked me that he would break up with me all of a sudden. Of course I had nothing in common with that boy, really, besides physical attraction. Not like me and my husband. My husband is my best friend. Which would make it much worse if he abandoned me.

3. My mother and I went to visit my brother's new baby today. Afterwards, we had lunch and got to talking about stages that babies go through. She said I went through one stage where I would cry hysterically every time she walked out of the room. My mother always took good care of me, but with two other kids to watch she had to leave me alone sometimes. She said that the other kids never reacted so violently when she left the room. Maybe that was the beginning of my fear of abandonment. Maybe every time she walked out of the room, I felt abandoned, helpless.

4. I think my fear of abandonment could also be a fear of losing control. Like when I was a baby and I couldn't control my mother walking out of the room. Or when I was a teenager and I had no control over what that boyfriend did. And of course my husband doesn't like to be controlled. He's usually pretty cooperative, but he's always made it clear that he doesn't like it when I get too controlling. I need to affirm that I can be safe without always being in control. I can let go of the people I love and need and they won't abandon me. I'm going to add some affirmations along those lines to my meditation practice.

INSIGHT AND EXERCISE FOR EMOTIONAL FITNESS

Exercise for Emotional Fitness tends to spark an increasing sensitivity to the interaction between physical activity and emotions. It provides you with firsthand experience of how strength, flexibility, and energy influence your psychological state. This evokes a greater sensitivity to and respect for the mind-body interface.

As you engage in aerobic exercise, you will also find that it stimulates your problem-solving capacity, often resulting in spontaneous Insights. It's not always necessary to focus on a particular problem or issue when you are working out. The Insight or solution rises to the surface of your consciousness without undue concentration or force. The rhythmic nature of the exercise, coupled with the increased blood flow to your brain and throughout your body, evokes fresh ways of thinking.

Flexibility exercises that are also essentially meditative, such as stretching and yoga, can also encourage Insight. As your muscles and joints loosen up, your mind opens up to new ideas that pave the way for Insight. Your thinking, along with your body, will become more fluid and flexible.

EFC ACTION EXERCISE: SETTING YOUR INSIGHT GOALS

1. In your Emotional Fitness Journal, name two or three areas of life in which you have had long-standing struggles. These might include expressing your needs in relationships, Assertiveness in job situations, or taking on specific types of new challenges.
2. How are these struggles affected by your Emotional Template and your personal mythology?
3. How could you envision making progress in these areas by developing greater Insight?

As you gain Insight skills through EFC training, you may find that you break through blocks and make progress with some of your deepest issues.

---

six

Assertiveness

THE FOURTH CORE COMPONENT OF EMOTIONAL FIT-
NESS IS ASSERTIVENESS. THIS CRUCIAL SKILL BEGINS
with a realistic, balanced view of your reasonable rights and
needs. It also requires consideration of other people's legitimate rights. With this frame of understanding, you can assert yourself in a healthy, appropriate manner. You can set
personal boundaries and take a well-defined stand in your
attitude and behavior.

Many people have mixed feelings about Assertiveness
because they confuse Assertiveness with aggressiveness.
They may believe that Assertiveness involves self-centered,
demanding, strident behavior. In fact, aggressiveness and
selfishness are antithetical to healthy Assertiveness.

Aggression intrudes on someone else's rights, while assertion does not. The assertive attitude fosters equality,
while aggressiveness is self-absorbed, tactless, and insensitive to the needs of others. And although aggressiveness can
sometimes move people to the "front of the line" in certain
fields and endeavors, it has negative overtones and harmful
repercussions. Aggressiveness negates Empathy and breeds
more aggression. It is often a sign of emotional immaturity
and imbalance, not fitness.

Assertiveness is positive in its approach, creating a

"win-win" situation whenever possible. It promotes equality in human interactions and is mindful of the rights of others as well as yourself. Assertiveness empowers you to stand up for your legitimate rights and express feelings honestly, through empathic communication and action.

The differences among Assertiveness, aggressiveness, and passivity become apparent when you think about a common activity such as driving. If you're trying to pull onto a busy highway and you passively wait for every single car in sight to go by, you'll never get anywhere. The cars behind you will get very annoyed, and you could cause an accident through your hesitation. If you're overly aggressive and you cut into the lane when another car is too close, that is also hazardous. To turn on to that highway safely, you have to make an informed judgment and move into the lane assertively.

The key to Assertiveness is a healthy sense of entitlement rather than either narcissism, which is an elevated level of entitlement, or co-dependency, which is an underdeveloped sense of entitlement. A healthy sense of entitlement means that you have a balanced view of what you need, want, and warrant. This understanding enables you to be considerate and positive while you are assertive, instead of abrasive, strident, or obsequious.

Imagine a long line of customers waiting for service in a crowded post office. A woman storms in and rushes to the front of the line. She tells the postal clerk that she just needs a quick book of stamps and no one will mind if she gets them first. When the clerk tells her she has to wait on the end of the line, she insults him and leaves in a huff.

Clearly, this is an illustration of an unhealthy sense of entitlement. This woman was entitled to want to get her stamps quickly, but she was not legitimately entitled to ignore the rights of other people waiting in line. If she had greater emotional sensitivity, she might have asked the other people in line if they minded if she quickly purchased a book of stamps. She might have elicited their Empathy by explaining her time pressure and gotten what she wanted.

Instead, by acting with inappropriate entitlement, she ended up causing resentment and sabotaging herself.

Although this woman may have thought she was merely being assertive, she was actually being aggressive, even though there was no physical or verbal violence involved. Aggressiveness tramples on the rights of others, in one way or another. And in a civilized society it usually produces the opposite of what is intended.

In EFC Training, all the Core Components work together to help you establish a balanced sense of entitlement. Your Empathy training deepens awareness of other people's feelings, so that you can avoid infringing on their rights. Insight enhances your understanding of how your Emotional Template and upbringing shape your Assertiveness style. Feelings Identification and Tolerance lets you recognize your possible discomfort yet continue to act assertively.

EFC ACTION EXERCISE: IDENTIFYING YOUR LEVEL OF ASSERTIVENESS

1. In your Emotional Fitness Journal, write a paragraph on your general impression of your current level of Assertiveness.
2. Rate yourself in the following areas, on a scale of 1 to 10, with 1 being nonassertive or passive, 5 being assertive, and 10 being unreasonably demanding or aggressive:
   How would you rate your assertiveness level in your career?
   In your close personal relationships?
   In your casual interactions?

   You may notice a difference in your level of Assertiveness in your personal and professional lives. Some people find it more difficult to be assertive in close relationships than in the world at large, while for others it is just the opposite. The variations are typically due to our earliest familial experiences and their impact on our Emotional Templates.

THE ORIGINS OF ASSERTIVENESS

The struggle to achieve a healthy sense of Assertiveness usually becomes most apparent around the age of two, during the infamous "terrible twos." However, the roots of this emotional skill, as with the other Core Components, are evident during infancy.

Infants have a primitive awareness of their own set of needs, involving sensory and physiological experiences related to pain, pleasure, comfort, discomfort, and survival. The preverbal infant tries to make his needs known, frequently at a high volume. Assertiveness allows the infant to ask for feeding, changing, comforting, and other requirements of early life. Without this innate capacity for Assertiveness, the infant's survival could be in jeopardy.

As the baby grows, gestures and preverbal vocalizing related to Assertiveness increase in complexity. Throughout this process, parents or primary caregivers are hopefully able to interpret what the child wants and meet these needs in an appropriate way. A balanced, consistent response encourages a healthy sense of Assertiveness by letting the young child know that she will get what she deserves.

Overresponsiveness, underresponsiveness, or highly inconsistent responsiveness to the infant's needs can lead to the beginning of difficulties with Assertiveness in the developing personality. Overresponding to the infant's every expression can create an exaggerated sense of entitlement. Underresponding can cause either a passive or aggressive personality to develop. Inconsistency tends to lead to a child who is highly uncertain about what to expect from others while also being inconsistent and unpredictable in his own responses.

As with other personality traits, genetics also certainly play a role in the propensity a child has toward Assertiveness, aggressiveness, or shyness. For example, researchers have found that people with the longer variety of a dopamine-4 receptor gene are more likely to be daredevils because this gene makes them less sensitive to pain. These individuals have been referred to as "Type T," or thrill-seeking personalities. A child with this type of gene might be prone to pounding his fist into hard objects, which could be construed as aggressive behavior. However, given strict boundaries, this same child can learn to modulate his behavior. Upbringing continually affects genetics, and vice versa, in the ongoing dance of development.

Dr. Jerome Kagan, a developmental researcher at Harvard University, identified signs of shyness in babies even before they were born. He found that children who turned out to be shy had faster heartbeats than other babies in the womb, indicating they were already highly reactive and prone to anxiety. However, after monitoring over five hundred children for seventeen years, Kagan found that these predispositions could often be overcome if parents gently but firmly desensitized children to anxiety-causing situations.

In a normal developmental pattern, by age two a child can express her Assertiveness through language. Temper tantrums, crying, screaming, hitting, and other aggressive gestures might also be part of the child's repertoire.

Fundamentally, the struggle that goes on between the adult and child during this period is also about boundaries. The toddler is trying to define himself as a separate person with needs, feelings, ideas, and actions all of his own. The caregiver's responsibility is to set limits on what behavior and expressions are socially and culturally desirable.

At the same time that verbal Assertiveness explodes, there is an increasing pressure on the child to conform to the dictates of the socialization process. The child must learn to use the "potty," refrain from hitting, biting, and spitting, share toys with other children, and a number of other demands. Inevitably, this sets up a boundary conflict, where the child attempts to assert his will to get what he wants, when and how he wants it.

During this stage, parents seem to be endlessly saying, "No," to teach the child what is safe and acceptable. At the same time, the child might be saying in essence, "No, I don't want to do this or that," "No, I don't like this or that," in an exasperating display of willfulness. At this critical juncture of emotional development, Assertiveness is linked to the child's attempt to define herself as a separate person through this process of seemingly endless self-assertion.

If the parent responds to the child's budding assertive behavior with patience and Empathy, the child learns that a certain amount of Assertiveness is acceptable. If, at the same time, the adult sets reasonable limits to prevent the child from unfairly infringing on others' rights, he is likely to grow up to be assertive rather than aggressive.

Unfortunately, many children don't have caregivers who are consistent and appropriately responsive to their assertive efforts. Another factor is that children tend to model adults' Assertiveness styles. If the parent characteristically exhibits aggression or passivity, the child might model this behavior in her own relationships. Among the range of personality styles, these early difficulties with Assertiveness can contribute to the development of two basic types, the narcissistic and the co-dependent emotional styles.

NARCISSISTIC ENTITLEMENT

Basically defined as "self-love," *narcissism* derived from the Greek myth in which Narcissus is condemned to contemplate his reflection in a pool of water for all eternity. Self-love in itself can be healthy, in the sense of legitimate and reasonable self-interest and solid self-esteem. However, when used in regard to narcissism it has the negative connotations of egotism and selfishness.

Emotional Fitness requires a balance between self-love and Empathy, meaning that you are concerned about your own needs but also sensitive to the feelings and rights of other people. Selfishness or narcissistic entitlement is a single-minded focus on one's own needs and desires, with little or no regard for others.

We've all come across people who tend to be demanding to an unreasonable degree, self-absorbed, and insensitive. Typically, these individuals were overindulged by their caregivers. They were led to believe that the world centered on them and their needs. Their parents probably had difficulty setting and keeping reasonable boundaries and struggled with saying "no" and meaning it.

Children can also develop narcissistic entitlement by modeling adults' behavior. They might grow up thinking they have to "watch out for number one" to get what they want from other people and from life. The demanding personality can also be a form of compensation for too little attention and responsiveness from self-centered parents.

Although narcissists may appear to be highly egotistical, this attitude is often a flimsy facade covering an interior life of insecurity and low self-esteem. For this reason, narcissistically entitled people can be prone to alcoholism, substance abuse, and behavioral addictions such as compulsive shopping or gambling. Since their narcissism stems from a desperate fear that they can never actually get what they need, they turn to addictions to fill up the emptiness and avoid confronting their own insecurities. They become blindly focused on trying to fill their neediness by feeding their addictions, with little regard for how their behavior hurts other people.

In addition to the addictive personality, there are many other narcissistic types, some of whom even attain high levels of success in the material world. There is the pushy, demanding, relentless individual who gets ahead through intimidation and callousness, the so-called "Type A" personality. There is the "temperamental artist" who uses creative talent as an excuse for self-absorption and emotional abuse of others, while constantly craving public affection and approval. On the extreme end, there is the criminal type who believes that ruthless aggression is the only way to get what he wants.

Narcissistically entitled people often exude a great deal

of energy, drive, and charisma. They can create a buzz of excitement and attraction that draws admirers into their orbit. People with difficulties in the area of self-esteem and Assertiveness are often drawn to narcissists like moths to the flame.

CO-DEPENDENCY

Originally, the term "co-dependent" was used to refer to a person involved in a relationship with an alcoholic or substance abuser. These relationships typically centered on the addicted partner's problems, with the co-dependent's needs submerged and diminished. The co-dependent "enabled" the addicted partner by covering up the addiction, keeping him or her financially afloat, and making other efforts at accommodation, leaving the co-dependent emotionally frustrated and drained.

In Emotional Fitness Conditioning, the term *co-dependent* refers to people who consistently subjugate their needs in their primary emotional relationship to their own detriment. The co-dependent's primary partner may be a narcissistically entitled but seemingly well-functioning person, or may have an addiction or other blatant problem that hinders the relationship.

These relationships are often an attempt to re-create and resolve unbalanced emotional relationships from childhood. The co-dependent's background usually includes at least one parent who was highly self-absorbed, narcissistically entitled, and/or had an addiction. The child grows up feeling that she must please and support the narcissistic caregiver to keep the relationship alive.

Because of her Emotional Template, she believes that she does not deserve unconditional love and her needs are not important. She must win and keep love by suffering and giving more than she gets in return. She believes that giving, enduring, and suffering are the price of love and are necessary in order to obtain and sustain a much-needed emotional tie.

The child of an alcoholic might be accustomed to subjugating his emotional needs to pacify his abusive father. In adulthood, he easily slips right into the role of co-dependent to a drug-addicted spouse. Or the son of a narcissist who modeled this behavior is attracted to a woman he can easily dominate.

The variations are endless, but the basic dynamics are the same. One side has weak personal boundaries and a basic belief that her needs will not be met. The other side is all-too-ready to step over those boundaries and absorb the codependent's energy into his endless emotional needs.

These types of relationship can be very passionate, powerful, absorbing, and even addicting. But they are ultimately demeaning, draining, frustrating, and rife with emotional pain. The narcissistic partner is rarely grateful for or satisfied with the co-dependent's efforts. In fact, the co-dependent's attempts at caregiving and control often provoke resentment and rage. And since co-dependents' personal boundaries are easily violated, they can become the target of verbal or physical abuse.

If you are involved in a co-dependent relationship with a partner who has an addiction disorder, or who has inflicted any type of abuse, I strongly urge you to seek help from a professional counselor or therapist. Peer support groups such as Al-Anon are also extremely beneficial in these types of circumstances. The EFC Program alone is not sufficient to cope with these situations. However, the EFC Training Techniques can be a strong support mechanism as you seek outside help.

ASSERTIVENESS IN INTIMATE RELATIONSHIPS

Many people have subtle issues with Assertiveness in their relationships, without falling into the category of frank co-dependence. For example, you may have trouble asking for the emotional support you want from your partner. Perhaps your relationship is generally happy, so you are afraid to "rock the boat" and instigate changes that might deepen your intimacy. Or you may find it difficult to express honestly your needs in the bedroom.

Many people who are quite assertive in the outside world still struggle with Assertiveness in the delicate area of romantic and sexual relations. They may focus on the negative aspects of Assertiveness: risk of rejection, damaging their partner's ego, or not getting what they want even if they ask for it. Even with partners they love and trust, many people find it difficult to be completely honest about their true sexual needs.

If you have Assertiveness issues related to intimacy, EFC Training can help you overcome barriers to honest communication. Through journal writing, visualization, and other techniques, you'll gain confidence in your ability to ask for what you want. And quite often, expressing your needs in an empathic and forthright manner is all that is required to elicit the desired change.

Another way in which certain people manifest difficulty with Assertiveness is by frequently feeling they must submit sexually to win approval, acceptance, and love. This often starts during the teenage years and can undermine young people's developing self-esteem and assertiveness style. It may result in becoming involved with a high number of sexual partners or participating in sexual activities they actually find disturbing. By building Assertiveness through EFC Training Techniques, many individuals find the strength they need to break out of self-destructive sexual behavior.

One case involved a woman in her mid-thirties who was in a ten-year relationship with a narcissistic man who was preoccupied with pornography and sexual variety. She had become enmeshed in the co-dependent role and tried to please him by participating in "kinky" sex acts which she found distasteful and demeaning. When she became involved in the EFC Program, the Training Techniques increased her sense of personal boundaries, leading to assertive action.

In this extreme situation, it was necessary for the woman to move to another state to get away from her consuming relationship and restart her life. She found the Training Techniques to be a profound source of strength during this difficult period. When she joined a women's support group, she encouraged her peers to use EFC activities, including visualization and journal writing, in their efforts to become more assertive.

EFC ACTION EXERCISE: ASSERTIVE ISSUES IN RELATIONSHIPS

1. In your Emotional Fitness Journal, write about your closest personal relationships in terms of narcissistic/co-dependent dynamics. Are there elements of these roles in your relationship? How strong are these elements? Which role do you tend to take?

2. If you have a tendency to be narcissistically entitled, write about how this impacts on the person with whom you are involved. Are you ready to relinquish some of this imbalance and focus on your partner's needs more often?

3. If you are involved with someone who is demanding and self-absorbed, list three steps you could take to change your relationship to a more equitable one.

4. What perceived risks or fears are keeping you from taking these steps?

Keep in mind that taking reasonable and healthy risks in relationships will build your self-esteem, even if it "rocks the boat" or puts the relationship at risk to some degree.

PERSONAL BOUNDARIES

Being emotionally fit in the area of Assertiveness means that you have firm personal boundaries and are willing to take a stand to protect them. You do not allow yourself to be ignored, insulted, trivialized, demeaned, or degraded. You know how to take reasonable and civilized action to prevent your personal boundaries from being violated. At the same time, you are aware and respectful of the personal boundaries of other people.

Lawrence, a thirty-six-year-old systems analyst, had been married for eight years to Jessica, who was highly controlling and demanding. She belittled Lawrence and gave him lots of "digs" throughout the day, along with constant commands. Friends and relatives were embarrassed to hear Jessica order her husband around and criticize him, and wondered how he could stand this treatment.

In reality, there was another side to the relationship that the couple concealed. Every month or two, Lawrence would go on a drinking binge and vent his rage at his wife with a torrent of verbal abuse. Then he would sleep off the binge and return to being passive, hopeless, and resigned. His personal boundaries were blurred and his sense of healthy entitlement was too weak to assert himself in any productive manner.

Initially, Lawrence entered therapy and became involved in the EFC Program because his wife was alarmed by his drinking and angry outbursts. But it soon became clear that the drinking was the symptom rather than the cause of the problems that plagued their marriage. Underneath the surface of his compliance, Lawrence was filled with rage at his wife and at his mother, who had nagged his father through fifty years of a miserable marriage. Lawrence was also mad at himself for being submissive and feeling a lack of healthy self-esteem.

In his EFC Training, Lawrence focused on Assertiveness. He used his Emotional Fitness Journal to identify and clarify his legitimate entitlements in his marriage. He began to use Fitness Focused Meditation to reduce his stress level, which lessened his urge to drink.

Much to his wife's shock, Lawrence joined a club without asking her and started playing racquetball three times a week as his Exercise for Emotional Fitness. This gave him a sense of taking control of his own time and boosted his self-image as he became more physically fit. Through Fitness Guided Visualization, he imagined scenarios in which he stood up for his reasonable rights with his wife. He also started reading books on assertive communication techniques, which he found useful.

At first, Jessica was disconcerted by Lawrence's attempts at assertion and tried to undermine his efforts. But Lawrence stood his ground and let her know that there had to be changes in their marriage or it would be over.

Gradually, Jessica learned to modulate her tone of voice when she spoke to him and be somewhat less demanding. It was slow going, but Lawrence's own self-esteem steadily gained ground as he demonstrated healthy Assertiveness instead of passive-aggressive behavior. He was motivated to continue to take healthy emotional risks to improve his marriage and encouraged his wife to explore her own unresolved issues.

HEALTHY EMOTIONAL RISKS

Assertive action entails asking for what you want and standing up for what you believe in, even if this means risking rejection, conflict, or change. The risk might require asking your partner for a change of behavior, thereby revealing that you're not totally satisfied in your relationship. It might be telling your employer that you're ready to take on more responsibility at work and you deserve a salary raise. It might involve letting your children know that you simply won't tolerate certain types of behavior, and risking their rebellion.

The risks that you take as you become more Assertive may meet with initial resistance and cause discomfort or anxiety on both sides. Sometimes these "growing pains" are unavoidable and necessary to advance your personal or professional life.

As a psychologist, I have always been intrigued that in Chinese calligraphy, the symbol for "change" combines the symbols for two other words: "danger" and "opportunity." Change inherently has elements of both opportunity for growth and danger of conflict and pain. A preoccupation with the danger side can lead to avoidance and keep you stuck in one place. As you gain Assertiveness, you'll learn to focus on the growth and opportunity aspect of change instead. This perspective will propel you to move ahead with positive expectations. I've seen this happen time and again with people who participate in the EFC Program, and I've experienced it in my own life.

When I was a graduate student, long before I started practicing the EFC Training Techniques, I had a great struggle with feeling entitled to ask for what I wanted. This problem reached its zenith when I was preparing for my doctorate. I was required to assemble a dissertation chairperson and committee who would guide, supervise, and judge my work. This meant asking brilliant, busy scholars, some of whom I did not know very well, to give me their time, attention, and support. With my fragile sense of self-esteem at the time, I anticipated that they would all turn me down.

Ultimately, I acted through my fear and forced myself to approach the finest people I knew of in the Department of Psychology. I ended up having a highly supportive and nurturing committee, which began to bolster my Assertiveness and sense of self in the professional arena.

Nearly twenty-five years later, I faced another milestone challenge when I brought my EFC book proposal to the publishing world. I had been practicing many of the Training Techniques of EFC for nearly a decade and had systematically reshaped areas of my Emotional Template that had been imprinted with expectations of failure. Throughout the process of writing the book proposal, I had been actively using Fitness Guided Visualization and other techniques to create an expectation of success.

Without the EFC Training Techniques, I doubt I would have the courage and conviction to market my book to the publishing world. Once again, as I had done with my dissertation, I was putting my best effort on the line. But this time, I entered the endeavor with an anticipation of success instead of failure.

We all have expectations built into our Emotional Templates that guide our actions. Sometimes, these preconceptions create paralysis or fear when it comes to asking for what we want. We may feel that we'll never get it, so it's safer not to ask.

As you attain a higher level of emotional strength through the EFC Program, you'll be able to move beyond your self-imposed limitations. Feelings Identification and Tolerance will help you identify your discomfort when making certain legitimate demands, yet forge ahead with Assertiveness. Insight will give you information about the source of your struggles with Assertiveness and dissipate their emotional hold. Empathy will help you understand your adversary's point of view in situations that require Assertiveness.

ASSERTIVENESS TRAINING AND EFC

In the 1970s, Assertiveness Training became extremely popular as the human-potential and women's liberation movements gained momentum. As women entered the workforce in greater numbers, many were drawn to Assertiveness Training to learn new ways of handling themselves in the professional world and moving beyond the gender roles they had been taught as "proper" young ladies.

In a sense, Assertiveness Training was a natural progression from the civil rights and liberation movements that transformed our society in the sixties and seventies. These movements ensured equal rights in the eyes of the law and society in general. Assertiveness Training taught people how to implement the civil and human rights that had been won.

Also during the 1970s, influential work on the cognitive aspect of Assertiveness was presented by Albert Ellis, a pioneer and guiding light of the cognitive behavior modification movement. In his 1973 book *Humanistic Psychotherapy: The Rational Emotive Approach*, Ellis listed positive mental health goals as including such traits as: 1) self-interest, 2) self-direction, 3) tolerance, 4) acceptance of uncertainty, 5) flexibility, 6) scientific (rational) thinking, 7) commitment, 8) risk taking, and 9) self-acceptance. In essence, these goals relate to a healthy sense of entitlement, self-esteem, and Assertiveness.

Ellis established the idea that taking care of yourself and your own needs without becoming overly narcissistic was a legitimate therapeutic goal. Ellis's School of Rational Emotive Therapy emphasized the cognitive and behavioral aspect of Assertiveness: changing limiting thoughts so that you can change your behavior.

From the EFC standpoint, Assertiveness is fundamentally an emotional skill. Before you can assert yourself appropriately, you need a healthy sense of entitlement on the emotional level. You need to understand how your upbringing and experiences have shaped your expectations and Assertiveness style. You require a firm and realistic comprehension of your reasonable rights and legitimate needs. Then you need a sufficient core of self-esteem to believe that you are fully deserving of having these needs met.

For example, if you are a working woman you might already know that under the Equal Pay Act, a Federal law, you are entitled to the equal pay for doing the same work as a male colleague. But unless you consider yourself a valuable employee, you might not have the confidence to ask for a salary increase. Similarly, if you experience inequities in a close relationship, you need to feel emotionally secure before you take the risk of pursuing change.

The EFC Training Techniques focus on the emotional strength that is the prerequisite for true Assertiveness. Through EFC Training, you will do much more than learn the technical skills of assertive behavior and communication. You will build your Assertiveness on a solid foundation of Emotional Fitness.

ASSERTIVENESS AND FITNESS FOCUSED MEDITATION

Initially it may appear that meditation and Assertiveness are antithetical. Quiet meditation involves "letting go" or a passive stance, while Assertiveness requires direct action. Yet under the surface, meditation is indeed an assertive activity.

Taking time out to sit down and meditate on a regular basis is in itself an assertive act. By setting aside this time for yourself, you are paying attention to your needs and exhibiting a healthy sense of entitlement. You are making a statement that despite the demands on your time, you can set firm personal boundaries and make a worthwhile investment in yourself.

Another aspect of Fitness Focused Meditation that fortifies Assertiveness is the use of specific affirmations, or positive goal statements. Your affirmations specifically state what you want for yourself and believe you deserve. The intensified suggestibility afforded by the meditation process allows these affirmative statements to become internalized. You will begin to exhibit more Assertiveness in action once you have firmly established belief in your self-worth and legitimate needs.

An additional bonus of meditating is that it helps you take control of your anger instead of letting it spill over into aggressive behavior or remain stifled and repressed. When you are in a situation that requires Assertiveness, you can utilize the rhythmic deep breathing you practice in meditation as an anger- or anxiety-management technique. This can serve to safeguard your physical as well as your emotional health.

Research has indicated that the healthiest response to anger is appropriate Assertiveness, rather than aggression or suppression. The Western Collaborative Group Study followed over three thousand men ages thirty-nine to fifty-nine to gather information on the role of personality in heart disease. This study found that the competitive, impatient "Type A" personalities who were more prone to heart attacks frequently overexpressed their anger.

At the other end of the spectrum, studies have shown that patients who developed rheumatoid arthritis, fatigue, and depression often had a marked inability to access or express anger. Clearly, the best path is balanced Assertiveness, which the practice of meditation and other EFC Training Techniques can help you to achieve.

FITNESS GUIDED VISUALIZATION AND ASSERTIVENESS

Fitness Guided Visualization allows you to work on specific goals in the area of Assertiveness. It provides a safe venue for rehearsing assertive actions you want to take with specific people and settings in your life and gather confidence in their expression. Once you have seen yourself acting assertively in your visualizations, you will find it becomes easier to transfer similar responses to your real-life interactions.

Visualizations can be customized to apply to any interaction in which you recognize that you need more Assertiveness, from an intimate relationship to a friendship to work situations. Emily, a thirty-two-year-old legal secretary, used this EFC Training Technique to deal with a common work issue: learning how to say no to unfair demands from a supervisor.

Emily worked for two different lawyers in a corporate law firm and was often overloaded with tasks from both bosses. She routinely worked late, disrupting her family plans and feeling resentful. To rehearse asserting herself in this situation, she created the following Fitness Guided Visualization.

I am typing up a long brief for Michael which has to be finished by the end of the day. I also have a number of letters from him I have to transcribe from dictation. I already feel topped out when Justin comes in with another long document to put into the computer. He tells me he needs it by the end of the day, plops it on my desk, and goes back to his office without even asking me if I can do it.

I feel my anxiety level rising. It moves up from my stomach, a queasy, nervous kind of feeling, and my heart starts beating faster. I promised my son I would go to his T-ball game at 5:30 and I just can't stay late today.

First, I need to cool down. I take off my glasses for a minute and close my eyes. I sit up straight and put my hands on my stomach. I breathe into my stomach, inhaling for a count of eight, exhaling for a count of eight. I do this eight times.

When I stand up, my heartbeat is back to normal and my body feels cooler. I knock briskly on Justin's door and go in, carrying his document. I sit down across from him so I can establish eye contact. I sit tall. I feel strong.

In a calm, pleasant voice, without any hesitation, I explain to Justin that Michael has already given me a number of priorities that will take up the rest of the day. I can put his document on the top of my list for tomorrow, but I can't stay late today because I have something planned with my son. I do not apologize. I know that I am entitled to a personal life.

Because of my tone of voice, my posture, and attitude, Justin accepts this explanation respectfully. I go on to suggest that a solution for avoiding this type of problem in the future might be to hire a junior part-time secretary, since the firm is doing well and we're busier than ever. He says he'll consider my suggestion.

When I return to my desk I feel strong and energized. It's easier to concentrate on the rest of my work now. I feel competent and in control.

ASSERTIVENESS AND THE EMOTIONAL FITNESS JOURNAL

The Emotional Fitness Journal directly accesses and evokes your deepest aims, desires, and feelings. It offers a safe haven for expressing your most truthful self. Through your journaling, you can survey your personal boundaries and clarify your legitimate entitlements. You can write about inequities in your relationships and plan how to remedy them. You can also explore the ways in which your personal mythology and the lessons you have learned from your upbringing may be inhibiting your Assertiveness.

Assertiveness requires strong yet sensitive communication skills. Many people who lack Assertiveness either have difficulty with expressing themselves honestly or tend to express themselves in a harsh, inappropriate manner. Either way, the Emotional Fitness Journal offers a chance continually to strengthen and refine communication abilities.

Assertiveness is about expressing the truth as you see it, in a tactful and Empathic fashion that also considers others' legitimate rights and feelings. Your Emotional Fitness Journal is a place where you can practice this type of healthy expression and hone your Assertiveness skill. You can play with different ways of expressing yourself and gain knowledge about the most productive methods to communicate assertively.

ASSERTIVENESS AND EXERCISE FOR EMOTIONAL FITNESS

Assertiveness demands emotional strength as well as truthful self-expression. Since the mind and body are intricately connected, exercise builds emotional power as it strengthens your physical self.

Since the 1970s, federal law has mandated equal opportunities for female athletes in public schools. In addition to promoting physical fitness, many educators believe that this initiative also encourages emotional growth in girls, particularly in the area of Assertiveness. When females participate in athletics, their competitive spirit is cultivated and their right to be strong and assertive is affirmed. When girls and young women gain a sense of mastery over their bodies, there are important emotional repercussions. Athletics are a powerful antidote to the myths of female weakness and vulnerability that can undermine Assertiveness.

Whether you are female or male, young or old, athletic or sedentary, exercising will amplify you capacity for Assertiveness. First, taking the time out to exercise shows a healthy sense of entitlement. It is a statement that you deserve to expend time and energy to ensure your own well-being.

Exercise is also a tool for achieving a good balance on the Assertiveness spectrum. It can be a healthy outlet for those who have a tendency toward anger and aggressiveness. And it can foster a perception of power in those who tend toward passivity and repression of strong feelings.

Once you commit to an exercise program, you will begin to build your physical strength and sense of presence in the world. You'll gain conviction in your ability to persevere through challenges. You'll experience a sense of accomplishment and mastery that builds your self-esteem, which is both a source and an outcome of Assertiveness. All these empowering qualities of exercise will put you in a stronger position to demonstrate Assertiveness in the key areas of your life.

EFC ACTION EXERCISE IN SETTING YOUR ASSERTIVENESS GOALS

1. List your three most important emotional needs. Briefly discuss how these needs are or are not met by the people who are important in your life.
2. Write down ways in which being more assertive might result in having your emotional needs met more often.
3. Write down three major goals related to your career or other endeavors.
4. How could developing Assertiveness help you to achieve these goals?

Assertiveness empowers you to take action and healthy risks to achieve your goals. It is instrumental in achieving satisfaction in love and work.

---

seven

Starting Your Emotional Fitness
Conditioning Program

E MOTIONAL FITNESS CONDITIONING IS AN ACTION-
ORIENTED SYSTEM OF BUILDING BOTH AWARENESS
and strength in the emotional realm. Understanding the
Core Components and how they affect your inner and outer
lives is only the beginning. The next step is to move beyond
the sphere of intellectual understanding into the proactive
world of EFC training.

This is where you take charge and create substantial
changes in the way you think, feel, and interact. You begin
to reshape areas of your Emotional Template, leave behind
negative aspects of your personal mythology, and break
through limitations. You progressively expand your Emotional Fitness through systematic practice of the Training
Techniques.

The EFC Program provides a structure for practicing
the Training Techniques and fortifying the Core Components of Emotional Fitness. It is a comprehensive workout
plan for your emotional self, with a number of positive side
effects for your physical body.

Like any worthwhile endeavor, building Emotional Fitness requires a certain amount of time and consistent effort.
However, the Program is designed to fit into a versatile,
busy lifestyle without being overly arduous. It requires a

total of approximately three to four hours per week, including physical exercise. This represents a very moderate investment of time for a potentially rich reward.

READY, SET, START

The initial plan is for a Pre-Program Week followed by the four months of the EFC Program. Begin by setting a firm date to start. If possible, schedule your starting date during a period when you don't have any unusual disruptions or distractions. But don't wait until you're completely free of stress and responsibility, since this time may never arrive.

Once you have set a date, write it down in bold print on your calendar, in your date book, and in your Emotional Fitness Journal. You might want to draw up a contract with yourself, making a commitment to start the EFC Program on a certain date and to practice the Training Techniques consistently. Consider your starting date to be a firm engagement and responsibility. Treat it with the same attention that you would any important appointment and try not to postpone your commitment unless extreme circumstances intervene.

EFC ACTION EXERCISE: YOUR ATTITUDE TOWARD CHANGE

If you find yourself postponing your starting date for the EFC Program, you need to look at your attitude about change and toward yourself. Ask yourself these questions:

1. How do I really feel about exploring my emotional life?
2. Does it make me uncomfortable to think about change?
3. Do I believe that it's best to "let sleeping dogs lie" when it comes to emotional issues?

4. Am I worried about how the EFC Program might affect my relationships?
5. Am I afraid that I'll find out information about my emotional self and/or my family of origin that is too painful?
6. Do I really believe the EFC Program will work for me?

Thinking about or writing your responses to these questions may allow you to identify and work through any resistance. Or, your answers may reveal that you could benefit from supportive psychotherapy during the EFC Program. There may be aspects of your past or your current emotional state that are too painful or complicated to handle on your own. Try to assess if seeing a therapist would make the EFC Program seem more manageable to you.

Several of the Core Components may be involved in your struggle to start the Program. Feelings Identification and Tolerance is paramount to this process. Very often, we avoid certain tasks or steps because we perceive them as being uncomfortable, difficult, painful, or anxiety producing. Procrastination arouses more discomfort, and anxiety mounts. Frequently, this fear is largely without basis in reality. The task itself is not as difficult as the anxiety produced by anticipation.

Take a minute to think about your FIT skills and your attitude toward starting the EFC Program. Perhaps you can write a few paragraphs on this topic in your Emotional Fitness Journal. Is it the thought of the Training Techniques themselves and the time involved in practicing them that arouses resistance to starting? Or is it the idea of confronting emotional issues in your life, exploring your Emotional Template, and perhaps changing the balance of power in some of your relationships?

Once you have identified the feelings that the EFC Program arouses, the second element of FIT comes into play: Tolerance of Feelings. In order to get started you might need to affirm that you have mixed feelings about EFC, but you're determined to tolerate your discomfort and move ahead. Even if the idea of starting the Program makes you feel somewhat nervous, uncomfortable, or overwhelmed, you can gather your emotional courage to withstand those feelings and begin the Program anyway. By taking this action to begin training, you begin the process of boosting your FIT capacity through the activation of the Fitness Reinforcement Loop.

Another Core Component that is involved in starting and staying with the EFC Program is Assertiveness. By setting aside the time required for the Training Techniques, you are asserting your reasonable rights. By taking a stance that Emotional Fitness is a worthwhile endeavor, you are demonstrating awareness of your legitimate needs and taking action toward fulfilling those needs.

If you find yourself procrastinating about starting the Program or protesting that you don't have the time, you need to look at your Assertiveness issues. Wouldn't you encourage someone you love to take time out for healthy, fulfilling activities? If the program were necessary for the wellbeing of someone in your family, wouldn't you find the time for it? Are you begrudging time for yourself that you would easily spend on someone else?

If you find it impossible to begin or keep up with the Training Techniques because of other people's demands, you may need to demonstrate more healthy Assertiveness regarding your schedule. It may be necessary to set limits either with your employer or your family regarding your time. With an added degree of Assertiveness, you should be able to carve out three to four hours a week for an endeavor that can profoundly change your life for the better. And it will improve the lives of those around you as well.

In case the Program sounds like a chore or another pressure, be aware that the Training Techniques are inherently gentle and gratifying. They can even be called fun and pleasurable much of the time. Their repetitive, rhythmic nature nourishes and soothes your mind and body. Once you get into the flow and rhythm of the Training Techniques, you'll find yourself looking forward to your practice time.

As you become more proficient at the Training Techniques, the Fitness Reinforcement Loop will take effect. You'll be encouraged by the upswing in your level of Emotional Fitness and a surge of strength and awareness. You'll become more assertive about your legitimate right to spend this time on your self-development. You'll be motivated to continue by the pleasure of the practices and the results you manifest.

TIME IS ON YOUR SIDE

When I recommend the Training Techniques to clients, the initial response is often, "But, Dr. Bergman, I'll never find time." While I acknowledge that many people have hectic schedules and juggle a great many responsibilities, I simply will not accept the "time excuse." With careful planning and commitment, it is possible to fit the Program into virtually any lifestyle.

Whether you are very busy or not, I suggest that you sit down during the Pre-Program Week to plan exactly how and when you will fit the Training Techniques into your schedule. For the first few weeks of the Program, it may help to write down in your date book the hour for EFC activities for each day. These "EFC Appointments" will give you a definite plan for training, so that you don't find yourself procrastinating or putting every other responsibility first.

Here are some suggestions for finding time in your busy schedule for the EFC Training Techniques:

—*Wake up twenty minutes earlier than usual so that you can start the day with a meditation session. The enhanced mental clarity and concentration you gain from meditation will more than compensate for a little less sleep.*
—*On alternate days, when you are practicing visual-*

ization instead of meditation, set your alarm twenty minutes earlier to practice Fitness Guided Visualization. This will reduce stress, help you cope with your responsibilities and stresses, and set a positive tone for the rest of your day.

—*You may want to get up forty minutes or an hour earlier than usual to fit in an Exercise for Emotional Fitness session after meditation or visualization. This will increase your energy level and you'll feel less fatigued throughout the day even if you're getting a little less sleep.*

—*Some people find it rejuvenating to practice one of the EFC Training Techniques at lunchtime or midday. This is a terrific way to recharge and avoid "midafternoon slump."*

—*A favorite time for the Training Techniques is after work, but before dinner. An exercise session, followed by meditation or visualization, can clear out the tension of the workday and set a new mood for your evening. This may also be a good time to write in your Emotional Fitness Journal.*

—*Journal writing can be done anytime, including right before bed. You might want to carry a diarysized journal with you and write when you're commuting on a bus or a train, or waiting for an appointment.*

—*If you're extremely pressed for time, consider giving up your daily newspaper or nightly news broadcast for the first few months of the EFC Program, so that you can spend that time on a training session instead. This can be an opportunity for you to focus inward instead of being distracted by the problems and tragedies of the outside world. If this sounds selfish, remember that you can do much more good for the world through Empathy than you can by passively absorbing an endless litany of news, particularly of the tabloid variety.*

> —*Identify other nonessential ways in which you spend your time. These might include watching TV, talking on the phone, or shopping. This is not to say that you should give up your entertainments and worldly pleasures, by any means. It is simply to suggest that you might squeeze twenty minutes here and there out of your day to direct toward EFC Training, which will ultimately give you more satisfaction than many other activities.*

Parents of young children often face the greatest time crunches. Whenever possible, practice your Training Techniques while your child is napping, playing with friends or siblings, or at a class or outside activity.

Another idea is to set your child up with a worthwhile video, a coloring project, or a game, and make it clear that you need a little bit of time to yourself while she has fun on her own. There's no need to feel guilty about asserting your right to devote some time to yourself occasionally. This can be an opportunity for your child to see an example of healthy Assertiveness and learn to react with Empathy. Remember, an emotionally fit parent is more likely to raise emotionally fit children.

If possible, use your Assertiveness to ask your spouse to take care of the children for the short period that the EFC Training Techniques require. In an empathic manner, explain that you know he is busy and works hard, too, but you would really appreciate this chance to do something that is very important to you. In addition, the time that you devote to EFC Training will ultimately make you less anxious, more patient and loving, and benefit the whole family.

A WORD OF CAUTION

To reiterate the important precautions stated earlier: *It is strongly advised that if any of the following conditions apply, you should undertake Emotional Fitness Conditioning only under the supervision of a mental health professional or physician. These conditions include but are not limited to:*

> —*Severe depression; suicidal thoughts*
> —*Serious or chronic physical illness*
> —*Taking medication for emotional problems*
> —*Patterns of severe physical, mental, or sexual abuse*
> —*A diagnosis of obsessive-compulsive disorder*
> —*Severe anxiety/panic disorder*
> —*Any diagnosed major mental illness, such as schizophrenia or bipolar affective disorder (manic-depression)*
> —*Drug or alcohol addiction or extreme behavioral addiction, such as sex addiction*
> —*Eating disorders such as anorexia or bulimia*
> —*Post-traumatic stress disorder.*

If you have any of these conditions, the Training Techniques can still be extremely useful as an adjunct to professional therapy and care. You should not be discouraged from participating in the EFC Program. Many of my clients have used EFC Training Techniques in conjunction with psychotherapy and/or psychoactive medications and have shown remarkable progress.

However, if you have any of the above conditions or other unusual circumstances, it is crucial to consult with the appropriate physician or therapist prior to beginning the program. You should also continue to consult with your doctor periodically throughout the course of your EFC Program. The EFC Program is not and should never be considered a substitute for appropriate medication for physical or mental illness, nor is it a substitute for ongoing therapy when needed.

USING THE EFC PROGRAM WITH A SUPPORT SYSTEM

If you are in psychotherapy but none of the cautionary conditions apply, it's usually helpful to let your therapist know about the EFC Program. You may want to have your therapist assist you in identifying issues and goals for the Program. You may decide to show your therapist sections of your Emotional Fitness Journal, or discuss your Fitness Guided Visualizations. I often encourage clients to talk about their EFC journals and visualizations, just as they would discuss their dreams in traditional analysis.

The EFC Program can help you gain optimal value from your therapy and accelerate your advances. And the Training Techniques can be valuable tools for facilitating progress in your chosen course of therapy.

The mental health care professionals with whom you might work on the program include psychiatrists, psychologists, psychotherapists, clinical social workers, and types of licensed counselors. Try to ascertain that the therapist is supportive of the Program and is open to the idea that the Training Techniques can be useful. If you meet with skepticism or negativism, you might let your therapist read the book so that it becomes clear the EFC Program is based on sound psychological principles and clinical experience. If the negative attitude persists, you might want to practice the EFC Program as a separate experience from your therapy sessions.

Outside of mental health care professionals, you can elect to seek support for specific elements of the program, although this is certainly not necessary. The chapters on the Training Techniques will teach you all that you need to know to participate in the Program. But if you have the desire and resources for a support team, there are several options.

Yoga teachers often include meditation in their classes and can also guide you in your Exercise for Emotional Fitness. Be aware, however, that the type of meditation you'll be practicing in yoga classes will differ somewhat from your EFC Fitness Focused Meditations.

Holistic physicians are interested in the emotional aspects of physical health and the connection between mind and body. A holistic doctor might help you direct some of your EFC meditation, visualization, and journaling practices toward healing physical and emotional ailments. Acupuncture can also be a useful adjunct during the EFC Program.

Personal fitness trainers who work at gyms or come to your home for private sessions can be highly motivating in the area of Exercise for Emotional Fitness. Group exercise instructors and aerobics and dance teachers can help you establish and keep up an exercise routine.

You can also supplement your EFC Program with videos, audiotapes, and books. Libraries and bookstores offer a great wealth of books on topics that relate to EFC, such as psychology, human potential, assertiveness, emotional development, meditation, relaxation, visualization, affirmation, positive thinking, the mind/body connection, dietary strategies, and various forms of therapy and exercise. For suggestions, you can refer to the "EFC Resources" list at the end of this book.

As the EFC Program stimulates your appetite for self-development, you might decide to supplement your training with classes, workshops, seminars, and lectures. You might be inspired to further your awareness of psychological topics and techniques, spiritual matters, relationship issues, communication skills, or business development skills. Delving into related topics can broaden your EFC experience and give you a chance to interact with people who share some of your interests.

If you are involved in any type of peer support group, you might find it helpful to discuss the program with your peers, when appropriate. Several EFC Program participants with whom I've worked have elected to introduce members of their women's support groups and recovery groups to the Program.

Friends and family members can also provide a support team for your EFC Program. However, it's best to approach them with care and sensitivity. You might meet with resistance, defensiveness, skepticism, or derision when you initially bring up the Program. There are many diverse reasons for negative reactions. Some people are cynical about the potential that human beings have for self-improvement. Others have a negative attitude toward self-help books in general. Or the person you approach might feel threatened by the idea of exploring emotional issues or the possibility of change.

If you meet with ambivalence but feel that your friend or family member is open-minded, you might suggest that he or she read about Emotional Fitness Conditioning before making a judgment. However, if you meet with stubborn resistance and a highly negative attitude, I recommend that you drop the subject with that individual. Pressuring other people about EFC will only create more defensiveness. It's not your job to manipulate or force other people into either accepting or participating in the EFC Program. Instead, use the energy to empower yourself and let others be convinced by the example of your growth.

If you have a friend or family member who is genuinely enthusiastic about the EFC Program, you might want to invite her or him to start the program at the same time and use the "buddy system." You can support each other, discuss your emotional growth and difficult issues that arise, and encourage each other to keep up with the Training Techniques. You and your buddy can:

· Set up a regular schedule for Exercise for Emotional Fitness.
· Work together on setting the Goals in your Core Components.

- Lead each other through Fitness Guided Visualizations.
- Check in with each other at a certain time each evening to see how you have done with your Training Techniques.
- Encourage each other throughout the Program.

Keep in mind that although using the buddy system or working with a therapist on the EFC Program can provide welcome support, it is not usually necessary. The Program is designed to be self-guiding and an independent effort. The only person you need to rely on is yourself.

THE EFC PROGRAM ON YOUR OWN

In the absence of any of the conditions listed in the "Word of Caution" section, you may opt to begin the EFC Program on your own. The types of issues, situations, and tendencies that you might want to address include the following:

1) An inclination toward having anxious or depressive feelings
2) A tendency to do things impulsively, without thinking them through
3) Procrastination and avoidance
4) Difficulty with anger management; internalizing anger or adult tantrums
5) Tendencies toward using substances, alcohol, food, or inappropriate sexual activity to manage feelings
6) Problems in persisting toward meaningful goals
7) Difficulty talking about feelings
8) Difficulty delaying gratification or present pleasures in order to achieve future gains
9) Tendency to be overly critical of others
10) Impatience, intolerance, and being judgmental

11) Not well liked by others; seen as harsh and self-righteous
12) Interpersonal problems, especially in the areas of closeness and intimacy
13) Overly self-absorbed
14) Job and/or career frustration
15) Not living up to your potential
16) Confusion about one's motivations
17) Stubborn, emotionally closed
18) Blaming others for problems
19) Marital, family, and parenting difficulties
20) Difficulty making or keeping friends
21) Health problems caused primarily by lifestyle
22) Confusion about reasonable needs and interpersonal entitlement
23) Characteristically subjugate needs in relationships
24) Often insensitive to other people's needs and feelings
25) Chronic self-esteem problems
26) Afraid to take emotional risks in order to grow
27) Relationship dissatisfaction
28) Inappropriately aggressive; bossy and demanding
29) Lack of interest in underlying reasons for thoughts, feelings, and behavior
30) Contempt for and denial of the importance of the world of emotions in your life

As you're reviewing this list, keep in mind that is not all-inclusive. EFC has been shown to address a very broad range of inevitable human problems and realities. In addition, EFC is not a symptom-oriented program; it is about wellness. Even if you do not relate to any of the issues listed above, EFC will make your life's journey more meaningful and satisfying. The EFC Program is beneficial wherever you begin on the spectrum of Emotional Fitness.

THE PRE-PROGRAM WEEK

Once you set your starting date, you may want to discuss the Program with your family and friends, to let them know what you will be striving to achieve. You may want to show this book to selected people in your life to allow them to understand what will be involved in your EFC Program. On the other hand, you may prefer to keep your EFC Training a private effort. It's your personal decision how and with whom you share it.

The Pre-Program Week is also the time to let your therapist learn about the EFC Program, if you have decided to do so. You can work with your therapist on goal setting and discuss any anxiety or uncertainty that the Program may arouse.

On the physical side, it is recommended that you go for a medical examination during the Pre-Program Week. The reason for this precaution is to determine if there are any physical conditions that might affect your ability to participate in Exercise for Emotional Fitness. Discuss with your physician what type of exercise you plan to do, the frequency, duration, and intensity. Your physician should be able to alert you to any medical restrictions or conditions that would affect your exercise choices.

Once you have checked in with your physician, you can select your Exercise for Emotional Fitness activities and set yourself up to start. This may entail joining an exercise class, getting new sneakers or workout clothes, or obtaining exercise equipment. Chapter 11 provides a "menu" of exercise activities that are appropriate for different fitness levels.

Another element of the Pre-Program Week is to begin practicing basic breathing meditation, to become acquainted with the breathing technique and the act of sitting quietly and stilling your thoughts. Practice basic breathing meditation for ten to twenty minutes during the Pre-Program week, at least three times and preferably every morning. Instructions for basic breathing meditation are given in chapter 8.

CHECKLIST FOR THE PRE-PROGRAM WEEK

1. Tell your close friends and family about the EFC Program, if you wish to do so.
2. Discuss the EFC Program with your therapist, if you have chosen to do so.
3. Spend some time to define your EFC Goals, either by talking with your therapist or by using the EFC Action Exercises in chapters 3 through 6.
4. Visit your doctor for a physical examination. Discuss your exercise choices with your physician to ascertain that they are appropriate.
5. Select your Exercise for Emotional Fitness activities and make any necessary preparations to start.
6. Practice basic breathing meditation for ten to twenty minutes, three or more times this week.

THE BASIC TRACK

The following four chapters will teach you what you need to know to practice the four Training Techniques of EFC: Fitness Focused Meditation, Fitness Guided Visualization, the Emotional Fitness Journal, and Physical Exercise for Emotional Fitness. The Basic Track provides a simple schedule for consistently engaging in each of these practices.

You are certainly not required to follow this schedule exactly. However, especially for the first few months, it is recommended that you stick with a plan and a structure. If you allow yourself too much leeway, you may find yourself missing too many sessions. And if you don't practice the techniques often enough, you won't see substantial progress and the Fitness Reinforcement Loop will be less likely to take effect.

Remember, you can't tone your muscles by looking at a gym or thinking about exercise. You have to put in the work to see the progress. As with practically any endeavor in life, consistent effort is required for achievement. You cannot attain Emotional Fitness by osmosis or even by reading this book. You have to add action to knowledge to manifest results. So try your best to stick with the Basic Track Schedule for the first four months. And if you want to practice the techniques more often or for longer periods of time, more Emotional Fitness power to you!

It's entirely your choice how you prefer to space out and structure your EFC activities, provided you do them each at least three times a week. You might want to do Fitness Guided Visualization directly after meditation, a combination that works well. Or you can alternate, practicing visualization one day and meditation the next. You can write in your EFC Journal any day or evening of the week. Exercise for Emotional Fitness can be done every other day, or more often.

For the first few weeks at least, it's a good idea to write down in your date book or on your calendar what activities you'll be doing on specific days. Do your best to keep these EFC "appointments" and make them a priority. Remember, devoting only twenty or forty minutes to your emotional health can make a tremendous difference as the effects accumulate.

During the first two months of the EFC Program, you'll be giving equal attention to all four of the Core Components, even if your Self-Assessments indicate that you're already stronger in certain areas. The reason for this approach is that all the Core Components work together to create and sustain Emotional Fitness. The first two months of the Basic Track will give you a solid foundation for the Customized

Track, during which you will shift your emphasis to selected Core Components.

EMOTIONAL FITNESS CONDITIONING PROGRESS CHART

You may find it helpful to make copies of this chart and use it each week of the EFC Program to keep track of your progress.

Mark an "X" or "check" for each EFC activity performed on each day. Strive for at least three marks per week per activity.

Week of: _____

M   T   W   Th   F   Sa   Su

Fitness Focused Meditation

Fitness Guided Visualization

Emotional Fitness Journal

Exercise for Emotional Fitness

Schedule for the First Two Months of the EFC Program: The Basic Track

FITNESS FOCUSED MEDITATION

Practice three times a week, ten to twenty minutes per session.

During the Pre-Program Week, practice basic breathing meditation without affirmations.

During the first eight weeks of the Program, repeat affirmations regarding one of the four Core Components of Emotional Fitness before and after the meditation session.

WEEK	CORE COMPONENT FOR FOCUS OF MEDITATION/ AFFIRMATIONS
Week 1:	Feelings Identification and Tolerance
Week 2:	Empathy
Week 3:	Insight
Week 4:	Assertiveness
Week 5:	Feelings Identification and Tolerance
Week 6:	Empathy
Week 7:	Insight
Week 8:	Assertiveness

After the first eight weeks, you have the option to repeat the Basic Track schedule or go on to the Customized Track schedule, as explained in the next section.

Fitness Guided Visualization

Practice three times a week, twenty minutes per session.

During the first eight weeks, the visualization scripts provided will concentrate on one of the Core Components each week, progressing through all four and then repeating the pattern.

WEEK	CORE COMPONENT FOR CONCENTRATION OF VISUALIZATIONS
Week 1:	Feelings Identification and Tolerance
Week 2:	Empathy
Week 3:	Insight
Week 4:	Assertiveness
Week 5:	Feelings Identification and Tolerance
Week 6:	Empathy
Week 7:	Insight
Week 8:	Assertiveness

After the first eight weeks, you have the option to repeat the Basic Track or move on to the Customized Track schedule.

EMOTIONAL FITNESS JOURNAL

Write in your journal three times a week, for fifteen to twenty minutes each session.

During the first eight weeks, it is recommended that you emphasize one of each of the four Core Components each week in your journal writing. However, if you find this too limiting and prefer to write in a "stream of consciousness" or free-flow style, follow your instincts.

WEEK	CORE COMPONENT FOR EMPHASIS OF JOURNAL WRITING
Week 1:	Feelings Identification and Tolerance
Week 2:	Empathy
Week 3:	Insight
Week 4:	Assertiveness
Week 5:	Feelings Identification and Tolerance
Week 6:	Empathy
Week 7:	Insight
Week 8:	Assertiveness

After the first eight weeks, you have the option to repeat the Basic Track schedule or go on to the Customized Track.

Exercise for Emotional Fitness

In order to experience the emotional benefits of exercise, try to exercise at least three times a week, for a minimum of twenty minutes per session. If you have not been physically active, you are likely to notice a difference in your emotional and physical sense of well-being from this duration of exercise. However, you may need to devote more time to working out if you want to noticeably tone and strengthen your body. If possible, gradually increase the duration of your exercise sessions to thirty to forty minutes.

If exercise is new to you, it is likely that you will need to concentrate on coordination and endurance during the first month. During the second month, you may be able to bring affirmations and creative thinking on the Core Components into your exercise sessions. Focus on one Core Component each week, using affirmations from your Fitness Focused Meditation.

Week 1:	Regular exercise
Week 2:	Regular exercise
Week 3:	Regular exercise
Week 4:	Regular exercise
Week 5:	Focus on Feelings Identification and Tolerance
Week 6:	Focus on Empathy
Week 7:	Focus on Insight
Week 8:	Focus on Assertiveness

After the first two months, you can move onto the Customized Track for your Exercise for Emotional Fitness.

THE CUSTOMIZED TRACK

The Customized Track enables you to work on individualized goals and issues and further your progress in selected Core Components. It provides a deeper, more specific, and personalized EFC experience. You can adapt the program to whatever is happening in your life through your choice of Primary and Secondary Core Components and by creating your own meditation affirmations and visualization scripts.

In general, I recommend selecting two of the four Core Components and working on each one for a month. However, if you feel strongly that there is one particular area on which you need to concentrate, you can work on this Core Component for two months consecutively or longer.

There are several ways to select your Core Components

for the Customized Track. If you are in therapy, you may want to talk to your psychotherapist about your areas of emotional strength and those in which you exhibit the most difficulty. For example, you may feel that your Insight is already being honed during therapy and you're innately empathic. However, you may find that Assertiveness is a struggle and you have difficulty tolerating stress. To address these issues, you would select Assertiveness and FIT with a focus on stress tolerance for your Customized Track.

Another way to choose the Core Components for personalized training is by doing your own Self-Assessment. List the four Core Components on a page in your Emotional Fitness Journal. Next to each Component, rate yourself on a scale from 1 to 10, with 1 denoting that you have extreme difficulty in this area and 10 being a position of strength. If you prefer, instead of a numerical scale, you can assess yourself with the words "Extreme Difficulty," "Some Difficulty," "Average," "Somewhat Strong," "Very Strong."

Of course, this should not be viewed as a judgmental exercise. If we're honest with ourselves, virtually everyone on earth has some vulnerabilities in the emotional arena. This evaluation is merely an optional method for identifying emotional areas in which you find yourself less developed so that you can strengthen them through EFC Training. The area with the lowest score is your Primary Core Component for Customized Training; the second lowest is the Secondary Core Component.

Another option is to retake the Basic Self-Assessments that were included in chapter 2. This time you will be using a numerical score to illuminate which Core Components should be selected for your Customized Track.

Answer each item using the following system:

1. Always or usually true/strongly believe
2. Sometimes true/believe somewhat
3. Occasionally or rarely true/believe rarely

4. Occasionally or rarely false/disagree a little
5. Sometimes false/disagree somewhat
6. Always or usually false/disagree completely

Write the number that applies next to each question.

Basic Self-Assessment for Feelings Identification and Tolerance

1. I tend to be guilty of procrastination or avoidance too often.
2. I often find myself reacting strongly to a given situation without really knowing why.
3. I'm generally viewed as someone who is impatient or intolerant.
4. It's usually not good to feel things too intensely.
5. I'm the kind of person who likes to be in control most of the time.
6. Strong feelings usually make me uncomfortable.
7. It's usually better to make decisions with your head, not your heart.
8. The axiom "Persistence pays" is often a strategy for failure.
9. It's usually safer to keep feelings in check and toned down.
10. I've been known to have a problem with my temper.

Basic Self-Assessment for Empathy

1. If I feel something strongly, and believe it deeply, it probably means it's true.
2. Given an opportunity, most people would take advantage of you if you let them.
3. I'm not very interested in what makes people tick.
4. A lot of people would like you to feel sorry for them.

5. Emotionally speaking, children are just "mini-adults."
6. Relationships tend to go better when each person works to have his or her own needs met.
7. Talking about my problems with others has rarely done me much good.
8. Listening to other people's troubles is too upsetting.
9. I think my needs are somewhat different from those of most people I know.
10. I envy other's success.

Basic Self-Assessment for Insight

1. My childhood was close to being perfect.
2. My past can't be too important as far as my life goes now.
3. I'm pretty much aware of everything going on in my life.
4. Children are so resilient that they can bounce back from adversity without much long-term impact.
5. I'm nothing like either of my parents.
6. Heredity is a much stronger influence on you than environment.
7. What happens to you in your life is largely a matter of luck, either bad or good.
8. If I'm not aware of something about myself, it can't be affecting me very much.
9. I really don't believe I have too many personal flaws.
10. My personality now is nothing like it was when I was a child.

Basic Self-Assessment for Assertiveness

1. If I'm angry, I'll usually keep my mouth shut.
2. I often find myself unsure of what my real needs are.
3. In life, it's the aggressive people who tend to get what they want.

4. My belief is that speaking your mind will get you in trouble.
5. Going out on a limb for what you believe in will unnecessarily complicate your life.
6. I view those who are always asking for what they want as pushy and demanding.
7. If getting what I want hurts someone else's feelings, then it's probably not worth it.
8. I'm rarely sure that I'm right.
9. It's hard for me to trust my feelings because they are always changing.
10. In relationships, whoever has the power makes the rules.

Add up your scores for each of the four Basic Self-Assessments. Lower scores, or more "True" answers, indicate greater difficulty in this particular Core Component. Higher scores, or more "False" answers indicate that you already have greater strength in this area. The area with the lowest score will be your Primary Core Component; the area with the second lowest score will be your Secondary Core Component for the Customized Track.

SCHEDULE FOR CUSTOMIZED TRACK

Fitness Focused Meditation

Three times a week, 10–20 minutes per session
Weeks 9–12: Focus on Primary Core Component
Weeks 13–16: Repeat focus on Primary Core Component or move on to the Secondary Core Component.

Fitness Guided Visualization

Three times a week, 15–20 minutes per session
Weeks 9–12: Focus on Primary Core Component with your customized visualizations.

Weeks 13–16: Repeat focus on Primary Core Component or move on to the Secondary Core Component.

The Emotional Fitness Journal

Write three times a week, 15–20 minutes per session
Weeks 9–12: Focus on Primary Core Component
Weeks 13–16: Repeat focus on Primary Core Component or move on to the Secondary Core Component.

Exercise for Emotional Fitness

Exercise at least three times a week, for a minimum of 20 minutes per session
Weeks 9–12: Select activities that are conducive to building the Primary Core Component and direct your thoughts to this Core Component during activity, if possible.
Weeks 13–16: Continue with the Primary Core Component or move on to the Secondary Core Component for your activity choice and mental focus.

THE EFC GOAL-SETTING PROCESS

In addition to using the Training Techniques to elevate your overall Emotional Fitness, the EFC Program involves setting specific goals within each Core Component. These goals personalize the training and address particular issues in your life.

For example, a reasonable goal for FIT might be to overcome a pattern of procrastination regarding an important task, such as studying or exercising, that you perceive as being potentially unpleasant, frustrating, or boring. A meaningful goal for Empathy might be to pay more attention to seeing areas of conflict from your spouse's point of view. An Insight goal might involve understanding the connection between your relationship with your father and a frustrating pattern in your adult relationships. For Assertiveness, an attainable goal might be to assert yourself with a dominating or narcissistic person in your life.

Other possible EFC Goals include:

Feelings Identification and Tolerance

1. To manage anger more appropriately and productively.
2. To function through feelings of anxiety in a particular situation.
3. To cope with stress without lasting physical or emotional impact.
4. To overcome feelings of inadequacy and low self-esteem.

Empathy

1. To become more sensitive to your partner's feelings and needs, especially when they differ from yours.
2. To improve understanding in a difficult parent-child situation.
3. To deal more empathically with an aging parent or relative.
4. To treat colleagues and subordinates at work with greater Empathy, even when they don't measure up to your standards.

Insight

1. To understand how your Emotional Template might set the stage for dysfunctional or frustrating relationships.
2. To clarify how your family or origin affects your anxiety level and issues of control.
3. To understand how your personal mythology is inhibiting growth in your current life.
4. To understand how your upbringing affects your style of anger expression/repression.

Assertiveness

1. To enhance your self-esteem, paving the way for more Assertiveness in a co-dependent situation.
2. To deal with an oppositional or aggressive person with appropriate Assertiveness.
3. To show loving Assertiveness in intimate relationships.
4. To moderate an overly aggressive or abrasive style into a empathic yet assertive manner.

Although these goals are stated in broad terms, when you set your own EFC Goals, try to be quite specific. Here are some examples of personalized EFC goals:

"Control my anger when the kids are bickering."

"Put my anxiety about work deadlines into perspective and learn practical ways to manage my career stress."

"Show my mother more Empathy even though she can be so stubborn about resisting change."

"Try to talk with Joe when he is rested instead of pouncing on him when he comes home from work. Remember to really listen to him even when things are hectic."

"Understand why I am attracted to narcissistic men in love relationships; how this relates to my parents' marriage."

"Learn why I have this fear that I can't compete on a fast track in business and how my personal mythology is holding me back."

"Be firm with the kids about needing a little bit of time for myself. Be more assertive with my husband about taking over with them so I can have a break."

"Let my wife know that I will not tolerate being spoken in that shrill, demanding way. Help her to

*become more aware of her tone of voice and learn
to speak to me in a way that doesn't make me mad."*

During the Pre-Program Week, sit down with your Emotional Fitness Journal and create a written list of goals for yourself in each of the Core Components. You can do this by speaking with your therapist, or by working on your own.

The EFC Action Exercises in Goal Setting in chapters 3 through 6 can be a useful guide. You can reexamine your answers to these questions and distill them into concise goals.

Start with one to three goals for each of the Core Components, listed in order of priority. When you are crafting your affirmations and visualizations, you can look to these goals for direction.

How long you work on each goal will vary. The guideline is to work with the specific goal for at least a month, then assess your progress. You may decide to stay with it for another month or two or to shift your focus to another goal. Move on to another goal when you have seen some progress, even if you have not necessarily achieved the first goal 100 percent.

For example, perhaps your goal is to develop your Feelings Identification and Tolerance Skills so that you don't overreact to criticism. You want to be able to accept criticism without it undermining your self-esteem and sapping your energy. After a month of focusing on this goal in your meditation and visualization practices, and writing about it in your journal, you find that you are beginning to be able to tolerate criticism well. Occasionally, however, you still overreact with a flood of self-doubt.

This doesn't mean that you haven't achieved your goal or that you need to stay with that particular EFC goal until you react to criticism with confidence every single time. Very few emotions or reactions in life are absolute, and we all ebb and flow in our feelings. If you have noticed an upward trajectory and movement toward your goal, you can consider this an achievement. You can continue to work on this issue or choose to move on to another goal, depending upon your priorities and needs.

SHOW YOURSELF EMPATHY

The path of Emotional Fitness Conditioning does not always go steadily upward; there are often dips and plateaus. There will be times when you find yourself stymied regarding certain goals, or when you make progress and then regress. This is all a part of the natural process of true, lasting self-development. It doesn't happen overnight, and it isn't always obvious or absolute.

It is vital that you be as empathic and loving toward yourself as possible during these ups and downs. Very often changes in the emotional realm are slow and subtle. If you keep practicing the Training Techniques, the desired changes and results will come at a pace you can handle.

Another common occurrence may be that you work at the EFC Program with gusto and commitment initially, then find yourself slacking off in your practice. The simple solution to this problem is to keep doing as much as you can manage. Even if you miss many of your training sessions and are unable to maintain the schedule, continue to practice the Training Techniques whenever you can. Doing something—anything at all—to nurture your Emotional Fitness and generate positive momentum is better than doing nothing.

The schedule set forth in this chapter is optimal, not mandatory. Don't waste energy berating yourself or feeling guilty if you find yourself straying from the agenda. Do what you can and be creative. You can juggle the training sessions around and adapt the schedule however you wish. Keep doing as much as you can, and as the Fitness Reinforcement Loop takes firm hold the practices will become second nature.

CHECKLIST FOR STARTING THE EFC PROGRAM

1. Select a starting date.
2. Plan exactly when and how you will fit the Training Techniques into your schedule.
3. Decide whether you will do the Program on your own or with a therapist or other support person.
4. Discuss the Program with your therapist, support team, and/or any friends or family you choose.
5. Have a medical examination and discuss your exercise choices with your physician.
6. Prepare yourself for your Exercise for Emotional Fitness if necessary by joining classes, buying equipment, etc.
7. Begin practicing Basic Breathing Meditation.
8. Choose a Primary and Secondary Core Component for focusing on during the Customized Track. (If you prefer, you can wait until the eighth week of the Program to make your selection.)
9. Write down one to three specific goals in each of the Core Component areas.
10. Start your EFC Program and congratulate yourself for having the courage and enthusiasm to make this effort!

eight

Fitness Focused Meditation

THE FIRST TRAINING TECHNIQUE OF EMOTIONAL FIT-NESS CONDITIONING IS FITNESS FOCUSED MEDITATION, which brings a personalized EFC approach to the universal practice of meditation. Through Fitness Focused Meditation, you can channel the power of the meditative state toward strengthening the Core Components of Emotional Fitness.

Meditation meets all the requirements of an ideal Training Technique. It is rhythmic and repetitive, the type of activity that instinctively satisfies the human nervous system. It allows you to move beyond the busy "mind talk" of everyday existence into a clear, calm, receptive state. Meditation has a beneficial influence on your body as well as your mind. And it can be practiced by anyone, anywhere, without incurring cost of any kind.

Meditation in itself encourages emotional wellness and spiritual growth. But Fitness Focused Meditation takes this natural outcome a step further, by instilling specific ideas about the Core Components of Emotional Fitness. While this technique requires no special talent and little training, with consistent practice it can have a potent effect. And you don't need any equipment, or special talent to participate: only the willingness to try.

In the past you may have considered meditation too

mystical for your personal predilections, or you may have tried the practice at some point. Whatever your preconceptions and past experience regarding meditation may be, I urge you to be open-minded—quite literally.

There are many types of meditation with a wide range of applications and purposes. Meditation can be used to seek enlightenment, to relax, to enhance mental capacities, to lower blood pressure, or to enhance immune system function. It is a versatile tool that can be used by all types of individuals, from spiritual seekers to skeptics and everyone in between.

FROM THE MOUNTAINTOPS TO THE MEDICAL INSTITUTE

In Eastern civilizations, meditation has been practiced for many thousands of years by followers of diverse religions. Some of the most ancient and well-known forms of meditation include the Zen Buddhist practice of "sitting Zazen" and the Indian Hindu practice of yoga.

The word *yoga* comes from the Sanskrit term which means "union" or joining of the physical, mental, and spiritual elements. It also refers to the uniting of the human being with the Higher Force, God, or cosmic consciousness, which goes by many names. Both a spiritual discipline and the original holistic health system, yoga is concerned with the connection between the mind and body. In almost all the various schools of yoga, meditation is a path to mental/ spiritual growth.

Across the globe and throughout the centuries, various forms of meditation have been employed by the spiritually inclined. Devotees of Judaism, Christianity, and Islam intermingle repetitive prayer and meditation in the pursuit of spiritual knowledge, redemption, and enlightenment. In many of these practices, a certain prayer or phrase from a holy book is repeated to evoke the meditative state.

In Europe and the United States, esoteric groups of spir-

itual seekers and advanced thinkers have practiced meditation during the last two centuries. But these practitioners
were generally considered to be outside the mainstream, as
science and conventional medicine dominated Western
thought. Meditation was familiar only to a small percentage
of the population until Transcendental Meditation (TM) was
introduced by the Indian guru Maharishi Mahesh Yogi in
the 1960s.

With a little help from high-profile friends such as the
Beatles and other sixties celebrities, the Maharishi and TM
took the counterculture by storm and meditation began to
be practiced *en masse*. Transcendental Meditation, which is
derived from an Indian Vedic tradition, involves sitting for
twenty minutes twice a day with eyes closed, concentrating
on a "mantra" or specific sound or word.

Much of the scientific research involving the effects of
meditation over the last three decades has involved TM
practitioners. A study at the Meru Research Institute in
Britain scored 147 TM meditators on abilities that usually
decline with age: motor speed, reaction time, creativity, and
visual memory. Given similar backgrounds of age, education, and gender, the individuals who had practiced meditation the longest showed the higher scores in these abilities.
Other research at the same institute found that meditators
scored an average of seven years younger than normal when
they were tested for such age indicators as hearing, visual
acuity, and systolic blood pressure. These studies inspired
some proponents to claim that meditation slows the aging
process itself.

Meditation may also enhance mental capabilities regardless of age. A study at the University of California at
Irvine found that Transcendental Meditation increased the
blood flow to the participants' brains by an average of 65
percent. A University of Washington study found that people who had practiced TM for more than a year had superior
tone perception skills. Other research has indicated that

long-term meditation can decrease mental anxiety, help people withdraw from addictions, and facilitate progress in
psychotherapy.

On the physical side, a study by Dr. David Orme-
Johnson of 2,000 TM meditators found that they were
healthier overall, with 44 percent fewer visits to doctors and
53 percent fewer hospital admissions than nonmeditators.
The collected data showed an 87 percent reduction in heart
disease and nervous system disorders, 55 percent reduction
in tumor occurrences, and 30 percent reduction in infectious
diseases in the meditating group. The researcher attributed
the results to lower blood pressure, lower cholesterol levels,
reduced effects of stress, and less use of alcohol and ciga-
rettes among the regular meditators.

While researchers sought to establish the legitimate
benefits of meditation, the practice still had a somewhat
counterculture "aura" among many factions of the general
population and the scientific community. This began to
change dramatically with the groundbreaking work of Dr.
Herbert Benson, a Harvard Medical School researcher with
impeccable credentials.

Originally trained as a cardiologist, Dr. Benson began
studying the effects of biofeedback and meditation on blood
pressure in the late 1960s. In clinical experiments, he identified dramatic physiological changes during meditation. In
contrast to a simple resting state, meditators consumed 17
percent less oxygen while meditating, and breathing slowed
from fourteen to fifteen breaths per minute to ten to eleven
breaths. The level of lactate, a bloodstream chemical associated with stress and anxiety, dropped precipitously. In addition, brain wave patterns slowed during meditation,
producing more low-frequency alpha, theta, and delta
waves, which are associated with rest and relaxation, instead of the high-frequency beta waves of the normal waking state.

Dr. Benson went to on coin the term "The Relaxation
Response," and publish the landmark book by the same

name. This book presented a simple, secular method of evoking the relaxation response by sitting in a relaxed but alert posture, relaxing the muscles, and repeating a focus word or brief phrase for ten to twenty minutes, once or twice a day.

Unlike TM, which assigns a specific mantra during a training course, Benson's method encourages the practitioner to select a focus word that is in keeping with his or her belief system. A religious person might use a brief repetitive prayer, while others feel more comfortable with a word such as *one* or *peace*.

Regardless of the focus word or phrase that is used, Dr. Benson found that meditation elicits many of the same physiological results: lower resting levels of oxygen consumption, heart rate, breathing rate, and muscle tension; with a shift to a pattern of predominantly slower brain waves.

This relaxation response can also be reached with certain forms of yoga, autogenic training, progressive muscle relaxation, and hypnosis accompanied by suggested deep relaxation. In EFC Training, it is evoked by the practice of Fitness Focused Meditation.

In 1988, Dr. Benson and his colleagues founded the Mind/Body Medical Institute at the New England Deaconess Hospital and the Harvard Medical School, the first major institute to study the effects of meditation, relaxation training, nutrition, exercise, and cognitive therapies on a wide range of medical conditions. Research at this innovative institute has found that stress-management techniques, including meditation, can have impressive results in helping people with high blood pressure (hypertension), stress-related muscle aches, headaches, and insomnia, among other conditions.

Most significantly for the EFC Program, studies have also shown that there is a decrease in anxiety, anger, hostility, and depression among people who meditate or use other relaxation methods on a regular basis. This indicates that the regular meditators are achieving greater Emotional Fitness.

There are specific physiological explanations why meditation has these remarkable effects. Stress sends the body into a fight-or-flight state which includes increases in blood pressure, faster heart and breath rate, more blood flow to muscles, and greater release of adrenaline (epinephrine) and noradrenaline (norepinephrine). Meditation creates many of the opposite effects, thereby exerting a protective mechanism against the physical wear-and-tear of stress.

Interestingly, research by psychophysiologist John Hoffman and his colleagues at the Harvard Medical School found that when people practice meditation or relaxation training, their bodies are less responsive to the stress hormone noradrenaline throughout the day. Apparently, meditation has a protective effect that lasts far beyond the period of practice.

While meditation in the EFC Program emphasizes Emotional Fitness, the potential effects of the practice on physical fitness are certainly a bonus. Meditation is one of nature's remedies, a tonic for your mind with positive "side effects" for your body.

LITTLE NEED TO WORRY

Very few precautions apply to meditation. The worst that will probably happen is that at first your thoughts will swirl around and you will find it difficult to concentrate on your breathing. If this occurs, don't fight it too hard. Just observe those thoughts floating away and return your attention to your breath.

In rare instances, meditation can arouse feelings of anxiety or anger to various degrees. Silencing the usual round of busy thoughts and tapping into the deeper consciousness can stir up painful feelings, sensations, or memories. If this happens, you may want to write about these feelings in your Emotional Fitness Journal. It is also helpful to do some Exercise for Emotional Fitness after meditation to dispel any vague sense of anxiety or discomfort.

If you experience extreme anxiety, anger, painful memories, or any type of unusual emotional stress when you attempt to meditate, this suggests that you may need psychotherapy as a support system during the EFC Program. There may be issues that you need to discuss with a professional before you can become comfortable with the solitary practice of meditation. If this is the case, discontinue Fitness Focused Meditation until you and your therapist feel that you are ready to try it again. Meanwhile, you can continue to build your Emotional Fitness level with the other three Training Techniques.

Fortunately, extreme reactions during ten-to-twenty-minute meditation sessions are quite rare. A little bit of boredom is probably the most negative response you'll experience, and that will dissipate when you begin to attain a true meditative state. Meditation is generally a soothing, yet pleasantly stimulating, activity.

BASIC BREATHING MEDITATION

During your Pre-Program Week, or even sooner if possible, begin to practice Basic Breathing Meditation at least three times a week. Try to schedule your meditation sessions at least an hour or two after eating any heavy meal, rather than when you are still digesting. It's best if your system is also free of caffeine and alcohol when you begin to meditate.

Meditating when you first wake up is often an optimal time, since your head is not yet buzzing with all the pressures of the real world. Meditating after work but before dinner can be very replenishing and set a pleasant tone for the rest of the evening. Any time of the day that you can fit in a meditation session is fine, with one exception. Try not to wait until so late into the evening when you're tired, or you might doze off instead of enjoying the meditative state.

When you are ready for your first meditation session, pick a quiet time and space where you will be uninterrupted for ten to twenty minutes. This means not answering the phone if possible, turning down the volume on the phone machine, and removing yourself from any sounds of television, radio, or talking.

You may want to play some soft music that has been composed especially for meditation and relaxation. Gentle, dim lighting is preferable to bright light, unless it is natural outdoor light.

Once you are accustomed to the practice, you may be able to emerge instinctively from your meditative state after an appropriate length of time. But in the beginning, it's helpful to use a timer or have a watch or clock within view. Otherwise, you might pop up in three minutes or spend the entire session wondering how long you've been at it.

Select a comfortable seat where you can sit with your spine in a vertical position without any physical strain. For some people this will mean sitting in a chair, while for others sitting cross-legged on a carpet, mat, or pillow is more comfortable.

If you are seated on a chair or sofa, be sure that you are adequately supported but not completely sinking into the cushions. You want to be undistracted by physical discomfort, yet not feel so cushy that you fall asleep. While some yoga classes finish with a lying-down meditation, for the beginning meditator the prone position is too easily associated with bedtime. What you want to achieve is a relaxed yet awake and aware state.

Sit with your hands on your thighs or in your lap. Close your eyes and keep them closed throughout the practice.

Begin to focus your attention on your breathing. Don't force your breathing in any way or even attempt to breathe deeply. Later, as you become more proficient, you may want to practice deep diaphragmatic breathing. But in the beginning, simply breathe naturally and normally. Attempt to follow the flow of your breath in and out of your body.

If you find it is difficult to concentrate only on your breathing, you can silently say "in" and "out" as you follow the movement of your breath. Or you can select your own mantra or focus word to say to yourself on each exhalation. This can be the word *one* or any word that helps you to concentrate and has positive associations.

If you have never attempted to meditate before, you will probably find that your mind and body are somewhat restless during your initial efforts. This is perfectly natural, since you're accustomed to being active. You're probably already terrific at juggling a lot of activities and keeping a multitude of ideas in your head at once. Stillness and complete concentration on the simple act of breathing may be radically new.

When you find yourself becoming distracted by thoughts, sounds, or physical restlessness, gently shift your focus back to your breath. Don't judge or reprimand yourself if your attention wavers. Just persist in calmly directing your thoughts back to your breath. With practice, you will find it easier to quiet your mind, and mediation will become second nature.

Be aware that you are unlikely to become a proficient meditator in the first week of practice. The acclimation process will continue after the Pre-Program Week when you are doing Basic Breathing Meditation, into the EFC Program when you are practicing Fitness Focused Meditation. There is no time frame that works for everyone. Some people find it easy to concentrate within the first few weeks, while for others it takes longer. It doesn't matter how quickly you adapt to the practice, only that you continue to make the effort.

Meditation is a prime example of how the Fitness Reinforcement Loop in EFC Training takes hold. At first, you may find that it's difficult to meditate for even ten minutes. Your mind is racing here and there, your body feels restless, and the meditation session feels endless. But if you gently keep shifting your thoughts back to your breath, you fall into the rhythm. It begins to feel very pleasant, natural, and relaxing. It's a delicious opportunity to let go, like sinking into a warm bath or stretching your tight muscles. Instead of a chore, meditation becomes a treat that you anticipate with pleasure. You will feel inspired to extend your meditation periods to twenty minutes.

Then you will start to recognize the rewards of the Training Technique, which can include a better ability to cope with stress, greater mental clarity, and a sense of inner peace. Your Fitness Focused Meditation creates a fertile ground for cultivating your Core Components. You will notice changes in the way you think, feel, and act as you gain Emotional Fitness.

Keep in mind that you can always return to Basic Breathing Meditation as a Training Tool, even after you have moved on to Fitness Focused Meditation. There may be times when you want to use meditation for relaxation purposes, instead of specifically to develop Emotional Fitness. Never hesitate to slip in a Basic Breathing Meditation at any time during the EFC Program. Going "back to basics" can be relaxing and rejuvenating at the same time.

Instructions for Basic Breathing Meditation

1. Pick a quiet time and space where you will be uninterrupted for ten to twenty minutes. If you wish, play some soft, meditative music. You may want to have a clock or timer nearby to check on the length of your meditation session.
2. Sit in a chair or position on the floor with your spine in a comfortable upright position. Place your hands on your thighs or in your lap. Close your eyes.
3. Focus on the natural flow of your breath in and out of your body. When you find yourself becoming distracted by thoughts, sounds, or physical restlessness, gently return your focus to your breath.

> 4. If you find it difficult to concentrate on your breathing, you can silently say "in" and "out" as you follow the movement of your breath. Or you can select your own simple focus word to say on each exhalation.

FITNESS FOCUSED MEDITATION: THE BASIC TRACK

After the Pre-Program Week, it's time to start Fitness Focused Meditation, which adds a personalized direction to your meditations. Before and after each session of Basic Breathing Meditation, you'll repeat statements regarding the Core Components of Emotional Fitness. These positive phrases, which are also known as affirmations, plant suggestions that the rhythmic act of meditation amplifies.

To affirm means to "make firm," or to assert or declare. Affirmations are concise positive statements that reflect desired reality. These statements do not have to be true already; rather, they can state a goal. For example, you can make the affirmation "I am assertive in my relationships," even if you currently struggle with passive tendencies. By stating the affirmation, you are giving yourself a message that will help you act assertively in the future.

Throughout the day, our minds are buzzing with an internal dialogue. We are constantly expressing our feelings, fears, hopes, goals, and opinions to ourselves. This interior conversation shapes many of our emotions, actions, and reactions.

This inner voice, shaped by our Emotional Template and personal mythology, can influence us to be upbeat or negative, optimistic or gloomy, confident or insecure, willing to take risks or fearful. The mind's monologue can be motivating, stimulating, and encouraging, but it can also foster anxiety, anger, and insecurity. How we talk to ourselves has a tremendous influence on how we perceive ourselves and others, how we are seen, and how we function in the world.

We've all met people who are unusually bold, happy, and confident, even though they don't seem to possess any special gifts or talents. To a large extent, this type of personality stems from an upbeat interior dialogue. These fortunate souls have an encouraging, optimistic voice in their own minds. That inner voice gives them the courage and self-esteem to act with positive force in the outside world.

Affirmations channel the influence of our "mind talk" toward healthy concepts and goals. This practice gradually helps to transform our Emotional Templates, which, in turn, influences the way we feel and act.

In the general practice of affirmations, positive statements can be recited silently, spoken out loud, written down, chanted, or sung. In a sense, many prayers or fervent wishes are akin to affirmations.

In the EFC Program, affirmations are joined with meditation to give them even greater momentum. First, you relax and implant positive suggestions into your mind with affirmations. Then you silence the usual stream of thoughts with Basic Breathing Meditation. Finally, when your mind is clear and refreshed, you state your affirmations again.

Try to repeat your affirmations with a positive attitude, even if they are not yet true in reality. If necessary, suspend your skepticism and allow yourself to believe in the possibility of change. Remember that most action starts as thought. Affirmations allow you to replace limiting or damaging thoughts with fresh ideas that lead to constructive actions.

The following sections offer suggestions for affirmations that you can use to advance your Emotional Fitness. Feel free to modify these phrases to reflect your own personal language style. While you want to retain the essential message, it's important that you feel as if you are speaking from your heart. You may find it helpful to write your affirmations on index cards until they are memorized.

SCHEDULE FOR FITNESS FOCUSED MEDITATION
Practice three times a week, 10–20 minutes per session.

During the Pre-Program Week, practice Basic Breathing Meditation.

During the next eight weeks, begin and end your meditation sessions with Fitness Focused affirmations regarding one of the four Core Components of Emotional Fitness.

Week   Core Component for Focus of Meditation/
         Affirmations

Week 1: Feelings Identification and Tolerance
Week 2: Empathy
Week 3: Insight
Week 4: Assertiveness
Week 5: Feelings Identification and Tolerance
Week 6: Empathy
Week 7: Insight
Week 8: Assertiveness

After the first eight weeks, you have the option to repeat the Basic Track schedule or go on to the Customized Track schedule.

INSTRUCTIONS FOR FITNESS FOCUSED MEDITATION
FOR FEELINGS IDENTIFICATION AND TOLERANCE

Seat yourself comfortably in your meditation position. Begin to concentrate on your breathing. Do the Basic Breathing Meditation for ten breaths.

Recite to yourself silently or out loud:

"I am focusing my emotional energy on being able to tune in to the inner world of my feelings. I want to learn to better identify, experience, and tolerate my feelings, to express them in productive ways. It is safe and healthy to identify and tolerate all my feelings."

After you have repeated these phrases three times, return to the Basic Breathing Meditation for ten to fifteen minutes. At the end of this time, with your eyes still closed, recite three times:

"I am learning to use my emotional energy to tune in to my feelings. I am learning to better identify and tolerate my feelings. I am learning to express my feelings in more useful and healthful ways."

After you have repeated these phrases three times, rise from your meditation gently. Repeat the Meditation for Feelings Identification and Tolerance three times during Week 1 of the EFC program, and again three times during Week 5.

INSTRUCTIONS FOR FITNESS FOCUSED MEDITATION FOR EMPATHY

Seat yourself comfortably in your meditation position. Begin to concentrate on your breathing. Do the Basic Breathing meditation for ten breaths.

Recite to yourself silently or out loud:

"I want to learn to be more understanding of other people's needs and feelings. I want to learn to be a more tolerant, empathic person who is mindful of others."

After you have repeated these phrases three times, return to the Basic Breathing Meditation for ten to fifteen minutes. At the end of this time, with your eyes still closed, recite three times:

"I am learning to be more attuned to others. I am learning to be more understanding of other people's needs and feelings. I am becoming a more tolerant and empathic person."

After you have repeated these phrases three times, rise from your meditation gently. Repeat the Meditation for Empathy three times during Week 2 of the EFC program, and again three times during Week 6.

INSTRUCTIONS FOR FITNESS FOCUSED MEDITATION FOR INSIGHT

Seat yourself comfortably in your meditation position. Begin to focus on your breathing. Do the Basic Breathing meditation for ten breaths.

Recite to yourself silently or out loud:

"I want to learn how better to understand the connections between my life as a child and the life I'm living now. I want to learn about my Emotional Template and my personal mythology. It is safe and healthy to go below the surface and gain Insight."

After you have repeated these phrases three times, return to the Basic Breathing Meditation for ten to fifteen minutes. At the end of this time, with your eyes still closed, recite three times:

"I am learning how better to understand the connections between my life as a child and the life I'm living now. I am learning about my Emotional Template and my personal mythology. I am learning to understand myself in a deeper way."

After you have repeated these phrases three times, rise from your meditation gently. Repeat the Meditation for Insight three times during Week 3 of the EFC program and again three times during Week 7.

INSTRUCTIONS FOR FITNESS FOCUSED MEDITATION FOR ASSERTIVENESS

Seat yourself comfortably in your meditation position. Begin to focus on your breathing. Do the Basic Breathing meditation for ten breaths.

Recite to yourself silently or out loud:

"I want to learn to recognize and assert my legitimate

rights, while still respecting the rights of others. I want to gain the strength to ask for what I want and take emotional risks. It is safe and healthy to act with Assertiveness."

After you have repeated these phrases three times, return to the Basic Breathing Meditation for ten to fifteen minutes. At the end of this time, with your eyes still closed, recite three times:

"I am learning to recognize and assert my legitimate rights, while still respecting the rights of others. I am gaining the strength to ask for what I want and take emotional risks. I am learning to act with greater Assertiveness."

After you have repeated these phrases three times, rise from your meditation gently. Repeat the Meditation for Assertiveness three times during Week 4 of the EFC program and again three times during Week 8.

FITNESS FOCUSED MEDITATION: THE CUSTOMIZED TRACK

After your have completed the Basic Track of the first two months of the EFC Program, you'll arrive at a crossroads where you have a choice of which way to go. If your Self-Assessments and your self-knowledge indicate similar levels of strength in all four Core Components of Emotional Fitness, you may want to repeat the Basic Track. You can also elect to repeat the Basic Track if you feel it's best to continue to work on all four Core Components because they support one another and/or you want more familiarity with the Basic Program.

The other choice is to shift on to the Customized Track of Training. The Customized Track requires that you select one or two Core Components to emphasize in your training efforts. These are your Primary Core Component and your Secondary Core Components.

During Weeks 9 through 12 of the EFC Program, you will concentrate on the Primary Core Component you choose. During Weeks 13 through 16, you can either continue to work on the Primary Core Component or move on to the Secondary Core Component.

Once you have identified which Core Components you want to highlight, you can opt to use the same affirmations that you used during the first two months of the EFC Program. Or you can tailor your own customized positive statements to deal more directly and specifically with your needs and goals.

CUSTOMIZED AFFIRMATIONS

When you invent your own affirmations, frame the statements in a positive, rather than a negative, way. Affirm what you want, rather than what you do not want, to achieve. For example, you can say, "I want to be more understanding of my wife's need to go to bed earlier than I," instead of "I don't get so annoyed about my wife wanting to go to sleep so early." Or you might say, "I am becoming more capable of being recognized and rewarded in my career," instead of "I don't feel so shy and self-conscious when I meet new people."

Even though you are stating the affirmation in the present tense, it does not have to be a reality yet. Hopefully, however, the statement has a good chance of becoming a reality. Try not to construct affirmations that are extremely unlikely to become true. "I am winning the lottery" is not an affirmation; it's a wish upon a star or a daydream. But you might say, "I am assertive about being recognized and rewarded in my career."

Never create an affirmation that has a negative repercussion for someone else. "I use my Assertiveness to get rid of that man who drives me crazy at work" is not appropriate. You could use the phrase "I assert my legitimate rights with my co-workers, and they treat me with respect." This creates the possibility of resolving problems with other people, without being vindictive.

Try to make your statements fairly short and simple. They can be general or situation-specific. Don't intellectual-ize or rationalize within your affirmation; simply declare what you want to attain. "I am learning to recognize how my parents' marriage, and their co-dependent/narcissistic roles influence the kind of people I'm attracted to and the way I act in relationships" is too wordy and explanatory. A more effective affirmation would be to say "My relationships are becoming healthier as I gain Insight into how my past affects the present."

FITNESS FOCUSED MEDITATION AND THE OTHER EFC TRAINING TECHNIQUES

Throughout the EFC Program, you can accelerate your progress by linking your various training activities to common themes. For example, during the week that you're concentrating on Empathy for your Fitness Focused Meditations, you can explore the same Core Component in your Fitness Guided Visualizations and your Emotional Fitness Journal. You might even carry your Fitness Focused Meditations into your exercise routine.

For instance, Denise is in her third month on the Customized Track, working on Empathy in her Fitness Focused Meditations. Her personalized affirmation for this Core Component is: "I am learning to be more patient and understanding with my mother."

During Fitness Guided Visualization, she imagines a scene in which her mother is worried about Denise's decision to leave a full-time job to become a freelance consultant. Instead of automatically feeling angry and defensive, Denise remembers her EFC Empathy training. She tells her mother that she appreciates her concern and reassures her that everything will work out well. As they hug affectionately, Denise smells the scented powder that her mother has always worn. The scent reminds Denise of being a little girl. But now she feels like the grown-up, wise and comforting. She feels a sense of pride that she can react to her mother's worries with Empathy instead of defensive anger.

Later that week, Denise writes an entry in her Emotional Fitness Journal related to the goal she has set forth in her Fitness Focused Meditations. She starts off with the affirmation, then writes frankly about the conflicts she has around this issue:

> *"I am learning to be more empathic with my mother. I understand that she means well, and I treat her with patience and Empathy."*
>
> *My mother has faith in me, but in such a limited way. She never seems to think that I can do something extraordinary or unusual. She has such limited scope. But I have to remember where she came from. When my mother was young, her parents were caught in the Depression and were out of work for a long time and could barely get by. So of course, she believes in the safe, secure route. It's easier for me to take chances because my dad was a good provider and I never had to worry about security when I was a kid. I have to remember that Mom is not really expressing her lack of faith in me; she's expressing her fear about the world in general. That's it!*
>
> *When I try something new and Mom gets all worried, it feels like she's saying I'm not good enough. That's what gets me so riled up. But her attitude is not really about me or my capabilities. It has to do with her personal mythology, not mine.*
>
> *Of course it's still going to annoy me. But I can talk about it with my friends; they understand. I have a right to express myself. But getting mad at my mother isn't really a constructive way to do that. It just makes me feel guilty, and it doesn't change the way she thinks at all. Being patient with her, showing Empathy, that works better for both of us.*

To complete her EFC focus on Empathy that month, Denise incorporates affirmations into her Exercise for Emotional Fitness sessions. She recites the affirmations to herself while power walking, and then again while she is stretching out and cooling down. She feels energized and confident after her workout, capable of showing her strength through Empathy.

LETTING GO

It may seem like a spiritual paradox to "let go" through meditation, while you are also focusing on a desired result through affirmation. But the two techniques can work hand in hand—as long as you don't try too hard or expect too much too quickly.

State your affirmations with conviction, believe in them, but don't expect the practice to be a magic genie in a bottle. Don't try to force yourself into a state of Emotional Fitness through sheer willpower. Let the process unfold at a natural pace. Look forward to personal growth and change, but don't judge yourself or be disappointed if nothing monumental happens right away. If you keep up the practice, you are soaking up the benefits on a deeper level, regardless of the immediate outward effects.

It's similar to a common pattern in the physical fitness world. Many people join health clubs because they want to lose weight and fit into a smaller size of clothing. But instead of pounds falling off quickly, they get stronger once they start working out. They reshape their bodies in attractive ways, but not in the way they expected. In addition, they may be gaining important health benefits, such as reducing the risk of heart disease.

If they are fixated on the weight-loss/clothing-size goal and it's not happening fast enough, they might quit exercising. However, if they appreciate the changes they are seeing, they will be inspired to continue to work out. Then they might reach an intensity of training where the pounds do, indeed, melt away.

The lesson here is that you can't always manifest quick or precise results with Fitness Focused Meditation or the other Training Techniques. But the Techniques are always working under the surface to clear the site, set the foundation, and build your Emotional Fitness. Sometimes progress is measurable; sometimes it is difficult to define. But whatever you do to nourish your emotional fitness will give you greater resources for an emotionally satisfying life.

CHECKLIST FOR FITNESS FOCUSED MEDITATION

1. Establish a meditation spot that is quiet, private, and comfortable.
2. Practice Basic Breathing Meditation at least three times during the Pre-Program Week, 10–20 minutes per session.
3. Practice Fitness Focused Meditation, three times a week, 10–20 minutes per session, according to this schedule:

Week 1: Feelings Identification and Tolerance
Week 2: Empathy
Week 3: Insight
Week 4: Assertiveness
Week 5: Feelings Identification and Tolerance
Week 6: Empathy
Week 7: Insight
Week 8: Assertiveness

4. During Week 8 of the EFC Program, decide if you want to repeat the Basic Track or move on to the Customized Track. If you are going on the Customized Track, select your Primary and Secondary Core Components and your customized affirmations.
5. During Weeks 9–12 of the EFC Program, practice Fitness Focused Meditation three times a week, 10–20 minutes per session, with affirmations regarding your Primary Core Component. Personalize these affirmations so they apply to your EFC Goals in special ways.

6. During Weeks 13–16 of the EFC Program, practice Fitness Focused Meditation three times a week, 10–20 minutes per session. Craft your own affirmations to focus on either your Primary Core Component, if you need more work in that area, or your secondary Core Component.

7. Throughout the Program, keep your Fitness Focused Meditations in mind as your practice the other Training Techniques.

nine

Fitness Guided Visualization

THE SECOND TRAINING TECHNIQUE OF THE EFC PRO-
GRAM IS FITNESS GUIDED VISUALIZATION, WHICH
allows you to strengthen your Core Components in distinct,
personalized ways. Visualization, which is also called imagery, involves the creation of specific mental images to
achieve a desired goal, response, or outcome. In EFC Training, these images are directed toward encouraging Emotional Fitness and nourishing the Core Components.

Fitness Guided Visualization, like meditation, is a
Training Technique that you can practice at home with only
a little preparation and no expense or equipment. You don't
need any special instruction or spiritual inclination to reap
the benefits of visualization. The practice draws on one of
our most natural, instinctive processes: imagining scenes in
our "mind's eye."

Everyone practices visualization on some level, although
not always productively. We all play imaginary scenes in our
heads, visualize various outcomes for the near and distant
future, picture ourselves interacting with people in any
number of situations.

Productive visualizations are one of the "secrets of success" of achievers in virtually all fields. The marathon runner visualizes herself moving ahead steadily during the race

and dashing across the finish line in a burst of glory. The successful salesman imagines himself warming up a prospective customer, making the pitch, and closing the sale. The account executive visualizes herself delivering the presentation, dazzling the potential client, and being handed the lucrative account.

Visualizations often revolve around relationships and personal issues, as well as achievement-oriented concerns. The teenager in love drifts through classes, picturing every detail of seeing her boyfriend after school. The wife who is mad at her husband imagines confronting him when he gets home and runs through the entire course of their argument before he walks in the door. The college student pictures meeting someone new at a party: what she will look like, smell like, her shape and feel when they dance.

Any scene that is "acted out" in great detail in our minds, with visual effects as well as a verbal script, can be called a spontaneous visualization. Whether the majority of our visualizations are encouraging or anxiety producing depends upon a number of factors: our Emotional Template, our personal mythology, our experience, and our basic disposition.

Take a minute to think about how you might already use visual imagery in your own life. Do you consciously employ it to instill positive expectations and energize your performance? Do your visualizations tend to sabotage your momentum? Do you usually imagine the best possible outcome, the worst, or a mixture, depending on the situation?

Like the mind's interior dialogue, spontaneous visualizations have the potential to give us great faith in ourselves and spur us on to excellence, or to sap our energy and drain our confidence. They have tremendous influence on our Emotional Fitness, as well as our actions in the world at large.

Guided visualization directs this influence toward specific goals. In the formal practice of visualization, a "scenario" is planned beforehand and a certain period of time is set aside to enact the imagery in the mind's eye.

Visualization has long been used for a variety of reasons, from spiritual enlightenment, to healing of physical problems, to attaining specific goals in the material world. In EFC Training, it is used to develop the Core Components as a whole and to work on specific issues and situations related to Emotional Fitness.

Through my own experience and that of many others who have used EFC, I can state with certainty that Fitness Guided Visualization can be a powerful training technique. Its potency stems from two sources: First, the Fitness Guided Visualizations that you create and practice will give you a valuable opportunity to see, hear, feel, and experience yourself responding with greater Emotional Fitness in various situations. Second, the practice makes you aware of how your unplanned, spontaneous visualizations affect your Emotional Fitness. You begin to gain control over your spontaneous visualizations and learn to channel them into more productive visions.

Guided imagery has been shown to be potentially valuable for both mental and physical health. The history of visualization as a therapy tool has some interesting parallels to the clinical study of meditation, to which it is closely allied. Both practices have been utilized by people of diverse world cultures for thousands of years. But only recently have they been adopted by the scientific community and given the additional seal of approval conferred by research.

THE OLDEST "NEW" HEALING ART

Using imagery for physical and mental health is hardly a new practice. Visualization was a mainstay of medical practices in Tibetan, Indian, African, and Native American and Eskimo cultures. Outside of formal medical practice, individuals in civilizations across the globe often used positive thinking, prayer, visualization, and the energy of their imaginations to heal and strengthen themselves and others.

In the contemporary Western medical community, visualization as a practical healing technique came to wider attention in the 1970s, as a facet of the new branch of study called psychoneuroimmunology (PNI). PNI focuses on the connections between the mind or emotions (psycho-), the brain (neuro-), and the immune system (immuno-).

Studies conducted by PNI researchers found that subjects who practice guided visualization were able to significantly increase their numbers of lymphocytes (a type of white blood cell), a finding that has wide implications for immunity. Exciting new developments regarding the role that guided imagery can play in health and healing continue to emerge from research centers.

Dr. Martin Rossman, a clinical associate in the Department of Medicine at the University of California, San Francisco and codirector of the Academy for Guided Imagery in Mill Valley, points out that the effects of imagery on healing are difficult to quantify and well-controlled studies are still rare. However anecdotal and clinical reports have indicated that guided imagery can be useful to help treat conditions that include chronic pain, allergies, asthma, cold and flu symptoms, high blood pressure, autoimmune diseases, and stress-related gastrointestinal, reproductive, and urinary problems.

In the world of psychotherapy, visualization has traditionally been included in several schools of formal therapeutic practice that evolved in Europe. The renowned practitioners who utilized forms of guided imagery included Robert Desoille, who developed the "directed waking dream" technique, Hanscarl Leuner, known for "guided affective imagery," and Carl Jung, who used an "active imagination" technique.

In contemporary therapy, guided fantasy is commonly used as a Gestalt technique, originally developed by Fritz Perls. Arnold Lazarus, a well-known psychologist and behavioral therapist who was awarded a Lifetime Achievement Award by the American Psychological Association, has written extensively about the use of guided imagery in the treatment of emotional problems. As part of a multimodal approach, visualization is sometimes used in the treatment of depression, insomnia, sexual dysfunction, and a variety of phobias and anxieties.

Well-known Canadian psychologist Donald Meichenbaum has suggested that guided imagery is effective for three basic reasons: 1) rehearsing positive images increases feelings of confidence and control, 2) images can create worthwhile shifts in internal self-talk, and 3) coping skills can be enhanced by rehearsing desired outcomes during visualization.

Even beyond the treatment of specific psychological conditions, imagery can be a tool for moving past blocks when therapy becomes "stuck." Imagery can clarify issues, allow repressed feelings to emerge and be expressed, and inspire creative, productive action. If words alone become a dead end, the addition of images can sometimes enable us to get past the barriers and move forward.

HOW VISUALIZATION WORKS

On the level of physical health, PNI researchers have found that various types of imagery can affect a wide range of bodily functions, including heart rate, blood pressure, respiration, brain wave patterns, and gastrointestinal functions. Visualization can also influence levels of various hormones and neurotransmitters. Imagery can directly activate the autonomic nervous system, which regulates bodily functions that are not usually within our conscious control.

You've probably already experienced these types of reactions through spontaneous visualizations. For example, you might start to salivate if you're hot and thirsty and you think about a piece of watermelon. Or you might feel a warm blush of blood flow when you picture your beloved—or expe-

rience a rush of adrenaline and a faster heartbeat if you visualize a large snake crossing your path.

The experiential evidence that guided imagery can be a
powerful force is all around us, but we have only a few clues
as to exactly how or why it works. We do know that imagery
has the potential to tap into right-brain function, which for
most people is visual, concerned with images, sounds, spa-
tial relationships, and emotions. Generally speaking, the
left brain is logical and verbal, while the right brain is sensitive to emotions. The right brain processes information simultaneously and synthesizes various elements, while the
left brain processes the information sequentially, breaking
it down into components.

The right brain is often credited with being more intuitive and emotional, capable of understanding the "larger
picture." Guided visualization, with its sights, sounds, and
feelings, activates this potential of the right brain and can
direct it toward healing and growth. When we add words
and dialogue to the visualization, the left brain is engaged
as well. Through Fitness Guided Visualization, we can go
directly to the source to strengthen our emotional capacities.

THE ELEMENTS OF GUIDED VISUALIZATION

There are certain key elements or qualities that differentiate a guided visualization from a fantasy or a spontaneous visualization. These factors need to be present to
maximize the value of the time you spend in your Fitness
Guided Visualization practice.

Before you begin, clarify and define your purpose for this
particular session. In you're in the first two months of the
EFC Program, working on the Basic Track, this intention
may be simply to strengthen one of your Core Components.
If you're on the Customized Track, the purpose may be more
specific; for example, to exhibit more Assertiveness with a
particular family member, or to build your Feelings Identi-

fication and Tolerance to withstand the pressure of managing multiple projects at work.

The next element of visualization is that it is planned and performed as a separate, deliberate activity. It's fine to enjoy pleasant imaginings when you're trying to fall asleep, or waiting for a friend. But Fitness Guided Visualization is a specific activity, a mind exercise for Emotional Fitness. During the EFC Program, you need to set aside time and make appointments for your visualization practice, so that you are certain to fit in three sessions per week.

Another very important distinction is that guided imagery follows a script which you decide upon beforehand. There's certainly room for improvisation and imagination within the script. But because you state the purpose of the visualization, you should know the general flow and the outcome of the imagery session.

Guided visualization expands upon the practice of affirmation by involving more of your sense memory. When we say there is a "script" for visualization, this does not suggest word-by-word character dialogue. The script or scenario is merely a structure for your creative flow. What you see, feel, and even smell in a visualization can be more impactful than what you hear or say. Try not to get overly involved with words during a visualization session. The visual images and the overall sensory scene can be more evocative.

When you are involved in your visualizations, imagine all the details of surroundings: lighting, smells, feel and texture of objects, any background music or sounds. These details bring the visualization to life and allow it to imprint a deeper impression.

PREPARING YOURSELF FOR FITNESS GUIDED VISUALIZATION

Fitness Guided Visualization is so closely linked to our natural imaginative processes that few precautions apply. However, in unusual instances, a visualization session can arouse anxiety, fear, anger, painful memories, or other uncomfortable feelings.

If you are in therapy, these seemingly adverse reactions can lead to fruitful insights if you discuss them with your therapist. On your own, you can explore any painful emotions, memories, or issues that may arise by writing about them in your Emotional Fitness Journal.

Finally, if any visualizations become too upsetting, you can simply break off the session. Calm yourself by focusing on some relaxed breathing, then get up and move around to release any tension. Guided Visualizations are not hallucinations or dreams that hold you in their thrall. You have control over the visualization and can always turn it off if it becomes too overwhelming or threatening. However, this is quite unlikely to occur, since you will be planning your scenarios to reflect Emotional Fitness and practicing with full waking awareness.

As with meditation, the typical problem that you'll probably encounter during visualization training is an initial difficulty in concentrating. If you find it hard to stay focused, bring additional sensory details into your visualization. If you find your mind wandering, gently guide it back to the imagery scene. Conjure up the specific colors of the setting, the lighting, the shadows. Imagine any smells that are present, any background sounds. These details should engage your mind and help to keep it from wandering.

Don't be dismayed if you're not immediately able to fully concentrate on your imagery scenarios. Like the other Training Techniques, Fitness Guided Visualization can take varying lengths of time to become familiar and comfortable. Just keep to your schedule, keep practicing, and the Fitness Reinforcement Loop will begin to activate. As time progresses, you'll find it easier to concentrate on your visualizations and imbue them with rich detail. You'll find the visualizations have growing relevance to your "real" life and vice versa. And you'll discover the ways in which you visualize yourself acting with greater Emotional Fitness begin to manifest in reality.

As with Fitness Focused Meditation, you don't need any special training, equipment, or talent to start Fitness Guided Visualization: just a commitment to practice on a regular basis. During the Pre-Program Week, write down EFC appointments for your visualization sessions for the first few weeks to keep yourself on schedule.

INSTRUCTIONS FOR FITNESS GUIDED VISUALIZATION

Find a quiet, private place for your visualization sessions. Seat yourself comfortably, but not in a position that encourages sleep. Before each session, read through the suggested scenario that is provided for the Core Component you are working on that week.

These scenarios are outlines or guidelines which you will fill in with your own personal details. You don't need to memorize the scenario; just read one through several times to capture the essence, then begin the visualization when it is fresh in your mind. Later, when you are creating your own scenarios, you can write them down beforehand in your Emotional Fitness Journal.

Some people prefer to record their own Fitness Guided Visualization tapes to guide them through the sessions. This would consist of your own voice, perhaps over the background of some meditative music, reading aloud the scenarios. You should pause between reading the phrases to give yourself ample time to work on the visualization. This pacing can be tricky, especially at the beginning. For most people, simply reading through the scenario a few times is easier and just as effective as recording.

Your Fitness Guided Visualization session should last from fifteen to twenty minutes. For the first few weeks or months, it's helpful to set a timer or have a watch or clock nearby in view. Of course, if you're deep into your visualization and you want to extend the session, feel free to do so.

Close your eyes and focus on your breath. Begin with a few minutes of Basic Breathing Meditation. When you are relaxed, you can begin the visualization. For the Basic Track, you will focus on the four Core Components consecutively for one week each, then repeat this pattern.

**SCHEDULE FOR FITNESS GUIDED VISUALIZATION:
THE BASIC TRACK**

Practice three times a week, 15–20 minutes per session.

Each week, use the visualization scenario that focuses on one of the four Core Components of Emotional Fitness according to the following schedule:

WEEK   CORE COMPONENT FOR FOCUS OF MEDITATION/
AFFIRMATIONS

Week 1: Feelings Identification and Tolerance
Week 2: Empathy
Week 3: Insight
Week 4: Assertiveness
Week 5: Feelings Identification and Tolerance
Week 6: Empathy
Week 7: Insight
Week 8: Assertiveness

After the first eight weeks, you have the option to repeat the Basic Track schedule or go on to the Customized Track schedule.

FITNESS GUIDED VISUALIZATION FOR FEELINGS
IDENTIFICATION AND TOLERANCE

Seat yourself in a meditation posture in a quiet place. Begin with a few minutes of Basic Breathing Meditation. If there are any areas of tension in your body, try to relax them with your breath.

When you are relaxed, deliberately begin to picture yourself in your mind's eye. See yourself in great detail struggling to identify a particularly difficult feeling or set of feelings. These might be feelings of anger, tenderness, excitement, helplessness, or other strong emotions. Picture yourself clearly experiencing these feelings in a specific situation with another person or persons. Imagine the details of the scene: the surroundings, the visual elements, the smells, what you are wearing, the texture of anything you are touching. Focus on any bodily sensations that these strong feelings arouse.

Now imagine yourself with a growing ability to label these emotions. Picture yourself with a strengthened ability to tolerate and talk about these feelings. Sense that their intensity begins to diminish as you gain mastery over them. Feel this now as you see it in your mind's eye.

Visualize yourself empowered by this activity. Fix the mental image of yourself now as a person with a wide range of powerful feelings and the ability to experience and express all of them in healthy ways. Picture these images with every fiber of your being.

After your visualization feels complete, spend a few minutes with Basic Breathing meditation before you open your eyes.

This scenario is a general outline that you'll need to customize to fit your own emotional issues and circumstances. Fill in details of your own life and whatever feelings you want to work on being able to identify and tolerate. The key is to make the visualization highly specific so that it has personal significance.

Here is an example of how one EFC participant customized his Feelings Identification and Tolerance visualization. This man, in his mid-forties and married for over twenty years, wanted to work on certain vague feelings of discomfort that his wife often unwittingly aroused in him.

It's the morning and I'm in bed with my wife. The sun is streaming in the windows through the white curtains, and I can feel its warmth on my face. Our cat is curled up between us and I'm petting her, feeling her soft fur. My wife opens her eyes and they look so pretty in the daylight, green with a little yellow around the edges.

It's nice and relaxing here, I still feel kind of dreamy, maybe like making love. The morning has always been our favorite time. But then my wife starts to talk about all the things we're supposed to do today, this weekend. Take the car in to the new mechanic, cut away some of those weeds, help our daughter sort through her college applications.

Now I can hear the kids downstairs, already watching music videos. The noise breaks the morning's quiet. I'm starting to get that feeling. What is it? It's that feeling that makes me want to turn over and go back to sleep and not face any of it.

But why, what is it that feels so difficult, when everything's really okay? Usually I'd just get up and start about my business. But this morning I'm going to go into the feeling deeper. What is it? It's not really anger or resentment . . . it's a feeling of weakness, of inadequacy. That I won't be able to be all the things I'm supposed to be to my family. The patient dad, the fixer of things, the good husband. I really want to be all these things and I know I can be. But on some level, somewhere inside, I still worry that I can't cut it. And when my wife starts with the litany of things to do first thing in the morning, I just feel like I don't have the strength.

I start telling my wife how I feel. She listens and as I talk she starts stroking my arm, soothing me with her touch. She says she feels the same way, sometimes. She says she'll try not to bombard me with too much early in the day.

She hugs me and her hair smells so nice. I've sometimes been afraid to admit any weakness to her . . . what woman wants a weak husband? But now I know that she doesn't see it that way. She respects me for talking about my feelings. She has faith in me. And I feel stronger, more capable.

I've identified something that was just lying there under the surface and now that I can see it, it doesn't seem as threatening. I feel a surge of energy as I hold my wife close. She's so soft but strong inside. I feel safe and accepted.

FITNESS GUIDED VISUALIZATION FOR EMPATHY

Seat yourself in a meditation posture in a quiet place. Begin with a few minutes of Basic Breathing Meditation. If there are any areas of tension in your body, try to relax them with your breath.

When you are relaxed, picture a specific person in your mind's eye who would benefit from your improved understanding and sensitivity. Visualize this person in precise details: his or her physical characteristics, mode of dress, and manner of expression.

Now see yourself in detailed interaction with that person. Imagine the time and the setting in as exact a way as you can. Visualize yourself engaging in behavior that is understanding, tactful, and sensitive. Clearly see the other person's appreciative response. Picture yourself feeling a sense of pride and achievement with your growing abilities. Imagine the feelings at this very moment as you form the scene in your mind's eye.

Visualize yourself now as a person with well-developed Empathy, connecting with others in a meaningful and understanding way. See all this clearly in your mind's eye. Visualize it with every fiber of your being.

When you have completed the visualization, spend a few moments with Basic Breathing Meditation before you open your eyes.

This visualization scenario can be customized to focus on whomever you want to show more Empathy. This might be a member of your family, a friend, neighbor, or someone with whom you work.

Here is an example of one personalized Empathy visualization. Joan, a regional sales manager, wanted to have a more empathic working relationship with a senior secretary who had been at the firm for a long time. This older woman was very resistant to change and seemed to complicate all the manager's attempts at implementing new office systems.

I go into the office and Arlene is already working at her desk. The windows are closed even though it's a beautiful day, and it smells musty. I say hello and open the window to breath in some fresh air.

Arlene has put a note on my desk saying we need to discuss my new system for tracking the salespeople's performance. I always get a little wave of dread when I see one of her little yellow notes. I sit down in the chair across from her desk, which is always perfectly neat. When I sit down, my suit skirt rides up and I suddenly feel self-conscious, young and snippy. I get a whiff of the lilac cologne she always wears. Arlene's hands are old and wrinkled as she picks up her old sales record book. No rings—she never married; all she had was this job.

She starts explaining in her very tedious way something about the old system versus the new one. She just can't accept that it's okay to use a computerized spreadsheet instead of the system she used for so many years.

But this is the key to why I need to show her more Empathy. I've come to realize that her critical style is probably based on insecurity. She probably feels threat-ened by me and my new methods.

Instead of getting all huffy and defensive, as I've done before, I thank Arlene for her comments. I assure her that the new way I'm keeping the sales records is per-fectly acceptable. I even throw in a compliment—telling her I think it's amazing that she kept the records manu-ally all these years, so accurately, but I'm not that experi-enced and I need the computer's help. This recognition pleases her and she seems satisfied.

I feel good that I've been able to connect with Empa-thy and move beyond my defensive posture. Now we can go through the rest of the day without tension and get to work without any more fruitless discussions. Empathy has proven to be more productive, as well as kinder and more mature. I feel calm and clear, instead of needlessly agitated. I dwell on the feeling of calm and control for a minute.

FITNESS GUIDED VISUALIZATION FOR INSIGHT

Seat yourself in a meditation posture in a quiet place. Begin with a few minutes of Basic Breathing Meditation. If there are any areas of tension in your body, try to relax them with your breath.

When you are relaxed, visualize yourself as you were as a child. See yourself and your family situation clearly in your mind's eye. Picture your parents, siblings, or whoever else was there with you. Observe your imagined surroundings in as precise detail as possible.

Recognize the profound connection between the child you see in your mind's eye and the person you are now at this moment. See this relationship between the past and the present. Feel its constant presence in your life. Imag-ine aspects of the child you were always being with you, even now.

Now visualize yourself being guided by these subtle forces. See yourself in your mind's eye interacting with another person, someone significant to you. Picture this in great detail. View yourself admitting to inevitable feelings of weakness and insecurity, feelings that evoke images of you as a child. Feel the sense of strength, liberation, and acceptance that comes with these admissions.

Now see your talents, resources, and abilities growing from your natural childhood curiosity and exuberance. See yourself using this energy in your life now. Visualize this clearly. Focus on these images with every fiber of your being.

When you have completed your visualization, spend a few moments on Basic Breathing Meditation before you open your eyes.

During your EFC Program, you'll customize this basic scenario to reflect your own experience as a child, your adult relationships, and emotional struggles and strengths. Here is an example of how a thirty-four-year-old EFC participant personalized his Insight scenario:

I'm eight or nine, and it's the first day of school. It's still hot like summer, but my father is dressed the way I always remember him being dressed, in a blue flannel suit. He puts on a hat when he's ready to go to work. He kisses my cheek and I get a whiff of his aftershave. He says "Have a good day at school, slugger."

That word "slugger" reminds me of baseball, getting picked last for the team. Suddenly I can't eat any more of my eggs. I feel nervous and queasy thinking about sports at school.

My mother sends me and my brother off with lunch boxes and kisses. She cares more about grades than sports, but my father expects me to be like my big brother. My brother doesn't wear glasses, like I do, and he's good at baseball. We're waiting outside for the school bus, and I feel sweaty and my stomach hurts. I spend a few min-utes feeling myself as this young boy, smart and very sensitive.

Now I visualize myself as an adult, at my job as in a pharmaceutical research lab. My boss is one of the ge-niuses who made a fortune before he was thirty, also has a gorgeous wife and is into mountain climbing. Even though he's younger than me, sometimes he makes me feel like I felt with my dad. I want to be like him, but I'm afraid I don't have what it takes.

I'm deep into a problem involving research for a new diabetes drug. My boss comes in, looking like one of those ads—lean, fit, tan, self-satisfied. He tells me that some of the "team" are going on a hike Sunday, would I like to come? I know a hike with him means a vertical challenge. I feel that dread in my stomach, that queasiness, like the kid in fourth grade is aiming the hardball right at my eyes.

But now I know who I am and what I'm worth. I give my boss some excuse about family obligations. I take a few deep abdominal breaths. I don't have to put myself in a situation where I'll be anxious or humiliated any-more. I'm not trapped into circumstances like when I was a kid. I can highlight my accomplishments instead.

I turn the boss's attention to my breakthrough on this new drug development. He's impressed with my creative thinking. I was always good at math and sciences when I was a kid; now I've directed my strengths into a success-ful career. I'll always carry the little boy who feels like a failure because he's not a good athlete inside. But I for-give and accept him, and my father does, too. I feel an enormous sense of relief, a weight being lifted from my stomach. I can breath all the way into it and feel good.

INSTRUCTIONS FOR FITNESS GUIDED VISUALIZATION
FOR ASSERTIVENESS

Seat yourself in a meditation posture in a quiet place. Begin with a few minutes of Basic Breathing Meditation. If there are any areas of tension in your body, try to relax them with your breath.

When you are relaxed, begin to visualize yourself in a scene with another person or persons in which you are standing up for your reasonable rights. See the interaction in precise detail in your mind's eye. Focus on what you're saying and feeling.

See yourself behaving in a legitimately entitled fashion, knowing you have no interest in hurting others or acting aggressively. View yourself asking for what you want and feeling more confident and strengthened about doing so. Picture yourself clearly stating your needs with greater comfort. At the same time, you can also visualize yourself being sensitive to others' rights as well.

In your mental images you can now see yourself behaving with quiet certainty, earning the respect of others, while showing respect for them at the same time. Visualize these scenes with every fiber of your being.

When you practice this visualization, add the details of any particular situation in which you need to be more assertive, whether it's professional or personal. Here is an example of how a young woman who had trouble being assertive with her boyfriend crafted her Assertiveness visualization:

I'm pacing around in my apartment and it's six-thirty and I'm waiting for Paul to call about whether or not we're having dinner tonight. I'm still in my business suit and I feel uncomfortable and restricted and I hear the clock ticking. I go and look into the fridge and eat some leftover pasta with my fingers. I'm hungry and restless and my heart is beating fast.

Why am I waiting for him to call instead of calling? Why am I buying into these stereotyped roles twenty years after women's lib? I still feel like I'm fourteen and waiting to be asked to dance at the junior high dance. I'm twenty-five; I can stand up before a roomful of people and make a presentation. I should be able to call.

I lie down on my bed and make the call, all the time wondering if I'll hang up if his machine answers. But he answers and he's glad to hear from me and wants to have dinner together at our usual Chinese restaurant. He seems genuinely not to think he did anything wrong by not calling.

We're at the restaurant now, each having a Chinese beer, refreshing but bitter. I'm still wearing my work suit, but without the jacket now, the blouse unbuttoned another button. Paul is in a dark blue suit and looks really handsome in the reddish glow of the restaurant's paper lanterns and he's talking about his day. He's a trial lawyer and his work may be more interesting than mine, but I still wish he'd ask about my day sometimes. I take a few deep breaths, inhaling all the smells of the food and seeing the other people eating around us, and I feel hungry but a little too jumpy to eat yet. I ask Paul if he'd like to hear about my day and he looks a little surprised but says sure.

I tell him I had a good day at work and did a big presentation that went well, but I would have been in a better mood if we had had a plan for dinner. He says it's hard for him to make plans on weekdays because he never knows when he'll finish work, if he'll be too beat to go out, etc. He starts nervously tapping his fingers on the table. But instead of letting him off the hook, I gently persist and I tell him that making a plan is important to me, or at least a phone call to say he'll let me know later. He says okay, he hears me, and he'll try. Then he starts studying the big maroon menu.

I don't know if he really means to change, but I feel that I've made a positive change just by speaking up. I'm proud of telling him what I want and feel that he'll respect me more for it, too. And if he doesn't, he's not the right person for me in the long run. I took a healthy emotional chance, and it feels right. I'm ready to enjoy my dinner.

FITNESS GUIDED VISUALIZATION:
THE CUSTOMIZED TRACK

After the first two months of the EFC Program, you can select whether to repeat the Basic Track schedule for your Fitness Guided Visualizations, or to move on to the Customized Track. If you decide to go on the Customized Track, it's most effective to work on the same Core Component that you have selected for your meditation practice. That way, your meditation and affirmations, your visualization, your journaling, and your exercise can all operate together to strengthen the particular Core Component you have chosen.

There are several criteria for selecting your Primary and Secondary Core Components. You can look at your original Self-Assessments and see if the scores indicate that you need more work in any particular areas. You can review related journal entries. If you're in therapy, you can include your therapist in the selection process. (The methods for selecting the Core Components to work on are discussed in detail in chapter 7.)

Once you have made your selections, use the Primary Core Component as your focus for visualizations during weeks nine through twelve. Then, based on your progress, decide whether you would prefer to continue working on the Primary Core Component or shift to your Secondary Core

Component during weeks thirteen through sixteen of the EFC Program.

This is also a good time to review your EFC Goals and see if you want to modify them. Try to incorporate these goals into the visualization scenarios you create for the Customized Track. For optimal results, focus on the same EFC Goals in both your Fitness Focused Meditation sessions and your Fitness Guided Visualizations.

Here is an example of how this process can work. After the first two months of the EFC Program, Jill decided to move onto the Customized Track. To select her Core Components, she reviewed her Basic Self-Assessment Scores. These clearly indicated that she was strong in Assertiveness, quite advanced in Insight (with the help of several years in therapy), but still had major struggles with aspects of Feelings Identification and Tolerance and with Empathy.

Jill, age forty, was married to Gregory when she was a college senior and had a child two years later. Her marriage gradually disintegrated, largely due to her husband's lack of success in his career. He tried to be a rock musician for many years, painting houses on the side to earn some money. Meanwhile, she went back to school, earned an MBA, and built a career in investment banking. The disparity between her and her husband's work styles, values, and earning power gradually created a bitter rift. They were divorced after twelve years.

Jill has a lot of anger at her ex-husband for "never growing up" and for "taking the best years of her life." In the years since the divorce, she has been too busy with her career and her daughter to devote much energy to meeting men or dating. Gregory, meanwhile, has remarried and had a baby with his much younger wife. Now Jill's sixteen-year-old daughter, Pamela, is rebelling against her mother's restrictions and favoring her more easygoing father.

In her Emotional Fitness Journal, Jill set down these goals for her EFC Program:

Feelings Identification and Tolerance Goals

1. To manage my anger at Gregory more effectively and find a productive, healthy outlet.
2. To be sure not to bring my frustrations into my relationship with Pamela.

Empathy Goals

1. To find more Empathy in my heart for Gregory.
2. To express and act with more Empathy toward Pamela.

Based on these goals, Jill practiced these FIT affirmations during her Fitness Focused Meditations:

"I am learning to manage my anger at Gregory more effectively. I use Exercise for Emotional Fitness to release my anger and resentment. I write honestly in my journal to let my feelings out."

To complement these affirmations, she created the following Fitness Guided Visualization:

> *I'm just back from work when the phone rings. It's Gregory, asking if Pam can drive by car over to see him this weekend because his truck is having trouble. I'm thinking of all the crummy cars he's had over the years and why he still can't get it together to have a car that runs. Then I hear his new baby crying in the background. That makes my jaw clench. He couldn't even take care of one family and now he goes and has another one. I start to tell him that I wanted to take the car to a party I was invited to Saturday night . . . maybe I'd like to get a personal life going, too. But he's already gotten off the phone, saying he has to get the baby's bottle..*
>
> *Now Pamela comes in. I can't stand what she's done to her beautiful hair, chopped it all off into a crew cut. I feel myself annoyed at the sight of her, enraged at Gregory, about to spill it all out. But I stop and try to relax*

my jaw so it doesn't start aching. I deserve to express my-
self, but is it really healthy to make my daughter feel
worse than she already does? No! I can identify this
anger and I can tolerate it. I can write about it tonight
in my journal. Maybe talk about it with my therapist to-
morrow. I don't have to lay it on Pam or keep it in my
clenched jaw.

I tell Pam that she's going to drive herself to Daddy's
this weekend because his car is broken. She looks happy
and hugs me, smelling faintly of sunscreen. She's still my
beautiful little girl when she smiles, even with that hair.
She asks what's for dinner.

I still feel wound-up though. I know if I just cook and
go through the usual routine, I'll be replaying my resent-
ments in my head all night. So I think of something dif-
ferent we can do. It's summer and stays light out until
late. So I suggest that we go Rollerblading. We can skate
to town and get a slice of pizza for dinner. Pamela taught
me how to Rollerblade and it's something we really have
fun doing together.

I change into shorts, stick money in my skate, and
get ready to go. We take off down the road. The wind feels
great, the rhythmic motion of skating feels fantastic. I
feel like a kid again.

After four weeks of concentrating on Feelings Identification and Tolerance in her EFC Program, Jill decided
to move on to Empathy for weeks thirteen through sixteen. She used these affirmations to reflect her Empathy
goals:

"I recognize that showing Gregory more Empathy is
healthier for all of us. I recognize the good in him. I take
time to understand Pamela's feelings and express Empathy
to her."

To reinforce these affirmations, Jill invented the following Fitness Guided Visualization:

I'm in the kitchen making dinner, cutting up vegetables for the salad. Pamela comes in and starts eating some pieces of salad out of the bowl. She's painted her nails black to match her lipstick. As usual, her appearance bothers me. I almost say that the nails look disgusting, but then I think about what she's trying to express. She's just trying to be cool, to be noticed, to create an identify for herself.

Didn't I do the same thing? I remember being back in my parents' kitchen. My mother's yelling at me for not wearing a bra and wearing the same worn jeans every day, for looking like a hippie. I remember how it made me feel like she didn't understand a thing about me. So why should I make Pamela feel the same way? Instead, I tell her that her nails look pretty cool.

Pamela tells me that her father invited her over for dinner. She says she'd rather go there than eat my chicken because his wife makes really good vegetarian food. This ticks me off and my jaw starts to tighten. I have to put the knife down and try to relax for a minute.

Instead of lashing out at Pam, I think about it for a minute. Gregory should have asked me ahead of time, but that's not his style. He's always been spontaneous. That was one of the things that made him exciting and fun when we were in love. All he's really done here is invite his daughter over for dinner, something that makes her feel good. I can let it go.

I tell Pam it's okay and I'll drop her off at her father's. She looks relieved. She's still a kid under that makeup.

I decide to freeze the chicken and just eat salad since I'm trying to lose weight anyway. I'll see if my friend wants to go to that coffee bar where they have live jazz. She said there are some interesting-looking men in there sometimes. I feel excited by the possibility of a free evening, without feeling guilty. Pamela can see her father and I can go out, maybe meet someone. I spend a few minutes picturing the possibility of meeting someone at the coffeehouse.

After a month of practicing Empathy affirmations and visualizations, Jill found that she was responding in healthier ways to small provocations from Pamela and Gregory that would have ordinarily set her off. She was often able to react with more Empathy and be less judgmental. Yet she still harbored a great deal of anger and resentment toward Gregory for the years of disappointment and their divorce.

As Jill continued with her EFC practice after the initial four months of the program, she focused primarily on Feelings Identification and Tolerance. She felt certain that as she learned to manage her anger more productively, she would have more energy to devote to establishing a new relationship.

FITNESS GUIDED VISUALIZATION FOR SPECIAL CONDITIONS

In conjunction with therapy and the other EFC Training Techniques, Fitness Guided Visualization can be used to advance treatment for conditions such as depression and panic/anxiety disorder.

Rebecca, a thirty-five-year-old communications executive, was in the process of recovering from a significant depression triggered by the loss of both her job and her love relationship. She had been involved with her boss, Brad, the married owner of her company. When he decided to end the affair, her job was also "downsized."

Through her Basic Track EFC work and psychotherapy, Rebecca realized that she had been denying a tremendous amount of rage, while simultaneously feeling helpless, powerless, and defeated. Here is an excerpt from a series of visualizations she crafted to address her anger and depression, and move toward greater Emotional Fitness. These types of visualizations can be a healthy, safe way to express anger and rage that cannot be expressed directly. They should be practiced only for a short amount of time and balanced with other types of visualizations and affirmations.

I see myself making a deliberate attempt to run into Brad at one of the after-work spots we used to go to. I feel very frightened about confronting him because he's always been able to manipulate and charm me, but I'm sure this is something I must do.

As I walk into the bar, I imagine the familiar scene, the smell of cigarette smoke, the people I recognize. My legs are a little wobbly, but no one seems to notice. A couple of people say hello to me like everything is normal. I see Brad standing at the bar, talking with a woman I don't know. I can feel the anger rise in me, like a volcano about to blow. I take a few deep breaths and continue toward him. He sees me now and looks very uncomfortable. I remember my therapist's words: "You've had an impact on him, too. It hasn't been a one-way street." It helps me remember that I have some power, too, not just him.

I move directly in front of Brad and feel anxious, yet calm at the same time, as if I'm sure of what I'm doing. I ask him for a few private words, and he reluctantly follows me into a corner booth. I see his face, look directly into his eyes as I'm talking. I tell him what a self-involved liar he is. I tell him it will all come back to him in the end. I tell him I'm glad we're through because he's a despicable human being. Then without waiting for him to say anything, I get up and walk away.

As I walk out the door, I feel lighter. I know the healing process is at work. I know I'm getting better and it feels right.

FITNESS GUIDED VISUALIZATION AND THE OTHER TRAINING TECHNIQUES

Fitness Guided Visualization and Fitness Focused Meditation work hand in hand. The visualizations serve as an extension of the affirmations that you use during meditation. In a sense, an affirmation is the photograph and a visualization is a motion picture. By adding visual elements, smells, sounds, and feelings, your visualizations make your affirmations and EFC Goals come alive.

You can also link your visualization practice to your Emotional Fitness Journal. You can use your journal to write down your visualization scenarios beforehand, to help set them in your mind. You can also write about the visualization after you have completed a session, when the imagery and feelings it evokes are fresh.

If you are in therapy, you might want to discuss your visualizations with your therapist. On the other hand, you might prefer to keep them as your own, very private property. Either way, you can use your EFC Journal to elaborate on the images, feelings, and themes that emerge from your visualization practice.

Fitness Focused Visualization can also play a role in your Exercise for Emotional Fitness. You can use the imagery process as you are warming up for your workout, to visualize the performance that you want to achieve. You can picture yourself walking to the top of that hill without stopping, making that smashing serve on the tennis court, running that extra mile. Visualization is a well-tested way to enhance desirable performance, used by professional athletes and dedicated amateurs alike.

Once you have gained the capacity to create and concentrate on imagery, you can use it for a myriad of positive purposes, in all the significant areas of your life: love, work, and play.

CHECKLIST FOR FITNESS GUIDED VISUALIZATION

1. Establish a visualization spot that is quiet, private, and comfortable.
2. Read the suggested scenario for the Core Component you are working on or review a scenario you have customized for your own situation.
3. Practice Fitness Guided Visualization, three times a week, 15–20 minutes per session, according to this schedule:

Week 1: Feelings Identification and Tolerance
Week 2: Empathy
Week 3: Insight
Week 4: Assertiveness
Week 5: Feelings Identification and Tolerance
Week 6: Empathy
Week 7: Insight
Week 8: Assertiveness

4. During Week 8 of the EFC Program, decide if you want to repeat the Basic Track or move on to the Customized Track. If you are going on the Customized Track, select your Primary and Secondary Core Components and clarify your EFC goals.
5. During Weeks 9 through 12 of the EFC Program, practice Fitness Guided Visualization three times a week, 15–20 minutes per session, with imagery related to your Primary Core Component and your EFC Goals.
6. During Weeks 13 through 16 of the EFC Program, practice Fitness Guided Visualization three times a week, 15–20 minutes per session. Craft your own imagery to focus on either your Primary Core Component, if you need more work in this area, or your Secondary Core Component.
7. Throughout the Program, keep your Fitness Guided Visualizations in mind as your practice the other Training Techniques.

ten

The Emotional Fitness Journal

T HE THIRD TRAINING TECHNIQUE OF THE EFC PRO-
GRAM IS THE EMOTIONAL FITNESS JOURNAL, WHICH
directs the process of keeping a journal toward exploring
and developing your Core Components. Like the other
Training Techniques, journal writing requires no special talent, training, or equipment. All you need to begin is the desire to become more emotionally aware and honestly express
your thoughts and feelings.

While journal writing is not as overtly repetitive as meditation, it does have a satisfying rhythm of its own and can
be a comforting ritual. Journaling offers a way to access
ideas and emotions regarding a particular person or situation in your life, past, present, or future. The journal also
provides a forum for self-dialogue about issues, struggles,
and solutions that arise in your daily life connected with the
Core Components. Above all, journaling is a tremendous release, a safe haven for expressing your innermost thoughts
and feelings.

Journaling capitalizes on the basic human urge to create
a record of our inner lives. Some of the most moving written
documents that have come down to us through the ages are
in the form of journals and diaries. There are examples of

journals written by statesman, royals, and commoners; intellectuals, professional writers, and ordinary people.

Many historic journals or diaries record details of activities, actions, and political events, in addition to private thoughts. But it is often the emotional content that continues to resonate over time because of the ways in which journals reveal the commonalties of human feeling.

THE THERAPEUTIC ESSENCE OF JOURNAL WRITING

Beyond the relatively small number of journals that have been made public through the years, there are countless private diaries that have been hidden from curious eyes and sometimes destroyed to maintain the privacy of their owners. Young people, navigating the intensity of youthful emotional life, are often compelled to write secret diaries.

Perhaps you kept a diary yourself at some point in the past. But chances are that as the demands of adult life took over, you let the practice lapse. While a small number of especially creative, introspective, or intellectual adults maintain diaries, most busy people don't take the time.

It's not as if we don't have plenty of emotional conflicts, concerns, and feelings to write about in our adult lives. It's just that we often believe it's our duty to put our emotions aside and concentrate on our work and family responsibilities. We may feel that it's immature and self-indulgent to "waste time" on journal writing when there is so much that needs to be done.

What happens to all the emotions and thoughts that we don't take time to write down? At best, we may have opportunities to express them verbally to a partner, friend, or relative. But even with those closest to us, there are thoughts we need to censor. Very few people have anyone with whom they can express all their thoughts, 100 percent of the time. No matter how emotionally honest we want to be, there is usually a layer of feeling that we cannot share.

Some of us, some of the time, may be able to set aside

those unexpressed feelings without any ill effect. But equally as often, it is the very emotions that remain unexpressed that have the most impact. They may play over and over again in our minds, taking up space that could be filled with more productive thoughts. They may manifest in physical symptoms, such as headaches, backaches, stomach distress, or fatigue. Unexpressed thoughts and feelings can also contribute to anxiety, depression, or phobias.

One of the reasons why psychotherapy is so popular and productive is that it offers a means of voicing the ideas and feelings that are too disturbing to discuss with anyone else. The therapist provides a nonjudgmental atmosphere where it is safe to voice and investigate what has previously been left unsaid.

As an adjunct to the self-expression inherent in talk therapy, many therapists recommend some form of journal writing. This practice has a long tradition stemming back to the Freudian dream journal. In modern psychotherapy, clients are often encouraged to record both their dreams and waking thoughts in their journals and to bring this material into the therapeutic dialogue.

In behavior therapy, journals are used to keep track of frequencies of target behaviors as well as accompanying emotions, moods, and thoughts. In Gestalt therapy, journaling is considered an important activity that extends the therapeutic process. Gestalt therapists have written extensively about the use of written journal exercises as "homework" between therapy sessions.

Written assignments between sessions and the keeping of journals are also commonly prescribed in other forms of individual, marital, family, and group therapy. This technique is especially useful in dealing with behavior-change and habit-control issues such as dieting, eating disorders, and smoking cessation. Several studies have supported the value of the writing technique as a way of extending the benefits of therapy and providing a sense of continuity and progress.

Another way in which the written word is used as a therapeutic tool is through letter writing. This involves writing a letter with no intention of ever sending it. Rather, the letter is a way to express thoughts that might be too painful, difficult, or impossible to actually transmit to the recipient. Letters can be written to people in current relationships, individuals from the past, or even those who are deceased. The goal is to put into words what has not been expressed more directly.

The Emotional Fitness Journal satisfies many of these therapeutic functions of journaling. If you are in therapy and want to share your journal, doing so can be a valuable means of accelerating your progress and opening up new avenues of discussion with your therapist.

If you are participating in the EFC Program on your own, your EFC Journal can be a form of talk therapy that you conduct with yourself, providing both release and direction.

EFC JOURNAL BASICS

Take a little time before you start the EFC Program to consider which format you prefer for your Emotional Fitness Journal. Think about what would be easy and comfortable for you, and what would make your journal special.

The first option is to write the old-fashioned way, by hand. If you want to handwrite your journal, select an attractive diary or notebook from a stationery store or bookstore. Try to choose a journal with a cover that appeals to you in terms of color and design. Of course you can also use any school-type notebook, but your journal assumes greater importance if it has a handsome cover. Many people also like to use a special pen that they reserve for journal writing.

Writing by hand has the advantage of separating the journal process from any business-related writing that you might do. Writing in a special book has a classic feel to it, connecting you with the centuries of people who have put pen to paper to express their private thoughts. Writing with a pen also reduces the urge to revise, edit, or correct your entries.

If you keep a handwritten EFC Journal, be sure to identify a secure, private place to store it. It's imperative that you feel uninhibited when you write and absolutely certain that no one will read your entries. If you write with the idea that someone else may read your journal, the process of investigating and fortifying your Core Components will be severely limited. Like a session with a psychotherapist, your Emotional Fitness Journal should be completely confidential.

The other option is to write your journal on a computer or a typewriter. The computer option is quite popular, although perhaps not as romantic as the handwritten journal with a clothbound cover. You can keep your journal in a file on your hard drive, put it on a diskette, or print the pages and keep them in a notebook.

Writing your journal on a computer can make confidentiality a little easier, particularly if you're clever enough to know how to apply password restrictions to your files. If you're not certain how to "lock" your files with a password, be diligent to ensure that no one will stumble upon your EFC Journal file in the hard drive while using your computer, or find the diskette. Be just as careful when storing your computerized journal as you would be with a handwritten copy.

One other precaution applies to writing your EFC Journal on a computer. You need to resist the temptation to heavily revise and edit. If you want to correct a few spelling mistakes as you go along, fine. But don't bother to revise your journal entries as you would ordinarily edit a document. It's more productive to spend your journal time letting your thoughts flow freely than cleaning up the entries. Editing creates a flavor of writing for work or school, preparing your words to be read by someone else. Journal writing is a completely different process.

The number-one rule of therapeutic journaling is: Don't judge your writing. It doesn't matter if it's rife with grammatical errors, redundancies, clichés, or whatever. Nothing matters, except that you state your feelings without inhibition. Just keep your pen moving across the page.

We are all ingrained from an early age through schooling to expect that our writing will be graded and corrected. Later, we worry about whether or not our writing at work is presentable, persuasive, or whatever it needs to be. It's sometimes difficult when we first start journal writing to realize that we can set aside this threat of someone peering over our shoulder, correcting, and judging our words.

Journaling is a completely different type of writing than any you might have done for school or work. It's even different than correspondence to a friend or relative. The EFC Journal is about the process, not the result. It doesn't matter how it reads because no one else is going to read it. All that matters is that you take the time to sit down, listen to your thoughts, and write them down honestly.

Knowing that no one will critique or even read your journal writing can be tremendously liberating. You might find that you truly enjoy this type of writing, even if you usually consider writing a chore.

If you generally do not like to write, think about why this is true. Perhaps what you really don't like about writing is the possibility of being judged or being considered a "bad" writer. When you're concerned about your writing being "good," it can drain the natural pleasure out of the process.

With the EFC Journal, the burden of judgment is entirely lifted. Journal writing is a liberated form with no threat of grades, critiques, or other people's reactions. Whatever you want to write is entirely right and perfect.

Finally, if you strongly dislike writing even with the knowledge that it will never be judged, you have the option of tape-recording your EFC Journal. This entails recording yourself for fifteen to twenty minutes while verbalizing your thoughts on the Core Component area you are concentrating on that week. If you record journal tapes, you need to secure them in a private place, just as you would a written journal.

The EFC Program involves writing (or recording) for fifteen to twenty minutes, three times a week. How much text this will produce depends on your writing speed and style, and is totally inconsequential. There are no required word counts or deadlines here.

For the first few weeks of the Program, it's recommended that you schedule your journal writing sessions, to ensure you put in sufficient time to benefit from the Training Technique. You can write in your journal any time of the day or night, as long as you do it consistently.

Many EFC participants find journal writing to be the easiest of the Training Techniques right from the onset. Journaling is likely to come more naturally than Fitness Focused Meditation or Fitness Guided Visualization, since it's not entirely new. But in case you do find journal writing to be a struggle, remember the Fitness Reinforcement Loop. The more often you practice the Training Technique, the easier it becomes. As it becomes comfortable and routine, it's more enjoyable. Then you begin to notice how it affects your abilities in the Core Components of Emotional Fitness. The results reinforce your desire and commitment to continue the Training Technique on a regular basis.

TWO TYPES OF JOURNALING

There are two basic styles of writing for your EFC Journal: Free Flow and Core Component Journaling.

The Free Flow technique gives you the freedom to write about any issues, thoughts, or events that relate to your Emotional Fitness. With this style, you do not decide beforehand exactly which Core Component you will be writing about. Instead, you let your thoughts flow about any emotional issue that concerns you. The Core Components that are involved will emerge on their own.

The second technique is Core Component Journaling. This is where you set out to write about topics related to a specific Core Component each week. Later, during the Customized Track, you can also write about selected EFC Goals.

You'll discover when you're journaling that almost all emotional issues involve more than one Core Component. For example, you might begin with a question of Assertiveness in a relationship and then find out that it also involves Insight and Empathy. Or you might want to write about an FIT struggle you have with anxiety, only to discover that your thoughts lead you back to Insight. The essential truth that all the Core Components are interwoven in our emotional lives constantly surfaces during journal writing.

For this reason, the Basic Track and Customized Track schedules for the EFC Journal should be viewed more loosely than the schedules for the other Training Techniques. You might be scheduled to write about one Core Component but find that your journaling gravitates toward others. Or you may have events or developments in your life that are crucial to write about from an emotional standpoint, even if they don't fit into that week's topic.

When journaling, personal adaptation from the suggested guidelines and Core Component themes are entirely acceptable. Write about whatever is on your mind and happening in your life as it relates to your Emotional Fitness. Don't be concerned about staying strictly with any specific Core Component as a theme if your thoughts go in another direction. The Basic and Customized Track schedules for journaling can be adapted in whatever way you choose.

It is not necessary—or even preferable—to try to find specific solutions to your emotional issues in your journal writing. Journal entries are not stories with a beginning, middle, and happy ending. Don't expect to have a breakthrough or tie up all the loose ends in every writing session.

In fact, it is the spontaneous, free expression inherent in

journaling that activates Emotional Fitness. This Training Technique will inspire your creative problem-solving ability and bring you a fresh perspective. Solutions and insights tend to surface naturally and spontaneously, but you can't control the process or force the outcome; simply let it evolve.

Ira Progoff, a New York–based psychologist, created a series of Journal Workshops in which thousands of people from different walks of life have participated. Progoff uses the metaphor that there is an underground stream of images and recollections within each of us that represents our interior life. When we enter this stream through journaling, we ride it to where the stream wants to go. The journal process is not analytic or insight oriented in the typical sense; it is a unique, life-changing event with its own momentum.

A FLEXIBLE SCHEDULE

The schedule for the Emotional Fitness Journal is the most flexible of any of the Training Techniques. At any time, you may choose to do Free Flow writing instead of focusing on a specific Core Component. Or you may change the emphasis to a different Core Component than the schedule indicates, or write about several elements in one entry.

SCHEDULE FOR THE EMOTIONAL FITNESS JOURNAL: THE BASIC TRACK

The Pre-Program Week: Write in your journal three times during the week, for about 15-20 minutes each session, using the Free Flow technique.

During Weeks 1-8 of the EFC Program, write in your journal three times a week, 15-20 minutes per session. You can loosely concentrate your writing on the following Core Com-

ponents, or you can do Free Flow writing or adapt the themes
in any way you choose.

WEEK	CORE COMPONENT FOR FOCUS OF MEDITATION/ AFFIRMATIONS
Week 1:	Feelings Identification and Tolerance
Week 2:	Empathy
Week 3:	Insight
Week 4:	Assertiveness
Week 5:	Feelings Identification and Tolerance
Week 6:	Empathy
Week 7:	Insight
Week 8:	Assertiveness

*After the first eight weeks you have the option to repeat the Basic
Track schedule, write in the Free Flow style, or go on to the Customized Track schedule.*

Following are examples of how some individuals have
utilized their Emotional Fitness Journal to explore their
Core Components during the Basic Track. These EFC Journal excerpts are intended to provide a taste of journaling,
not a recipe for writing. Your journal will record specific examples from your own life that relate to the key areas of
Emotional Fitness for you.

EFC JOURNAL EXCERPT: FEELINGS IDENTIFICATION AND TOLERANCE

*Today I found myself feeling uptight after a meeting
with my supervisor. I wasn't sure why. Then I fell into a
slump and I felt tired and listless the rest of the day.
Since I'm working on Feelings Identification and Toler-*

ance, I started to think more about this experience. So far I've figured out that I'm really very angry with my boss. He was subtly critical of me and I just let it go, even though it wasn't fair.

I'm starting to believe that I have a definite problem acknowledging when I'm angry—not just at work, where you can't always express it (without getting fired), but also in my relationships with women. I don't want to know it, feel it, or express it. Maybe that's why my girl-friend says I turn off sometimes, go into my shell like a turtle. Maybe it's because I'm afraid to feel how angry I am.

This seems important. I'm going to see if I can come up with some other examples of how I do this when I sit down to write again.

EFC JOURNAL EXCERPT: EMPATHY

My husband was being a real pain again last night. He saw some charge bills and hit the ceiling. Didn't even bother to really find out what they were for, like a suit I really needed for work, and some things for the kids. I felt attacked and got defensive. I called him cheap and controlling. I was really so mad. Then I remembered that I was trying to become better in the area of Empathy, always a tough one for me.

I had been visualizing being more understanding when my husband and I fight about spending, taking into account his pressures and worries, too. Thinking about this helped me back off and feel less attacked. I was even able to tell him that I understand he must be feeling very pressured about money.

Once I changed my attitude, his attitude did a 180. He even said he was sorry for blowing up. He's never apologized during one of our money fights before! Then we were able to talk about our budget some more, like partners instead of opponents.

I always felt that if you empathize with people too much, they just walk all over you. But now I'm starting to feel more positive about this Empathy thing. Maybe it really does work.

EFC JOURNAL EXCERPT: INSIGHT

I've been trying to improve my reactions to my wife. I react so strongly when I feel she's made a stupid mistake. Then I feel rotten for making her feel bad. It makes me feel guilty and that makes me resent her more.

I used to believe that I had a perfect childhood. A real "Leave It to Beaver" kind of family. But now I realize that my father was kind of critical, especially with my mother. But she never complained; she just swallowed it. I always thought it was because she was good-natured, but I guess there was more going on there. She must have had her own problems with Assertiveness and self-esteem.

Now I find myself doing the same thing with my wife, being too critical. Taking on my father's role as the one who's always right. The difference is, I guess I also identify with my mother, because I'm aware of the pain that being too critical causes my wife.

I'm hoping that this new awareness will help me be kinder, less critical. I'll think before I just start in. I don't have to keep repeating these patterns endlessly.

EFC JOURNAL EXCERPT: ASSERTIVENESS

I'm starting to realize that I attract friends who are very self-centered, who only want to talk about themselves. Even my oldest friend, Dee. She's always in some sort of crisis. And if there isn't one, she has to create one.

And she expects me to talk about it on and on, until her next crisis hits. I guess it's partly my fault for never making her stop and listen to me.

I want to be a good friend and a caring person. But I'm starting to realize that there's a difference between Empathy and letting someone else take over completely. I'm a person, too, and I have issues I'd like to talk about with Dee or another friend. I'd like to be the center of the conversation sometimes, instead of always being the good listener and sympathetic ear.

I'm not sure I can change the pattern with Dee, after all this time. But at least I can look for some new friends where the balance is more equal. I'd like some friends who can really listen to me, as well as talk. Maybe if I assert myself from the beginning that this is what I expect, the relationships will develop more equally.

THE CUSTOMIZED TRACK FOR THE EMOTIONAL FITNESS JOURNAL

Once you have completed Weeks 1–8 of the EFC Program, you have a choice of repeating the Basic Track schedule for the EFC Journal or working on the Customized Track. At any time, you can also return to Free Flow journaling or write about emotional issues that deal with several different Core Components.

If you select the Customized Track, begin by identifying your Primary and Secondary Core Components, according to the criteria discussed in chapter 7. The Primary and Secondary Core Components that you use for journaling should match the ones you are concentrating on in your meditation/affirmation and visualization practices. This allows the Training Techniques to support one another in fortifying your Emotional Fitness.

SCHEDULE FOR THE CUSTOMIZED TRACK FOR THE EFC JOURNAL

Write in your EFC Journal for 15 to 20 minutes per session, three times a week.

Weeks 9–12 of the EFC Program: Use your Primary Core Component as a theme for your journal entries.

Weeks 13–16 of the EFC Program: Continue to write about your Primary Core Component, or use your Secondary Core Component as the theme for your journal entries. Again, this selection should match the Core Component on which you're focusing in your other Training Techniques.

The basic thrust of your EFC Journal during the Customized phase is to dialogue with yourself about personal issues, struggles, and attempted solutions connected to your Primary or Secondary Core Components. You can write about the Core Components as they relate to relationships and events in your current life or in your past. The key is to concentrate on the emotional aspects of your experience, rather than merely recording events.

You can also write about your EFC Goals in your journal entries or elaborate on your Fitness Focused Meditation and Fitness Guided Visualization themes. Another option is to use the following journal exercises/questions related to the Core Components as a starting point. You may want to explore one question for a single entry or continue writing down your thoughts during another journaling session.

FEELINGS IDENTIFICATION AND TOLERANCE JOURNAL EXERCISES

1. Describe two situations that consistently frustrate you. Pay close attention to your feelings as you do

this exercise. Now write out potential solutions to these situations using your strengthened FIT skills.

2. How do you typically deal with angry feelings? When do they come up and how do you react?

3. Think about the emotions you find intolerable. How do you attempt to avoid them? What happens as a result of this avoidance? What would happen if you faced these feelings head-on?

4. What is the feeling that you fear most or find most unbearable? What evokes this emotion? How do you handle it now? How would you like to manage this feeling as you gain Emotional Fitness?

5. Do your feelings have a substantial impact on your quality of life and/or ability to function? Do you have a struggle with depression, acute anxiety, phobias, or compulsions? How can you envision that increasing your ability to identify and tolerate feelings might help to alleviate these problems?

6. How do you use food, alcohol, smoking, drugs, or other substances to cope with your feelings? How do your emotions influence your habits? How might this change if you were better able to tolerate and express all types of feelings?

EMPATHY JOURNAL EXERCISES

1. List two or three qualities or actions in others that particularly bother you. Assess yourself in light of these qualities or actions. If you were more empathic, how would you react differently?

2. List two or three qualities or behaviors in others that you admire. Assess yourself in the light of these qualities or behaviors. What can you do to exhibit them more frequently?

3. List three behaviors or emotional responses that you want others to show you. How can you go about exhibiting these responses to others more often?

4. To what type of person do you find it most difficult to show Empathy? If you were less judgmental, how would this change?

5. How does it make you feel when you are harsh and unreasonable with someone close to you? How would you, as well as the other person, benefit from developing more Empathy?

6. Imagine a scenario in which you are likely to have difficulty showing Empathy. How would the situation change it you looked at the issue from the other person's point of view, taking into account his or her concerns and needs?

INSIGHT JOURNAL EXERCISES

1. List four positive characteristics of each of your parents. Then list four of your own positive qualities. Compare these characteristics with your parents'.

2. List four negative characteristics of each of your parents. Then list four of your own negative qualities. Compare these characteristics with your parents'.

3. Find three areas where you have made a conscious effort to be like your mother. Identify three ways you have made a conscious effort to be different from your mother.

4. Find three areas where you have made a conscious effort to be like your father. Identify three ways you have made a conscious effort to be different from your father.

5. Describe the most basic struggle you experienced as a child. Try to find evidence of this struggle in your current life.

6. List two or three of the central defining events of your childhood. Try to find continuing evidence of the impact of these events in your contemporary life.

ASSERTIVENESS JOURNAL EXERCISES

1. List your four most basic emotional needs. Now briefly discuss how you do or do not operate in your life to have these legitimate needs met.
2. Describe the characteristics of someone you view as appropriately assertive. Now compare yourself in light of these traits.
3. Look at three close relationships in your life in regard to Assertiveness. How could these relationships become more meaningful if you intensified your healthy Assertiveness?
4. Identify an individual in your life who behaves in a narcissistically entitled fashion. List three steps you could take to make your relationship with this person more equitable.
5. List three of your own qualities or actions that involve unreasonable needs and/or demands you might make on others. How could working on a healthier balance of Assertiveness help you modify these behaviors?
6. Define the term *self-respect* as it applies to you and others. Assess how you have or do not have enough self-respect. Suggest how Assertiveness could help you gain more self-respect.

THE EFC JOURNAL AND SPECIFIC EMOTIONAL PROBLEMS

Modern cognitive and behavioral therapies have made extensive use of the journaling process in the treatment of depression, anxiety and panic states, obsessive-compulsive disorders, and certain other emotional difficulties. If you are prone to any of these conditions, the EFC Journal can be a useful adjunct to psychotherapy.

Following are examples of how the EFC Journal can be used to address specific emotional problems. In these cases, journal writing and the other Training Techniques were utilized as part of a multimodal approach that included professional counseling.

EFC JOURNAL EXCERPT: DEPRESSION/FEELINGS IDENTIFICATION AND TOLERANCE

Now that my depression has lifted a little, I'm becoming more aware of just how angry I've been with my ex-boyfriend and still am in a lot of ways. He really used me, fed me lines, and I was too vulnerable to resist.

Even as I'm writing this, I start to feel enraged and I'm literally shaking with anger. My usual way is to swallow my upset or try to minimize it in some way. But my doctor told me this could kindle and fuel depression for me. It's not good to hold that stuff in.

I know I don't ever want to feel that blackness again. So I've got to keep working at labeling my angry feelings and learning healthier ways to feel my anger and express it better. I'll tell you, it's not easy.

My doctor suggested that I write a letter to my ex that I may or may not mail and get all my feelings out. If I can do that, I think I'll be able to face him directly some time soon and tell him like it is.

EFC JOURNAL EXCERPT: EATING DISORDER/EMPATHY

I've been bulimic for over three years now. I stuff myself, then make myself throw up. It's really hurting my health now, and I have to do something. So I'm in this support group, and I'm also doing the EFC Program.

When I took the EFC Self-Assessments, I found my biggest problem was in the area of Empathy. Which kind of surprised me. I guess I never really thought about how much I think about other people before.

But it's interesting; last night in the group we went around the room and talked about when we're less likely to do our usual symptoms with food. I blurted out that when my boyfriend and I are close and getting along, I'm less likely to binge and purge. I still do it, but not as bad.

It's funny, but my boyfriend always complains that I'm obsessed with my food problems, and I guess, with myself. Maybe I do need to focus a little more on him and his feelings. I also want to try this with my best friend. She's always so good about listening to me talk about my eating disorder, but maybe I need to listen to what's going on in her life more. Maybe if I'm less involved with my own problems with food, it'll become less of a problem.

EFC JOURNAL EXCERPT: ANXIETY-PANIC DISORDER/ INSIGHT

My mother was always a major worrier. I always tell people that I grew up watching her shriek with horror about something or other all the time. I never felt safe.

My father seemed physically fragile, always tired and worried. He was constantly worried about dying, and one day he finally did die. I remember I was so sad, but I wasn't really surprised; it always seemed like something really bad would happen to us.

I'm always scared, and I never remember a time when I didn't feel this way. I'm always on edge. My therapist says this is the "fight-or-flight" response and it's been programmed into my nervous system from growing up in such a tense atmosphere.

Writing this could be helpful, but I'm still not sure how. Maybe understanding that there are reasons why I'm like this, always on edge, that it's not really my fault. It's like if you know how something works, then maybe you have a chance of fixing it.

EFC JOURNAL EXCERPT: SOCIAL PHOBIA/ ASSERTIVENESS

My therapist tells me I have issues about asking for what I want from other people. The truth is, I'm so sure I won't get what I want that I've mostly given up trying. I've pretty much been keeping to myself lately. It seems like the only way to stop getting hurt.

But the EFC Program says that you can't change by just thinking about your problems, or even talking about them, although that's part of the solution. You also have to actually do some things, take some action, to become stronger. In my case, I guess what I have to do is start reaching out to others and stop hibernating. My therapist calls it taking "calculated emotional risks."

It makes sense that if I stop approaching women, for instance, I don't even have a chance to be happy. I really don't want to be alone. I see all these people my age who already have a nice families, and I feel I'm missing out on so much. I know that I'm pretty miserable now and I have been for a long time. So what do I have to lose? I hear the words in my head: "Take a chance!"

Just writing this, I feel a little glimmer of hope. Like maybe I don't have to be stuck in one place. Maybe I can just reach out and take a chance.

EMOTIONAL FITNESS JOURNAL CHECKLIST

1. Decide on the format for your journal: handwritten, typewritten, or written on a computer. Purchase a journal, diary, or notebook and special pen if you prefer to write by hand.
2. Determine exactly how and where you will keep your journal safe and private.
3. During the Pre-Program Week, write in your journal three times during the week, for about 15 to 20 minutes each session, using the Free Flow technique.

4. During Weeks 1 through 8 of the EFC Program, write in your journal three times a week, 15-20 minutes per session. You can loosely focus your writing on the following Core Components, or you can Free Flow or adapt the themes in any way you choose.

WEEK	CORE COMPONENT FOR FOCUS OF MEDITATION/ AFFIRMATIONS
Week 1:	Feelings Identification and Tolerance
Week 2:	Empathy
Week 3:	Insight
Week 4:	Assertiveness
Week 5:	Feelings Identification and Tolerance
Week 6:	Empathy
Week 7:	Insight
Week 8:	Assertiveness

5. After the first eight weeks you have the option of repeating the Basic Track schedule, writing in a Free Flow style, or going on to the Customized Track schedule. If you select the Customized Track, determine your Primary and Secondary Core Components, which should match the areas you are working on in your meditation and visualization sessions.

6. If you're working on the Customized Track, write about your Primary Core Component during Weeks 9 through 12.

7. Write about your Secondary Core Component during Weeks 13 through 16 of the Customized Track.

8. Remember that you always have the option of writing about different Core Components as they relate to issues or events that come up in your life. Keep your journal writing relevant and fluid.

eleven

Exercise for Emotional Fitness

THE FOURTH AND FINAL TRAINING TECHNIQUE IS EX-
ERCISE FOR EMOTIONAL FITNESS, WHICH ALLOWS
you to channel the benefits of exercise into enhancing your
mental state and strengthening your Core Components. At
first, you may wonder why exercise is an integral part of
emotional health. If you have ever emerged from a workout
with a distinct change in your mood and mind-set, you'll understand. Exercise has the ability to galvanize your emotional energy, relieve stress, and lift your spirits—benefits
that add momentum to your EFC Program.

Exercise creates stamina, resilience, and confidence,
which, when translated to the emotional realm, relate to
Feelings Identification and Tolerance. The challenge of staying with an exercise plan gives you direct experience in tolerating and persevering through difficult feelings.

Empathy is enhanced by exercise through both direct
and subtle pathways. First, as you work through the initial
discomfort that may be involved in a new exercise regime,
you learn to relate to other people's physical limitations and
struggles. In addition, when you are hardier and energized
yourself, you have more emotional strength to give other
people. You have greater physical and emotional reserves to
draw upon when others need your Empathy.

The rhythmic nature of exercise encourages the Core Component of Insight. Repetitive movements, such as walking, jogging, and swimming, allow your mind to shift from surface concerns to a deeper state of clarity. As you become established in your exercise routine, you're likely to find that a workout sparks your problem-solving ability and enables you to move past surface explanations to in-depth explanations that are indicative of Insight.

Exercise also has the inherent capacity to fortify your Assertiveness ability. As you gain physical skills and stamina, you become more confident in the world at large and can act with healthier Assertiveness. When you finish a vigorous workout, you feel a sense of mastery that can be channeled into your interactions with others. In addition, building aerobic and muscle strength can lead to a general sense of empowerment.

BENEFITS FOR YOUR BODY AND MIND

The physical effects of exercise have been well documented and highly publicized. Exercise can improve the ability of your circulation, immune, and musculoskeletal systems to handle various types of stresses. It can fortify your autoimmune system and help to remove toxins from your body.

The circulatory and cardiovascular systems are especially activated by aerobic exercise, which can reduce the heart rate while it increases stroke volume. This means that the heart supplies more blood with each stroke, meeting your body's needs for blood supply with greater efficiency. This improved circulation regulates blood pressure and can prevent fatty acids from depositing in the arteries. It helps to prevent hardening of the arteries and the resultant risk of heart disease.

As the size and strength of the blood vessels increase with regular aerobic training, more blood flows to the organs and tissues, rejuvenating the cells. Aerobic exercise also increases blood supply to the brain, which has an influence on clarity of thinking and mood.

Another important benefit of regular exercise, if it is weight bearing, is to strengthen the musculoskeletal system. This can help to prevent osteoporosis, which is of particular concern to women after menopause.

A balanced exercise program should include stretching for flexibility, as well as weight-bearing aerobic exercise. Stretching helps to keep your spine aligned, your muscles fluid, and joints lubricated. It can counteract the effects of sedentary jobs and awkward postures, sometimes preventing or alleviating back and neck pain and stiffness.

One of the major reasons why exercise adds to Emotional Fitness is its capacity to provide you with more energy. As you become more fit, the number and density of the capillaries feeding the muscles increase. This enables the muscles to produce more mitochondria, cells that turn fuel into energy. When you have greater reserves of both physical and mental energy, your ability to strengthen your Core Components and respond with peak Emotional Fitness is substantially enhanced.

Physical exercise may actually prolong or extend life, as well as improve its quality. The Centers for Disease Control and Prevention has stated that if every American who is currently sedentary would engage in some physical activity for thirty minutes a day, there would be an annual decline in deaths of 250,000 a year.

Dr. Ralph Paffenbarger of Stanford University, one of the most renowned researchers in the exercise area, has published several studies concluding that moderate exercise in adult life can significantly increase life expectancy. His famous study of Harvard alumni found that men who participated in activities such as walking, climbing stairs, and sports, in which they used 2,000 or more calories per week, had death rates one-quarter to one-third lower than those who were less active.

Since the mind and body are essentially parts of one

whole, physical benefits of exercise can influence your emotional state. In addition, exercise has distinct mental/psychological results and is often associated with an upswing in mood. There are many reasons for this phenomenon, some well understood and others less so.

One of the mechanisms by which exercise alters brain chemistry is by activating the production of neurotransmitters such as endorphins. Endorphins can induce feelings of well-being, joy, and euphoria, sometimes called "runner's high." A more accurate term would be "exercise high," since any sustained aerobic exercise can produce this sensation. Exercise can stimulate the release of endorphins and other chemical messengers such as serotonin, producing a sense of euphoria.

Exercise has a relaxing as well as energizing effect, a delightful paradox. Aerobic exercise often relieves stress and tension, leaving you relaxed and invigorated. Stretching and yoga can induce even deeper states of relaxation.

During aerobic exercise, blood flow to the brain increases, which enhances the quality of your thought processes. Studies have shown that aerobic exercise has the potential to improve memory, concentration, verbal fluency, and creative problem-solving ability. These abilities produce greater resources for building your Core Components of Emotional Fitness.

In one study at the Longevity Research Institute in Santa Monica, a group of thirty-one volunteers, average age sixty, who had suffered from cardiovascular and other degenerative diseases, followed a diet and exercise program that included daily walks. After less than a month, volunteers scored substantially higher than they had previously on tests that measured specialization, self-control, tolerance, achievement, and intellectual efficiency.

Another interesting study followed a group of adults in their forties who took part in a walking/jogging program for ten weeks. Compared to the control subjects, who remained sedentary, the exercisers had a much better response on memory tests involving retention of numbers. This study seems to indicate that exercise can improve memory and other cognitive functions at any age.

Exercise has been indicated as a treatment for moderate psychological problems such as depression and anxiety. In a pilot study, Dr. John Greist of the University of Wisconsin Medical School found that a strenuous running program provided effective symptomatic treatment for some moderately depressed subjects. Several other therapists who were surveyed in Dr. Greist's article described cases in which depressed individuals improved when they began running.

There are several possible explanations for why some depression can be alleviated by running. One theory postulates that depression is caused by a deficiency of the hormone norepinephrine in the synapses of the brain. Vigorous aerobic exercise can stimulate a surge of the release of norepinephrine, along with endorphins. Other evidence suggests that the neurotransmitter serotonin, thought to play a key role in the regulation of emotions, is made more available in the brain with systematic physical activity.

Another possible explanation of the cognitive type is that exercise is a distraction from the repetitive negative thought patterns of depression, forcing the individual to notice the environment and other elements. Also, physical activity seems to counteract the feelings of helplessness so common in depression. In some situations, depression may actually be caused or exacerbated by physical inactivity and confinement because it seems to fuel feelings of helplessness.

Running has been used to treat anxiety and phobias, including agoraphobia (fear of open spaces) and claustrophobia (fear of closed spaces). While running and exercise alone are not cures for phobias, they can reduce irrational fears when combined with psychotherapy and visualization techniques.

When it comes to "everyday" anxiety, exercise is known to release pent-up tension and reduce worry while it builds confidence. One study found that even a fifteen-minute workout reduced anxiety levels among the participants.

A SAFE EXERCISE PROGRAM

Before you start any new form of exercise for your EFC program, it is strongly recommended that you visit your medical doctor for a complete physical examination. This should include a stress test, a blood workup, and other tests that your physician deems are necessary once you explain that you intend to start or accelerate an exercise regime. Be sure to discuss the specific physical activities in which you plan to participate and get your doctor's opinion as to their safety, considering your present physical condition.

Once you have started your exercise routine, you'll need to listen to your body and use your common sense. It's not unusual or necessarily dangerous to experience difficulty and mild aches and pains when you start a new activity. These "growing pains" can, in fact, indicate that your workout is sufficiently strenuous to build physical fitness. But if you experience any of the following warning signs or any other intense pain during or after your workout, stop immediately and check with your physician before you resume the activity. These warning signs include, but are not limited to:

· Sudden sharp pain
· Recurrent pain or pain that does not diminish after a day or two of rest
· Extremely rapid heart rate or irregular heartbeat
· Shortness of breath or difficulty breathing
· Dizziness or fainting

THE ELEMENTS OF EXERCISE

There are three main elements of a balanced exercise program:

· Aerobic or cardiovascular exercise
· Strength training or musculoskeletal development
· Stretching or flexibility exercise

Aerobic exercise conditions your heart to pump more blood with each stroke, resulting in a lowered resting heart rate and higher overall cardiovascular fitness. During aerobic exercise, cells throughout your body are oxygenated as a large volume of blood is pumped through your heart, lungs, and muscle groups. Aerobic exercise can also positively affect your metabolic rate, leading your body to operate more efficiently.

Forms of aerobic exercise include: walking, jogging/running, swimming, aerobic dance, step classes, biking, rowing, spinning (high-intensity exercise using stationary bike), and cross-country skiing. Other types of dance, various sports, and jumping rope can also be aerobic if they are performed nonstop for twenty to thirty minutes.

Aerobic exercise generally has a rhythmic quality, which makes it especially encouraging for the Core Components of Emotional Fitness. It produces a set of physiological changes that can evoke emotional effects such as elevated mood, confidence, creativity, and clarity of thinking. For these physical/psychological benefits, aerobic exercise is preferred as the primary choice during the EFC Program.

Strength training or musculoskeletal development, increases the strength, endurance, and flexibility of the skeletal muscles of the body. This is achieved through repeated movements in which the muscle is challenged, either by lifting your own body weight or an outside weight for resistance. As training continues, the amount of weight and the number of repetitions and sets can gradually be increased to continue building the muscles.

Strength training is especially good for developing Assertiveness. It can also assist with aspects of FIT, such as withstanding discomfort, overcoming shyness, and alleviating anxiety.

Moderate strength training has quite a different intent and effect than bodybuilding or weight lifting. Bodybuilding strives to develop and display massive, highly defined, symmetrical muscles through the use of heavy freestanding weights such as barbells and dumbells. Strength training works to firm, tone, and strengthen without developing exaggerated, bulky muscles.

Strength training can be performed with free weights or weight-resistance machines. You can also use your own body weight and gravity as a form of resistance, for example, when doing sit-ups and push-ups. Many aerobic dance, step, and other workout classes incorporate strength-training exercise into their routines. These classes can be a good way to gain the benefits of strength training, aerobics, and stretching in one session.

If you have never used weights or weight machines before, be sure to get instruction from a trainer (at your gym or one-on-one) to be certain you are using the correct form and the right level of weights or resistance.

Stretching, or flexibility exercises, work to keep your spine aligned, your muscles fluid, and joints lubricated. Stretching helps to maintain the full range of motion, prevent susceptibility to injury and back pain, and reduce aches, pains, and stiffness. It relieves muscle tension and can be quite relaxing. Stretching is helpful for nurturing Empathy and Insight.

Stretching can be done as a separate exercise session or it can be incorporated into an aerobic and/or strength training workout. In fact, flexibility exercises are recommended at the finish of most aerobic activities as a way to reduce muscle fatigue and tightness.

Yoga practice includes a great deal of stretching, along with muscle-strengthening and breathing exercises. Many stretches that are used in exercise classes of all types are based on ancient yoga postures.

SCHEDULE FOR EXERCISE FOR EMOTIONAL FITNESS IN THE EFC PROGRAM

During the Pre-Program Week or before, select one or two aerobic activities that you think you will enjoy and be able to do consistently. Have your physical exam and check with your doctor about the specific activities that you have selected.

Also during the Pre-Program Week or before, purchase any clothing or equipment you require, sign up for classes, join a gym, or do whatever else you need to do get ready to exercise.

For the first few weeks at least, it's a good idea to write down "exercise appointments" in your date book. Establish a firm schedule and stay with it.

The Basic Track:

During Weeks 1 through 8, do aerobic exercise at least three times each week, for 20 to 30 minutes per session. Include adequate warm-up and cool-down. If you are a beginner, you can break up the sessions into 10-minute periods with rest in between. As you build endurance, strive to continue for at least 20 minutes without stopping. If you want to increase the number or length of sessions, or add other activities, that's fine as long as you don't overdo it.

Depending on which activity you choose, you may need to concentrate on the movement itself, or you may have time to think about your EFC affirmations, goals, and themes. If you have an opportunity, focus on whatever Core Component you're working on in the other Training Techniques that week.

The Customized Track:

During Weeks 9 through 16, do aerobic exercise at least three times each week, for 20 to 30 minutes per session. Include adequate warm-up and cool-down.

Try to increase your duration to 30 minutes, or more if you're inspired. Gradually increase the intensity of your workout, also. For example, you can walk up hills, run faster, or try a more advanced aerobic dance class. Don't overwork your body, but keep challenging yourself. If you want to exercise more than three times a week, this will accelerate your EFC training as well as your physical progress.

You may want to continue with the exercise you started during the first two months of the Program, and/or try new, more demanding activities. You can also devote some of your sessions to those activities that nurture a particular Core Component. During your workout, if possible, and during the cool-down period afterwards, affirm your EFC goals and focus your thoughts on your Primary or Secondary Core Component.

THE FITNESS REINFORCEMENT LOOP IN EXERCISE FOR EFC

If you have not been exercising at all and feel that even twenty minutes at a time is too much, you can do two ten-minute sessions in a day instead. After a few weeks, you can probably progress to twenty continuous minutes, and after a few more weeks, go for thirty. This will ensure that you are exercising for a sufficient length of time to activate the Fitness Reinforcement Loop.

The Fitness Reinforcement Loop is readily apparent during Exercise for Emotional Fitness, since it is modeled on the training effect in athletic endeavor. For example, at first, running or fast-paced walking might greatly increase your heart and respiration rate, causing fatigue and physiologic stress. But as the training effect evolves over time and your body becomes conditioned, a stabilizing of these rates occurs and you develop tolerance for the demands of running. Once you gain physical strength and endurance, the activity no longer seems so arduous. It becomes a pleasure and a joyful outlet instead of an effort of sheer will.

Hopefully, you'll select a form of exercise that you enjoy from the outset, even if you do experience some degree of difficulty initially. But if you find exercise to be a chore no matter what you do, keep in mind the Fitness Reinforcement Loop. Your exercise sessions will inevitably become easier and more pleasurable. And you will experience a motivating array of physical and emotional rewards.

CHOOSING YOUR EXERCISE FOR EMOTIONAL FITNESS

Remember the sheer joy of physical activity when you were a child? Running, walking, biking, playing ball, swimming in the summertime, dancing . . . there was probably some type of exercise that you thought was pure fun.

This is the type of feeling we want to recapture with Exercise for Emotional Fitness. This is exercise that is just for you, not for a team, not for a score, not to impress anyone else. It's time to let go, to recharge, to play.

If you have been exercising regularly, you've probably already found an activity you like to do. If you're just beginning or resuming exercise, select an activity that is appropriate to your fitness level and your lifestyle and, most important, potentially pleasurable. The secret to avoiding "exercise burnout" is simple. If you derive joy from the process as well as the outcome, you're more likely to continue.

In 1994, decades after health experts began urging Americans to exercise for health, a study found that only 20 percent of the population was doing the minimum required for physical fitness. Clearly, the threat of heart disease, obesity, and other health problems is not enough to keep people motivated.

In most cases, it is not primarily discipline that keeps people going in an exercise program. The people who keep up with their exercise are the ones who enjoy it. Certainly they may be driven by the desire to stay in shape for reasons of health and vanity, but it's also likely that they delight in the exercise for its own sake as well as the results.

With so many forms of exercise to choose from, there is truly something for everyone.

If you haven't yet found an activity that you like, try something new. Be aware that there is a certain adjustment period, during which you need to master the skills and strengths that the activity requires. But once you do, you should find your exercise sessions fun as well as rewarding. If you don't, try another activity until you discover one that's right for your fitness and energy level, your temperament, and your tastes. If you prefer, you can participate in two or three different activities as part of your EFC Program.

Initially, select an activity that's not too taxing for your current physical fitness level, so you're not discouraged during first weeks of the EFC Program. Later, as you gain strength and endurance, you can move on to more challenging activities.

FINDING YOUR FITNESS LEVEL

Following are guidelines for identifying your basic Fitness Level. These guidelines are a starting point, but certainly not the last word on what's safe and what isn't for your particular condition. It's still imperative to have a checkup and ask your physician if you're ready for the specific form of exercise you select.

These levels are designed for people within the general age range of eighteen to sixty. If you're older, your level will depend on your exercise history and your health history, with special attention to cardiovascular factors. When you identify your level, be realistic and honest with yourself, but not judgmental. It doesn't matter whether you're a Level 1 or Level 4, as long as you exercise safely and consistently.

FITNESS LEVELS

Level 1:   Ideal weight
            Already participating in regular, vigorous exercise
            No health problems

Level 2:   Ideal to moderate weight
            Already exercising intermittently, and/or fairly
            active lifestyle
            No major health problems

Level 3:   Moderately or quite overweight, and/or
            no regular exercise, inactive lifestyle

Level 4:   Overweight and very sedentary lifestyle, no
            exercise
            Prexisting physical conditions such as severe ar-
            thritis, heart disease, hypertension, disabilities, or
            other significant physical limitations

*Note: Physical activities for Emotional Fitness can be adapted
for almost anyone, even those who are wheelchair bound.
Check with your physician for modifications of different
forms of exercise, if needed.*

AEROBIC ACTIVITIES FOR DIFFERENT FITNESS LEVELS

If you're currently at Level 3 or 4 and you find the aerobic choices limited, remember that you can build up to additional activities. This is achieved through a walking or swimming program, and weight loss when needed. An exercise trainer, teacher, or physician should be able to give you guidance on your progression.

Aerobic Activities

Jogging/Running: Level 1 to start.
                      Level 2 can start with fast walking and
                      build up to jogging.

Walking: All levels. Adjust distance and speed to
                      individual condition.
                      Not recommended for those with severe
                      arthritis in hips or knees, or certain
                      disabilities.

Swimming: All levels.

Aerobic Dance/   Levels 1 or 2. (Level 2 can start with be-
Step: ginner classes.)
                      Level 3 can work up to it with a walking
                      or swimming program.
                      Not recommended for people with injur-
                      ies or arthritis.

Other Dance: Levels 1 and 2.
                      Levels 3 and 4 can work up to it by start-
                      ing slowly.

Biking/Spinning: Levels 1 and 2.

Sports/Martial Arts: Levels 1 and 2.
                      Level 3 can build up to it after a brisk
                      walking program.

Rowing/Cross   Level 1; Level 2 can start with 5 minutes
Country Skiing/   and gradually add time.
Jumping rope:

Nonaerobic Exercise

Strength Training: Levels 1 and 2.
                      Level 3 can start slowly with guidance.

Stretching: Some form of gentle stretching can be
                      done by all levels, with attention to injuries
                      and physical limitations. Individual guid-
                      ance may be needed for Levels 3 and 4.

Yoga: Levels 1 and 2. Levels 3 and 4 can also
                      participate, with personalized attention
                      from a yoga instructor.

The best way to embark on a new exercise program is with a knowledgeable trainer or teacher. One option is to book a few sessions with a personal trainer, who can create and supervise a customized workout. Training can take place in a gym, health club, spa, in your home, or outdoors. Personal trainers are highly motivating and can often coax the most reluctant exerciser into moving, but they are expensive.

Less costly alternatives usually involve group classes, which are widely available through gyms and health clubs, dance schools, exercise salons, adult education programs, "Y's," and community schools. Classes offer a trained instructor, the fun of a group, and a structure and schedule to keep you on track. Exercise videos and books are other options.

Many people find it useful to have an exercise partner with whom they regularly schedule workouts. Partners can help you stay with your exercise schedule, since you have some explaining to do if you try to wriggle out of a session. They can also make the workouts more interesting, sociable, and fun. Canine companions can make excellent exercise partners for walkers and even runners, depending on the breed. You can check with your veterinarian to find out if your pet would be an appropriate running companion.

Following are some basic thoughts and hints about the most common forms of aerobic exercise to help you make your selection. You can learn more about safely performing whatever activity you choose from instructors, books, and videos.

WALKING

Walking comes naturally and is a safe, easy, and free form of exercise that almost anyone can do. While walking is relatively gentle, it still delivers measurable benefits. A study by the Institute for Aerobics Research found that brisk walking for a minimum of twenty minutes at least three times a week can substantially improve the body's oxygen uptake and cardiovascular strength.

Walking also strengthens muscles, particularly in the lower body. To add upper-body impact you can move your arms back and forth vigorously as you walk, carry light weights, push a carriage, or walk a dog on a leash.

Walking has been well regarded throughout the ages as a mental tonic as well as a physical boon. It helps to clear the mind, stimulate creative thought processes, and reduce tension. While walking can be done on a treadmill, in a mall, on a city street, or almost anywhere, a pleasant outdoor setting is especially refreshing to the soul.

Since it is entirely rhythmic and natural, walking is ideal for cultivating Emotional Fitness. You can let your thoughts flow freely during your walk or meditate on your EFC affirmations, goals, and progress.

Wear comfortable, climate appropriate clothing for your walks and a good pair of sneakers or walking shoes. Keep your neck and shoulders relaxed, your arms swinging, and your hips flexible. You can start with as little as ten minutes at a time if you're at Level 3 or 4 and gradually build up to twenty minutes, then thirty or forty.

Begin with five minutes of walking at a slower pace to warm-up. Slow down again for five minutes at the end to cool down. As you become accustomed to walking, you can gradually increase speed and duration to build fitness. Walking uphill also increases the aerobic effect. As you become more conditioned, you may find yourself spontaneously breaking into a jog.

JOGGING/RUNNING

Jogging or running is one of the most rewarding, intensive and even addictive forms of exercise. It produces a sense of exhilaration and achievement, which has an intense effect on Emotional Fitness as well as physical capacity. However, it's certainly not for everyone.

Since there are many precautions associated with running, it's critical that you have your doctor's go-ahead before starting. Even if you are of a healthy weight, free of injury, and fairly fit already, you'll want to start with a few weeks of brisk walking three times a week, then graduate to slow jogging. You can methodically increase the frequency, intensity, and duration of your runs, monitoring your rate to stay in the target zone.

You'll need high-quality running sneakers built for forward motion and light, layered seasonal clothing. If you run outside at dusk, dawn, or after dark, wear reflexive patches on your clothing.

If you run indoors on a treadmill, try not to get too engrossed in all the complicated readings found on the high-tech machines. Run at your own rhythm and let your mind flow for the EFC effect.

Running is never an entirely risk-free activity, but you can make it safer with sufficient warm-up and cool-down. Warm-up consists of mild stretching and a slower pace for the first five minutes of the run. Cool-down requires slowing the pace back down to a walk for the last five minutes, followed by gentle stretching. It's nice to take a long, hot shower to relax your hardworking muscles and joints afterwards.

SWIMMING

Like walking, swimming is a safe, natural form of exercise in which almost everyone can participate. As long as you know how to swim and do it in an area with a lifeguard, swimming brings little risk of injury. Wear goggles to protect your eyes from chlorine, and never swim alone or in rough surf or currents.

If you're at Fitness Level 3 or 4 you can start with ten minutes of swimming, then gradually build up to twenty minutes and then thirty. Once you've hit the twenty-minute marker, the cardiovascular benefits start to kick in. Swimming also strengthens the muscles and can be therapeutic for injured joints and for arthritis.

You can warm-up and cool-down for aerobic lap swimming right in the water, by slowly stretching along the sides of the pool. As alternatives to lap swimming, you can walk or run in a pool, or take an aqua aerobics class.

Swimming is a tonic for the emotions because of the sense of weightlessness, the rhythmic quality of the swimming strokes, and the immersion in water with its evocation of the womb. While you are swimming, you can repeat your meditation focus word and affirmations and even think of a visualization. Or you can allow your mind to wander and let the water do its magic.

AEROBIC DANCE AND STEP CLASSES

High-impact aerobics enjoyed a tremendous vogue, followed by a crash due to a high rate of injuries. Now, most aerobic dance classes are low impact, meaning that they minimize jumping, bouncing, and other high-impact movements to reduce the risk of injury.

If you're at Fitness Level 1 or 2, you can start with an appropriate-level class, depending on your experience. Aerobic dance classes are widely available, offered in health clubs, gyms, exercise salons, spas, "Y's," adult-education classes, and community schools. Before you sign up, ask about the instructor's experience and credentials, and, if possible, watch a class. Be sure that the instructor has a supportive attitude and a firm grounding in exercise safety.

Aerobics should be done on a well-cushioned health-club floor or wooden surface, while wearing supportive aerobic sneakers. If you have a history of joint injuries or arthritis, or if you are at Fitness Level 3 or 4, aerobic dance will be too demanding.

Many of these same guidelines apply to step classes, which use a step of varying heights to intensify the workout without adding impact. When stepping, keep your knees slightly bent, your shoulders aligned with your hips, and back straight. The step should be low enough to prevent knee pain and injury.

Step and aerobic dance classes often include upper-body strength work, along with stretching, warm-up, and cooldown. They can be an excellent way to include all three elements of exercise in one strenuous, thorough workout. The excitement generated by the music and a good instructor can be inspiring and produce an aerobic "high."

Aerobic dance and step classes have a strong rhythmic element and are conducive to strengthening the Core Components, particularly FIT and Assertiveness. Since the classes keep you busy with varied movements, they do not allow much time for contemplation. But they can still encourage Emotional Fitness by building self-esteem, along with a sense of mastery and control.

Other forms of dance are not strictly aerobic in nature, unless you keep moving for twenty to thirty minutes without stopping. Nonetheless, dancing oxygenates, strengthens, and limbers up the body, and offers an outlet for expressing emotions. Dancing is also an especially relevant activity for those looking to build social skills, an area encompassing all the Core Components. Whether you enjoy rock-and-roll dancing, belly dancing, ballroom, or ballet, follow your bliss.

BIKING

Bicycle riding, particularly outdoors, is a solid aerobic workout that builds Emotional Fitness as well as physical fitness. Indoor stationary bikes are an alternative for inclement weather or for those who don't feel secure riding on roads with cars. Either type of biking, when done for twenty to thirty minutes nonstop, provides cardiovascular conditioning and muscular strength, while delivering the emotional benefits of rhythmic exercise.

Biking is generally recommended for Fitness Levels 1 and 2, while Level 3 can prepare with a brisk walking program combined with stretching. However, if you have arthritis, knee injuries, or back pain, biking is not a safe choice, since it can put pressure on the joints and compress the spine. Also, if you're male, there is some evidence that prolonged time on a bike can affect your urogenital system, so you may want to check with your doctors regarding precautions.

Racing bicycles, which are ridden with the spine almost parallel to the ground, relieve spinal pressure but require a high degree of fitness to handle. Mountain bikes, hybrids, and regular bikes are better for beginners. Spinning bikes, a popular type of stationery bike, are generally used in gyms and high-energy classes.

To warm-up for biking, do some gentle stretching, followed by a period of slow riding. Stretching is also recommended after the ride to cool-down and maintain flexibility. Bikers need sneakers with a good grip, close-fitting biking shorts or pants, reflectors on the bike, and, above all, a safety helmet. If you're planning to take long rides, a bike pump, a spare inner tube, a repair kit, and a bottle of water are strongly recommended. Awareness of vehicles on the road and adherence to safety precautions at all times is imperative.

Unless you ride indoors on a stationery bike, you'll need to stay alert and won't have time to focus on your EFC goals or other distracting thoughts during the ride. However, biking can strengthen the Core Components, particularly FIT and Assertiveness.

SPORTS

Technically speaking, sports are a cross between aerobic and anaerobic exercise, since they usually involve short bursts of activity rather than sustained movement. But if a social, competitive game motivates you to exercise, sports can be a good option. You may want to include tennis, racquetball, basketball, soccer, volleyball, squash, baseball, hockey, or martial arts in your Exercise for Emotional Fitness program. If golf is your game, walk the course instead of riding in a cart to get a better workout.

Be sure that your Fitness Level, strength, and experience prepare you for whatever sports you want to play. Warm-up and cool-down for sports usually consist of gentle stretching and walking or jogging in place. Wear appropriate sneakers and any safety equipment that is suggested. Try to enjoy the sport for its own sake instead of fixating on the competitive aspect.

Sports don't allow you much time to think about the Core Components, nor do they have a rhythmic quality. But they can be a terrific release of anger, frustration, and other emotions, freeing you up to experience greater Emotional Fitness. Sports can fortify the Core Components, particularly FIT and Assertiveness.

ROWING/CROSS-COUNTRY SKIING/ROPE JUMPING

Rowing can be done outdoors or indoors on a stationery rower. To qualify as aerobic, it must be continued for at least twenty minutes without stopping. Rowing can provide cardiovascular training, as well as strengthening the upper body. It has a rhythmic quality that can nurture the Core Components, especially when in an outdoor setting. Of course, if you go canoeing, kayaking, crewing, or paddling, you must wear a life preserver and have someone along with you at all times.

Cross-country skiing can also be an outdoor sport or a gym activity. It provides a vigorous aerobic workout that strengthens the heart and muscles. Since outdoor cross-country skiing requires skill as well as basic fitness, be certain you have the right equipment and an experienced companion with you. Indoors or outdoors, cross-country skiing is rhythmic and can foster development of all the Core Components.

In general, both rowing and cross-country skiing are appropriate for Fitness Levels 1 and 2, with adequate warm-up and cool-down in the form of stretching and slower movement.

Jumping rope is intensive exercise, and only Fitness Level 1 participants are likely to be able to do it for a solid twenty minutes at the outset. Those at Fitness Level 2 can begin with five minutes and gradually build up, provided there is no history of arthritis or joint injuries. Wear supportive sneakers and jump rope only on a flexible gym floor or wooden surface. Warm-up and cool-down by stretching and walking in place.

Jumping rope can provide a sense of accomplishment along with the aerobic effects that help facilitate Emotional Fitness. However, you'll probably want to balance it with other exercise choices during the EFC Program.

STRENGTH TRAINING

Aerobic activities are a priority during the EFC Program, due to their unique combination of tangible mind/body effects. But you should not feel limited to aerobic exercise if you want to expand your fitness choices. Anything that you want to do in addition to your three sessions of aerobic exercise a week can only enhance your progress.

Strength training is a popular choice, either as a separate activity or incorporated into a fitness class or self-guided gym workout. Strength training is useful for developing Assertiveness and for many aspects of Feelings Identification and Tolerance. In the Insight area, strength training can help you overcome limiting personal mythologies. Many people find that building muscles is also empowering in an emotional sense.

In general, strength training is appropriate for Levels 1 and 2, while Levels 3 and 4 may be able to participate with the individual guidance of a skilled trainer or therapist.

STRETCHING

Stretching is an integral part of any aerobic exercise session, to help prevent injuries, aches, and pains, as well as elongate your growing muscles. Teachers, trainers, and exercise books and videos can show you the best stretches for your particular aerobic activity or sport. Don't shortchange yourself by skipping the stretching—it's one of the most important parts of your workout.

A stretching session after aerobics can be a powerful time to repeat your EFC affirmations and consider your progress in the various Core Components. You can then segue into deep breathing and a few minutes of restful meditation.

On days when you don't do any aerobic exercise, try to spend ten minutes stretching, in the morning, at the end of a workday, or whenever you can. You can create a routine of favorite stretches or work on special stretches for whatever body part feels tight. The release of physical tension will have its counterpart in a letting go of psychological tension, freeing your energy for Emotional Fitness.

The beauty of stretching is that almost anyone at any fitness level or age can do it. However, you may need personal guidance from a teacher or trainer to show you which stretches are appropriate for your condition. It's well worth the investment in some initial guidance to devise a stretching routine that you can continue to do on your own for years to come.

YOGA

While yoga is not strictly an aerobic activity, it is ideal for cultivating Emotional Fitness. Yoga emphasizes deep, rhythmic breathing and the connection among the body, the mind, and higher spiritual forces. With a history that stretches back for thousands of years, it is the original Exercise for Emotional Fitness, producing a profound influence on the mind as well as the body.

During the EFC Program, you may want to do yoga instead of some of your aerobic exercise sessions or in addition to them. If you're substituting yoga for aerobics, try to take a class that features a dynamic, active style of yoga practice. Yoga classes range from very mild and meditative to extremely challenging and kinetic. See if you can watch the class or speak to the instructor before signing up for a series, to determine that the style and pace are appropriate.

Yoga has the innate capacity to activate all the Core Components of Emotional Fitness. Its spiritual philosophy of "oneness" and altruism encourages Empathy. The meditation and deep breathing inspire Insight, while the practice of difficult poses strengthens Feelings Identification and Tolerance.

Yoga is generally appropriate for Fitness Levels 1 and 2, while Fitness Levels 3 and 4 can participate in beginner classes with personal attention from skilled instructors. Yoga is similar to Emotional Fitness Conditioning in that you can start at any level and continue to learn and grow throughout a lifetime.

EXERCISE CHOICES AND THE CORE COMPONENTS

While nearly all forms of exercise have general benefits that can be utilized in the enhancement of the Core Components, certain activities have special strengths. Once you've reached the Customized Track of the EFC Program, you may want to select types of exercise that support the Primary and Secondary Core Components on which you are focusing in your other Training Techniques. The following list provides general guidelines as to which Core Components various exercise activities tend to encourage.

FIT: Jogging/running, aerobic dance/step, outdoor biking, spinning, rowing, cross-country skiing, martial arts, strength training.

Empathy: Walking, swimming, aqua aerobics, cross-country skiing, some team sports, yoga, stretching.

Insight: Jogging/running, walking, biking, swimming, cross-country skiing, yoga, stretching.

Assertiveness: Aerobic dance/step, spinning, strength training, sports, martial arts, racing (including running, swimming, bicycling, and other types).

During your EFC program, you can mobilize the emotional energy and problem-solving ability that is generated by exercise to focus on specific issues around Core Components. For example, when I reached an impasse during the writing of this book, I would often let my thoughts flow freely around the subject while I was running. By the end of the run, I would have evolved several leads that would allow me to continue successfully. You can utilize a similar process to make breakthroughs in your EFC efforts during your own Exercise for Emotional Fitness sessions.

CHECKLIST FOR EXERCISE FOR EMOTIONAL FITNESS

1. Determine your Fitness Level and review the exercise choices. Decide on one or two activities in which you would like to participate.
2. Visit your physician for a complete examination. Tell the doctor specifically which types of exercise you plan to do and get the go-ahead.
3. Purchase any clothing or equipment you need, sign up for classes, join a gym, or do whatever else is necessary to prepare.
4. During Weeks 1 through 8, do aerobic exercise at least three times each week, for twenty to thirty minutes per session. Include adequate warm-up and cool-down.

5. During Weeks 9 through 16, continue to do aerobic exercise at least three times each week, for 20 to 30 minutes per session. Include adequate warm-up and cool-down. Try to gradually increase the intensity and duration of your workouts. Experiment with a few other activities if you wish, in "cross-training" fashion.

6. Whenever you have the opportunity during your exercise sessions, focus on your EFC affirmations, goals, and progress as previously discussed.

twelve

The Impact of Emotional Fitness Conditioning

I T'S PERFECTLY NATURAL TO WONDER WHAT CHANGES AND RESULTS YOU CAN EXPECT FROM THE FOUR months of the EFC Program. However, there is no one-size-fits-all answer. Emotional Fitness Conditioning has a wide range of potential benefits. Your attitude about change, your personality and expectations, and the life circumstances with which you start are some of the many factors that can influence the outcome.

Many participants experience dramatic changes in their external world as well as their inner lives during the course of the EFC Program. Other people have more subtle reactions, largely reflected in how they think and feel, which then gradually come to have an impact on the way they live in positive ways. Often, the seeds of change are planted during the Program, but it takes additional time for the full potential of EFC to be realized.

Another common question about the Program is whether Emotional Fitness Conditioning will make you happier. The only honest answer to this question is yes, no, and maybe. Everyone has a different definition of happiness. And everyone knows that happiness is an elusive, hard-to-define quality involving both perception and reality. It is impossible to quantify, measure, or universally define.

However, it is highly likely that Emotional Fitness Conditioning will have a positive effect on the four major areas that are key elements of happiness: self-esteem, relationships, job satisfaction/performance, and physical well-being.

EFC AND SELF-ESTEEM

Self-esteem is a successful outcome or "product" of systematically strengthening your Core Components. It is produced by engaging in specific patterns of both thought and behavior, which are directly influenced by EFC.

What is commonly termed "self-esteem" consists of three basic elements: self-image, body image, and ego ideal. Self-image concerns how you view, value, and feel about yourself. The goal here is to be able to see yourself as an essentially worthwhile person.

Of course, your own personal values about what qualities a worthwhile human being should possess will influence both your self-image and your self-esteem. Traditionally, most people value being good to their families, concerned about others, productive, honest, and dependable. Your own value system may be different; for example, you may believe it's imperative to be creative, attain a certain level of material success, or change the world.

However you define a worthwhile human being, your self-image will be enhanced by the EFC Program. Building the Core Components of FIT and Assertiveness will empower you to progress in your ongoing efforts to be the person you want to be and legitimately can be given your essential talents and resources. Meanwhile, Empathy and Insight will help you to acknowledge and forgive your shortcomings, instead of allowing them to undermine your self-image. At the same time, you'll see concrete progress in the qualities most of us have defined as important and worthy.

Body image, the second element of self-esteem, is your perception of your physical body. The goal here is to have a basic feeling of acceptance and comfort with your physical self. This includes approval of the way your body looks and feels, in its active and inactive states.

The Training Technique of Exercise for Emotional Fitness plays a major role in improving your actual level of physical fitness and your body image. Meditation, visualization, and journaling help you come to terms with your real or perceived physical shortcomings. The Core Components of Insight and Empathy enable you to be less judgmental and more empathic and realistic about your body image. The idea is to strive for a feeling of comfortable imperfection.

Ego ideal, the third element of self-esteem, concerns the way you would like to see yourself, if you could pick and choose your characteristics, attitudes, and behaviors. A healthy, mature ego ideal is constructive and largely attainable. Unhealthy, unrealistic, or antisocial ego ideals can cause chronic frustration, low self-esteem, self-hatred, and conflict with mainstream society.

For example, if someone's ego ideal is to be the cleverest con artist on the planet, this is clearly dangerous. More commonly, the ego ideal might be somewhat grandiose, such as becoming a famous rock star or ballerina. These types of ego ideals can be inspiring if the the roles are remotely attainable. But they can be detrimental for someone who doesn't have the training, talent, drive, connections, and luck to achieve his or her ego ideal.

Many of us have certain ego ideals in our youth, which are then modified and made more realistic as we get older. This doesn't mean that we've "sold out" or given up on our dreams; rather, it is a sign of emotional maturity to adjust the ego ideal to the conceivable reality. For instance, a woman who wanted to be a Broadway star at age ten might be satisfied with going to aerobic dance classes and being a successful businesswoman at age forty-five. A man who was convinced he had to be an astronaut at age twelve might modify his ego ideal to being a good provider and a loving parent.

These accommodations of ego ideal allow us to reconcile

our dreams with reality and to maintain a healthy level of self-esteem. They also lead to positive modifications in our Emotional Templates. Rather than selling ourselves short, we actually give ourselves an opportunity for satisfaction by adapting our ego ideals as our lives unfold.

Enlarging your Insight brings understanding of the origins of your ego ideal and how it affects your behavior, relationships, and self-esteem. Empathy allows you to accept and forgive that you might not have reached your original ego ideal. Feelings Identification and Tolerance and Assertiveness give you tools for withstanding the potential difficulty of shifting your ego ideal to one that is grounded in mature values and to pursue goals in keeping with your personal reality. As the ego ideal becomes more reasonable, you have a better chance of fulfilling it and enjoying the self-esteem that results when ego ideal more closely approximates reality.

Solid self-esteem gives us the ability to maintain our essential self-worth even in the face of disapproval, criticism, or rejection. Yet it is human nature to care deeply about how others react to us, value us, and love us. Inevitably, our relationships have an impact on our self-esteem. By fostering more satisfying relationships, EFC also serves to enlarge our self-esteem.

EFC AND RELATIONSHIPS

As you've seen from some of the stories of participants, Emotional Fitness Conditioning can have a profound effect on relationships. Relationships with intimate partners, children, other family members, and friends can be positively altered by EFC. Developing your Core Components also influences interactions with co-workers, acquaintances, and even strangers.

The EFC Program can bring many benefits to relationships: improved communication, a more equitable balance of power, stronger bonding, less fear and insecurity, deeper love and passion. How the EFC Program might affect your own relationships depends on many factors, including the current dynamics and the history of the relationship, the issues that need to be resolved, and receptiveness toward change.

First you need to consider your own attitude toward change when it comes to relationships. The prospect of change can be threatening, confusing, or overwhelming in a relationship that has settled into a certain predictable pattern, however frustrating that pattern might be. The changes that relationships go through once you expand your Insight and Assertiveness are sometimes difficult and painful. We often feel safer maintaining the familiarity of the "status quo," even if we are dissatisfied or unhappy.

This is where the basic Core Component of FIT becomes so essential. It allows you to withstand the discomfort and difficulty that may ensue when you start to open up new lines of communication and explore interpersonal issues. FIT gives you the emotional courage to go through the necessary work to build a healthier relationship. It enables you to experience change as opportunity rather than danger.

The attitude of the other person in the relationship is also critical. Some people are reasonably open to change, while others are extremely resistant, usually because they feel threatened.

You can never force other people to change through Emotional Fitness Conditioning. All you can do is change the way you think, feel, and interact. By treating others with a sensitive balance of Empathy and Assertiveness, you can encourage them to respond. But, ultimately, the only person you can count on to change and grow through the EFC Program is yourself.

Whatever the other person's particular state of Emotional Fitness and receptiveness to change, however, the relationship is certain to evolve as you develop your Core Components. How you perceive, react, and communicate will alter your experience of the connection and give you a sense of control. This does not imply that you control the other person. It relates to your ability to understand and control your own emotions and actions regarding the relationship.

The most effective way to help other people through the EFC Program is not necessarily by convincing them to use the Training Techniques themselves. If they express an interest, it's certainly a nice idea to share this book and let them decide for themselves if they would like to participate. But just as you can't force anyone else to diet or exercise, it's rarely worthwhile to try to talk other people into the EFC Program. The best approach is usually to show others how it works through your own example.

If you are a parent of young children, you may have a more direct opportunity to share your knowledge of Emotional Fitness. You can teach your children that it is safe to experience and express their full range of feelings and that they can learn to withstand even the unpleasant emotions (FIT). You can show your children the importance of recognizing other people's feelings and treating everyone with respect and tolerance (Empathy). You can transmit understanding about the connections between the past and the present and surface and depth experience, and also be mindful of what type of personal mythologies you encourage (Insight). You can help your children to be clear about their legitimate needs and rights and know how to assert them appropriately (Assertiveness) while respecting the rights of others.

These lessons have always been a part of good parenting. The skills of Emotional Fitness encompass basic human values and attributes that parents instinctively try to instill in their children. The EFC Program will help you strengthen these qualities in yourself, so you can share them with your children and others you love more easily and naturally.

EFC AND PHYSICAL WELL-BEING

The Training Techniques have a measurable positive impact on your physical health, as well as your emotional wellness. By addressing your emotional issues and working toward solutions, you free yourself from a great deal of stress that might undermine your well-being.

In some instances, EFC may even help to relieve physical symptoms. It's long been suspected that repressed and negative emotions can have a detrimental impact on physical health, exacerbating or inducing pain, illness, or lowered immunity. PNI researchers are currently gathering data on mind/body interactions, working to quantify these complex connections. While the results are far from conclusive, there are strong indications that emotions can have a profound impact on physical health in some cases.

This is not to imply that anyone causes or is to blame for her or his own illness or pain. The biological, genetic, structural, and environmental factors, as well as the random element of chance involved in health should never be underestimated. But regardless of the precise mechanisms of mental/physical interplay, it is safe to say that becoming more emotionally fit can't hurt your health; it can only help.

If you are interested in reaching a higher state of physical fitness than the norm, you can take EFC a step further and use the Training Techniques to strive toward peak athletic performance. Many professional athletes utilize meditation, affirmation, and visualization as training tools. You can become your own sports psychologist by using Fitness Focused Meditation and Fitness Guided Visualization to work on specific exercise or sports-related goals.

In addition, nourishing the Core Components in general can hone physical skills. For example, Empathy as well as Assertiveness is important in team sports. The ability to withstand uncomfortable feelings (FIT) is clearly essential for individual endeavors, such as marathon running, long-distance biking, or strength training.

However you define your personal goals in the physical realm, Emotional Fitness Conditioning can bring you greater physical balance, energy, and endurance. If you continue to practice the Training Techniques, you have the potential of enjoying a healthier, more satisfying life.

EFC AND JOB SATISFACTION AND PERFORMANCE

EFC is useful whether you're productively retired, self-employed, working in the home, or in an outside environment. Developing your Core Components through the EFC Program can produce many tangible results in the work realm. These changes take place in three major aspects of your career: job-related relationships, satisfaction, and performance.

For most people who work outside the home, the work environment is a complex "mini-family model" of relationships. Many of the emotional issues that tend to arise in family life are mirrored in the workplace, including authority struggles and sibling (co-worker) rivalries. Status and recognition issues, alliances, and animosities of various kinds are often played out in the work arena.

As you become more emotionally fit, you will notice shifts in how you relate to co-workers on all levels, including subordinates, peers, and supervisors. The Core Component of Assertiveness is the one most often associated with job-related interactions, yet it is far from the only factor. All your Core Components have an impact on work environment relationships in various ways.

Empathy will attune your sensitivity to the feelings and emotional nuances that underlie the behavior of co-workers, facilitating more effective communication. Insight will give you a better understanding of how your own and other people's Emotional Templates influence styles of relating in the workplace. Feelings Identification and Tolerance will help you identify how emotions affect performance, concentration, and reactions to stress on the job.

Assertiveness will empower you to express yourself effectively without resorting to either counterproductive aggressive or obsequious stances. Just as important, it will cultivate your awareness of other people's legitimate rights and needs in conflict situations.

Another way in which EFC can enhance your work experience is by actually helping you do a better job. Regular practice of Fitness Guided Meditation can sharpen mental clarity, creativity, and problem-solving abilities. Exercise for Emotional Fitness generates the mental energy to get the job done and can also heighten thinking processes. Fitness Guided Visualization and journaling can be used as techniques for dealing with work-related issues and encouraging creativity. Each of these Training Techniques can hone your concentration and discipline, increasing your potential for success and job satisfaction.

By strengthening your Core Components, you will gain mastery over emotional issues that may be distracting you from your work, sapping your energy, or blocking your goals. As you make breakthroughs in the personal sphere, additional mental energy will be freed up for your work. You're less likely to be held back or drained by unresolved issues or negative emotions.

Acquiring FIT skills will enable you to more readily withstand the inevitable stress of work. Insight will give you knowledge of how your past affects your feelings about work, bringing greater tolerance for the ups and downs of your career. Empathy will refine your interpersonal communication skills. Assertiveness will allow you to make legitimate demands and set reasonable boundaries, creating a more comfortable and rewarding work environment.

As with any other worthwhile endeavor, the path to fulfillment in work is not always an upward trajectory. Depending on what you do to earn a living and how you truly feel about it, you may go through a difficult adjustment period before you become more satisfied with your career. Gaining awareness of your feelings and giving yourself permission to express them can kindle dissatisfaction initially. It's possible that you'll finally let yourself fully acknowledge negative feelings about your job that were previously repressed.

This process is similar to the flow of personal relationships during the EFC Program. Self-knowledge and expressing your full range of emotions can bring up painful awareness. The key to getting through this stage is to recognize that awareness is progress, even when it isn't always easy or upbeat.

You may need to squarely face your negative feelings about your work to gain the motivation required to take steps to change your situation. Whether it's a matter of making adjustments at your current job, looking for another position, or even contemplating a complete change of careers, the first step is awareness. Then you can take sensible steps to move toward a job situation with greater potential for long-range satisfaction. First, you must be willing to look at your feelings honestly and explore them. Then you need to take action to bring about desired changes.

RATES OF PROGRESS

The EFC Program is structured as a four-month plan because this time period is generally long enough to discern progress if you practice the Training Techniques according to the schedule. However, the rate of progress and change is entirely variable and individual.

There are several ways to evaluate your progress. One approach is to retake the Basic Self-Assessments for the Core Components at the end of the four-month period. You'll probably find that some of your scores are different by this time, indicating results in key areas. You can also write in your EFC Journal about the progress you have made toward achieving your original EFC Goals.

When you are assessing your progress after four months, don't be too demanding or judgmental in your expectations. It's not fair to expect a complete turnaround in the way you think and feel. Nor is it realistic to expect that you can perfect every relationship or overcome years of ingrained thought or behavior patterns. These are all ongoing processes that take time and, in fact, may never be fully complete. We are all works in progress, in that sense.

Everyone has a different rate of change, depending on where you are starting, where you want to go, your Emotional Template, your personality, your life circumstances, and how you feel about change itself. Try to consider all these factors and evaluate with Empathy when you assess your progress.

If you have practiced the Training Techniques consistently during the four months of the EFC Program, there's great probability that you will be able to notice substantial improvements in your Emotional Fitness. Give yourself credit for the advancements you've made, even if they are not as extensive as you'd anticipated.

If you are seriously disappointed with your progress after four months and feel blocked in important emotional issues, you may need professional counseling as an adjunct to the EFC Program. There are many circumstances of the past and present that are simply too much for us to handle alone, no matter how bravely we might try. Often, the guidance of a skilled and empathic mental health professional is the only way to address complex or long-standing issues. This is not a failure on either your part or that of the EFC Program. Deciding to start therapy can itself be a major indication of progress.

LIFELONG EMOTIONAL FITNESS

The EFC Program provides a structure for starting to practice the Training Techniques regularly and strengthen your Core Components. But Emotional Fitness Conditioning is not merely a four-month program—it is a blueprint for lifelong emotional development.

After the initial four-month period, it's time to personalize your training further. Use the Self-Assessments and the questions throughout this book to select Core Components on which you want to focus. Set new EFC Goals for yourself. Keep the momentum going, and your emotional wellness will continue to grow.

If you don't continue with the Training Techniques, the self-knowledge you've gained will always be with you. But your ability to act and communicate with Emotional Fitness may diminish.

For example, imagine that you were a world-class tennis player. If you stopped playing and training, you would still retain your knowledge and experience of the game. However, without the action component of playing on a regular basis, you would gradually lose your ability to triumph on the court. Similarly, if you stop the Training Techniques, you will still have your emotional awareness, but your ability to apply this knowledge may be more limited.

If you find the EFC Program schedule too limiting or time-consuming, you can adapt it to fit your lifestyle after the four-month period. You may want to use Fitness Guided Visualization only once a week, or whenever you have a specific issues to address. You may want to write in your journal every day or just once a week. You may decide to sometimes incorporate Fitness Focused Meditation into your exercise sessions, instead of meditating as a separate activity. Exercise is a little less flexible, since three times a week is the minimum suggested by experts for maintaining physical fitness. But by the time four months have elapsed, you'll probably be "hooked" on exercise and want to do it more often, not less.

Even with the best intentions, there may be times in your life when you let one or more of the Training Techniques lapse. There may be periods when you do absolutely nothing to nourish your Emotional Fitness, although I hope not. But if you do have these ups, downs, or plateaus, remember that the Training Techniques are always available.

You can begin to utilize them again at any time, either gradually, or through the structure of the EFC Program.

Sometimes, if you find yourself going through a difficult emotional period, the best response can be to start with the first step again. Make a commitment to start the EFC Program again and set a firm date to begin. If you need additional support, consider seeing a psychotherapist. Give your emotional life the attention and nurturing that it requires. Try to include Emotional Fitness Conditioning as a permanent feature of your life.

One of the most exciting aspects of the EFC is that there are no limits. You can always deepen your capacity to understand and honor your feelings through FIT. You can continually spread your awareness and Emotional Fitness through greater Empathy. You can go on honing your knowledge of the connection between the past and present through Insight. And you can always augment your ability to act with healthy Assertiveness.

EFC can expand your life at any age. As you get older, you may find yourself with more time for the Training Techniques, greater patience, and fewer distractions. You may find that your Emotional Fitness naturally ripens with age. In fact, many of the qualities we call the "wisdom of age" are manifestations of a natural evolution of the Core Components.

The Training Techniques can be performed at any age, with special benefits during different life stages. As you get older, the practices can help keep your body well and your mind flexible. At the same time, they can impart the emotional strength and wisdom to meet the challenges of the aging process. Emotional Fitness Conditioning can be a lifelong journey, constantly enriching and broadening your world.

appendix:

EFC Self-Assessments and EFC Action Exercises and Emotional Fitness Conditioning Progress Chart

EFC Self-Assessments and EFC Action Exercises

SELF-ASSESSMENT FOR FEELINGS IDENTIFICATION AND TOLERANCE (FIT)

Respond to each item with either "True" or "False."

1. I tend to be guilty of procrastination or avoidance too often.
2. I often find myself reacting strongly to a given situation without really knowing why.
3. I'm generally viewed as someone who is impatient or intolerant.
4. It's usually not good to feel things too intensely.
5. I'm the kind of person who likes to be in control most of the time.
6. Strong feelings usually make me uncomfortable.
7. It's usually better to make decisions with your head, not your heart.

8. The axiom "Persistence pays" is often a strategy for failure.
9. It's usually safer to keep feelings in check and toned down.
10. I've been known to have a problem with my temper.

Two or more "True" answers indicate a need to work on Feelings Identification and Tolerance. The higher the number of "True" answers, the greater the need to work on this particular Core Component.

SELF-ASSESSMENT FOR EMPATHY

Respond to each item with either "True" or "False."

1. If I feel something strongly, and believe it deeply, it probably means it's true.
2. Given an opportunity, most people would take advantage of you if you let them.
3. I'm not very interested in what makes people tick.
4. A lot of people would like you to feel sorry for them.
5. Emotionally speaking, children are just "mini-adults."
6. Relationships tend to go better when each person works to have his or her own needs met.
7. Talking about my problems with others has rarely done me much good.
8. Listening to other people's troubles is too upsetting.
9. I think my needs are somewhat different from those of most people I know.
10. I envy other people's success.

Two or more "True" answers indicate a need to develop greater Empathy. The more "True" answers, the greater the need to work on this particular Core Component.

SELF-ASSESSMENT FOR INSIGHT

Respond to each item with either "True" or "False" to the best of your ability.

1. My childhood was close to being perfect.
2. My past can't be too important as far as my life goes now.
3. I'm pretty much aware of everything going on in my life.
4. Children are so resilient that they can bounce back from adversity without much long-term impact.
5. I'm nothing like either of my parents.
6. Heredity is a much stronger influence on you than environment.
7. What happens to you in your life is largely a matter of luck, either bad or good.
8. If I'm not aware of something about myself, it can't be affecting me very much.
9. I really don't believe I have too many personal flaws.
10. My personality now is nothing like it was when I was a child.

Two or more "True" answers indicate a need to work on Insight. The higher the number of "True" answers, the greater the need to work on this Core Component.

Note: If you have been in therapy and/or have already developed an unusual degree of Insight, it's possible that you have no "True" responses on this Assessment. But whatever your starting point, you can always benefit from deeper understanding of your Emotional Template and greater Insight!

SELF-ASSESSMENT FOR ASSERTIVENESS

Respond to each item with either "True" or "False."

1. If I'm angry, I'll usually keep my mouth shut.

2. I often find myself unsure of what my real needs are.
3. In life, it's the aggressive people who tend to get what they want.
4. My belief is that speaking your mind will get you in trouble.
5. Going out on a limb for what you believe in will unnecessarily complicate your life.
6. I view those who are always asking for what they want as pushy and demanding.
7. If getting what I want hurts someone else's feelings, then it's probably not worth it.
8. I'm rarely sure that I'm right.
9. It's hard for me to trust my feelings because they are always changing.
10. In relationships, whoever has the power makes the rules.

Two or more "True" answers indicate a need to develop Assertiveness skills. The more "True" answers, the greater the need to work on this Core Component.

EFC ACTION EXERCISE: IS EMOTIONAL FITNESS CONDITIONING FOR YOU?

To find out if the Emotional Fitness Conditioning is a viable program for you, ask yourself these questions:

1. Have you ever been interested in gaining the insights and benefits of psychotherapy?
2. If you are in therapy now, do you feel the desire to further your progress by taking action outside the sessions?
3. Do you ever wish you had more knowledge of how your emotions affect your life?
4. Are you seeking a better understanding of how your past affects your present?

5. Would you like to be able to manage your emotions more productively?

6. Could your relationships benefit from greater awareness of your emotional makeup and those of the people who matter in your life?

7. Would your relationships be enhanced if you could communicate with more Empathy, Insight, and healthy Assertiveness?

8. Would you like to teach your children or other young people how to manage their emotions more productively and build a foundation of Emotional Fitness?

9. Do you acknowledge that the state of your physical body influences your mental state?

10. Do you believe that knowledge plus action can result in positive change?

The key to this questionnaire is simple. If you have answered even one of these questions with a "yes," then the Emotional Fitness Conditioning Program is for you!

EFC ACTION EXERCISE: FEELINGS IDENTIFICATION AND TOLERANCE

1. In your Emotional Fitness Journal, list as many different words as you can for your feelings (up to thirty). Divide them into two columns, for positive and negative feelings.

2. Pick out the most prevalent negative feeling. Write down three ways in which this emotion impacts on your actions or life.

3. Next, write down a scenario where you develop the Emotional Fitness to prevent this negative emotion from impacting on your life. What can you do to channel the negative emotion more productively, or move through the feeling to the desired action?

You will find that the power of a negative emotion diminishes once you accurately identify it and gain confidence in your ability to tolerate it.

EFC ACTION EXERCISE: UNDERSTANDING PROCRASTINATION

1. In your Emotional Fitness Journal, write down three goals or tasks that you never seem to accomplish due to procrastination.
2. Next to each activity, write down the emotions that arise when you think about doing it. Don't settle for the surface reasons, such as "not enough time" or "don't have the right tools." Delve deeper and try to pinpoint the emotions that are standing in your way.
3. Evaluate these emotions. Are they based on something that happened in your past? On some belief system? On some reality?
4. If you could tolerate these feelings, is there anything else that would keep you from working toward accomplishing your goal or completing your task?

As you develop greater FIT skills, you will learn to tolerate difficult emotions and carry on with energy and conviction.

EFC ACTION EXERCISE: SETTING YOUR FIT GOALS

1. In your Emotional Fitness Journal, list your three top goals in life at this time. These could be related to your personal or your professional life.
2. How does your present capacity to identify and tolerate feelings help or hinder your present progress toward these goals?

3. How would an enhanced capacity for FIT help you achieve these goals?

As you practice the Training Techniques, you'll find that enhanced Emotional Fitness can give you the persistence to attain your most significant goals.

EFC ACTION EXERCISE: CULTIVATING EMPATHY

1. In your Emotional Fitness journal, list three qualities or behaviors that you would like other people to show to you more often (for example, patience, affection, or acknowledgment of achievements).
2. Pick three important people in your life. Write down how you can offer each one of these people more of the qualities/behaviors you want others to show to you.

Empathy has positive repercussions. It often flows back to you, in one form or another.

EFC ACTION EXERCISE: EMPATHY BEGINS AT HOME

1. In your Emotional Fitness Journal, write down the name of a family member with whom you need to exhibit more empathy.
2. Write down the two or three behaviors or characteristics of this individual that bother you most.
3. Imagine how you would approach a discussion about these behaviors with Empathy. Phrase your opening line in the most positive, supportive way you can. Continue writing what you might say to get the other person to understand your point of view.
4. How do you imagine he or she would feel about this approach and respond to it?

As you learn to communicate with greater Empathy, you'll find you get a markedly better response and break through many stumbling blocks in your personal relationships.

EFC ACTION EXERCISE: SETTING YOUR EMPATHY GOALS

1. In your Emotional Fitness Journal list your two or three most important relationships, leaving space between each name for additional writing.
2. Next to each person's name, write down ways in which you could show her or him greater Empathy.
3. If you could act with greater Empathy, how would it affect each of these relationships?

As EFC training increases your ability to act with empathy, you'll find that you also receive more of what you need from the people in your life.

EFC ACTION EXERCISE: SURFACE TO DEPTH EXPLANATIONS

1. List the one behavior pattern in your life you would most like to change.
2. List the surface reasons why you think you behave this way.
3. Write a paragraph on how this behavior started. How old were you? Did you learn it from someone or imitate someone who did it? When do you tend to behave this way now?
4. Free-associate about what might be the depth explanation, or possible psychological reasons why you continue to manifest this unwanted behavior.

Taking the time to look into your past will often give you the Insight you need to break out of destructive patterns in the present.

EFC ACTION EXERCISE: UNDERSTANDING YOUR PERSONAL MYTHOLOGY

1. In your Emotional Fitness Journal, write down three major elements of your personal mythology— the way you view, define, and limit yourself—that you feel may restrict you from achieving your goals.
2. How and when did the elements of this mythology begin to emerge? Did someone tell you you were a certain way?
3. Write about special times in your current life when you feel limited by these personal myths and how you might modify these myths to make them more supportive.

As you enlarge your capacity for Insight, you will be able to discard the limiting elements of your personal mythology.

EFC ACTION EXERCISE: SETTING YOUR INSIGHT GOALS

1. In your Emotional Fitness Journal, name two or three areas of life in which you have had long-standing struggles. These might include expressing your needs in relationships, Assertiveness in job situations, or taking on specific types of new challenges.
2. How are these struggles affected by your Emotional Template and your personal mythology?
3. How could you envision making progress in these areas by developing greater Insight?

As you gain Insight skills through EFC training, you may find that you break through blocks and make progress with some of your deepest issues.

EFC ACTION EXERCISE: IDENTIFYING YOUR LEVEL OF ASSERTIVENESS

1. In your Emotional Fitness Journal, write a paragraph on your general impression of your current level of Assertiveness.
2. Rate yourself in the following areas, on a scale of 1 to 10, with 1 being nonassertive or passive, 5 being assertive, and 10 being unreasonably demanding or aggressive.
   How would you rate your assertiveness level in your career?
   In your close personal relationships?
   In your casual interactions?

You may notice a difference in your level of Assertiveness in your personal and professional lives. Some people find it more difficult to be assertive in close relationships than in the world at large, while for others it is just the opposite. The variations are typically due to our earliest familial experiences and their impact on our Emotional Templates.

EFC ACTION EXERCISE: ASSERTIVE ISSUES IN RELATIONSHIPS

1. In your Emotional Fitness Journal, write about your closest personal relationships in terms of narcissistic/co-dependent dynamics. Are there elements of these roles in your relationship? How strong are these elements? Which role do you tend to take?
2. If you have a tendency to be narcissistically entitled, write about how this impacts on the person with

whom you are involved. Are you ready to relinquish some of this imbalance and focus on your partner's needs more often?

3. If you are involved with someone who is demanding and self-absorbed, list three steps you could take to change your relationship to become more equitable.

4. What perceived risks or fears are keeping you from taking these steps?

Keep in mind that taking reasonable and healthy risks in relationships will build your self-esteem, even if it "rocks the boat" or puts the relationship at risk to some degree.

EFC ACTION EXERCISE IN SETTING YOUR ASSERTIVENESS GOALS

1. List your three most important emotional needs. Briefly discuss how these needs are or are not met by the people who are important in your life.

2. Write down ways in which being more assertive might result in having your emotional needs met more often.

3. Write down three major goals related to your career or other endeavors.

4. How could developing Assertiveness help you to achieve these goals?

Assertiveness empowers you to take action and take healthy risks to achieve your goals. It is instrumental in achieving satisfaction in love and work.

FEELINGS IDENTIFICATION AND TOLERANCE JOURNAL EXERCISES

1. Describe two situations that consistently frustrate you. Pay close attention to your feelings as you do

this exercise. Now write out potential solutions to these situations using your strengthened FIT skills.

2. How do you typically deal with angry feelings? When do they come up and how do you react?

3. Think about the emotions you find intolerable. How do you attempt to avoid them? What happens as a result of this avoidance? What would happen if you faced these feelings head-on?

4. What is the feeling that you fear most or find most unbearable? What evokes this emotion? How do you handle it now? How would you like to manage this feeling as you gain Emotional Fitness?

5. Do your feelings have a substantial impact on your quality of life and/or ability to function? Do you have a struggle with depression, acute anxiety, phobias, or compulsions? How can you envision that increasing your ability to identify and tolerate feelings might help to alleviate these problems?

6. How do you use food, alcohol, smoking, drugs, or other substances to cope with your feelings? How do your emotions influence your habits? How might this change if you were better able to tolerate and express all types of feelings?

EMPATHY JOURNAL EXERCISES

1. List two or three qualities or actions in others that particularly bother you. Assess yourself in light of these qualities or actions. If you were more empathic, how would you react differently?

2. List two or three qualities or behaviors in others that you admire. Assess yourself in the light of these qualities or behaviors. What can you do to exhibit them more frequently?

3. List three behaviors or emotional responses that you want others to show you. How can you go about exhibiting these responses to others more often?

4. To what type of person do you find it most difficult to show Empathy? If you were less judgmental, how would this change?

5. How does it make you feel when you are harsh and unreasonable with someone close to you? How would you, as well as the other person, benefit from developing more Empathy?

6. Imagine a scenario in which you are likely to have difficulty showing Empathy. How would the situation change if you looked at the issue from the other person's point of view, taking into account his or her concerns and needs?

INSIGHT JOURNAL EXERCISES

1. List four positive characteristics of each of your parents. Then list four of your own positive qualities. Compare these characteristics with your parents'.

2. List four negative characteristics of each of your parents. Then list four of your own negative qualities. Compare these characteristics with your parents'.

3. Find three areas where you have made a conscious effort to be like your mother. Identify three ways you have made a conscious effort to be different from your mother.

4. Find three areas where you have made a conscious effort to be like your father. Identify three ways you have made a conscious effort to be different from your father.

5. Describe the most basic struggle you experienced as a child. Try to find evidence of this struggle in your current life.

6. List two or three of the central defining events of your childhood. Try to find continuing evidence of the impact of these events in your contemporary life.

ASSERTIVENESS JOURNAL EXERCISES

1. List your four most basic emotional needs. Now briefly discuss how you do or do not operate in your life to have these legitimate needs met.

2. Describe the characteristics of someone you view as appropriately assertive. Now compare yourself in light of these traits.

3. Look at three close relationships in your life in regard to Assertiveness. How could these relationships become more meaningful if you intensified your healthy Assertiveness?

4. Identify an individual in your life who behaves in a narcissistically entitled fashion. List three steps you could take to make your relationship with this person more equitable.

5. List three of your own qualities or actions that involve unreasonable needs and/or demands you might make on others. How could working on a healthier balance of Assertiveness help you modify these behaviors?

6. Define the term "self-respect" as it applies to you and others. Assess how you have or do not have enough self-respect. Suggest how Assertiveness could help you gain more self-respect.

EMOTIONAL FITNESS CONDITIONING PROGRESS CHART

You may find it helpful to make copies of this chart and use it each week of the EFC Program to keep track of your progress.

Mark an "X" or "check" for each EFC activity performed on each day. Strive for at least three marks per week per activity.

Week of: _____

M   T   W   Th   F   Sa   Su

Fitness Focused Meditation

Fitness Guided Visualization

Emotional Fitness Journal

Exercise for Emotional Fitness

Resources

The EFC content area is noted in parentheses following each resource listed.

Key: FIT=F   Fitness Focused Meditation=FFM
      Empathy=E   Fitness Guided Visualization=FGV
      Insight=I   Emotional Fitness Journal=EFJ
      Assertiveness=A   Exercise for Emotional Fitness=EX

1. *The Assertive Woman*. Nancy Austin and Stanlee Phillips, Impact Publishers, San Luis Obispo, Calif., 1997.(A)

2. *Meditation Training: Basic, Advanced, Esoteric* (6 audio-tape series). Azoth Institute of Spiritual Awareness, 13994 Marc Drive, Pine Grove, Calif. 95665, 1991. (FFM and FGV)

3. *Co-Dependent No More*. Melodie Beattie, Hazeldon Foundation, Center City, Minn., 1992. (A and I)

4. *The Relaxation Response*. Herbert Benson, M.D., with Miriam Klipper, Avon, N.Y., 1976. (FFM and FGV)

5. *Making Peace with Your Parents*. Harold Bloomfield, M.D., with Leonard Feder, Ph.D., Ballantine, N.Y., 1996. (I)

6. *Minding the Body, Mending the Mind*. Joan Borysenko, Ph.D. Bantam, N.Y., 1988. (FFM, FGV, and F)

7. *Taking Responsibility*. Nathaniel Branden, Ph.D., Simon & Schuster, N.Y., 1996. (F, I, and A)

8. *The Simple Abundance Journal of Gratitude*. Sara Ban Breathnach, Warner, N.Y., 1995. (EFJ, E, and I)

9. *Living, Loving and Learning*. Leo Buscaglia, Ph.D., Ballantine, N.Y., 1982. (E, I, and F)

10. *Random Acts of Kindness*. Conali Press Editors, Conali Press, Berkeley, Calif., 1993. (E)

11. *The Power of Meditation and Prayer*. Larry Dossey, M.D., et al. Hay House, Carlsbad, Calif. 1997. (FFM and FGV)

12. *Anger: How to Live With It and Without It*. Albert Ellis, Ph.D., Citadel Press, N.Y., 1977. (F and A)

13. *Resilience*. Fredrich Flach, M.D., Hatherleigh Press, N.Y., 1997. (F and I)

14. *The Psychopathology of Everyday Life*. Sigmund Freud, M.D., Nixon, N.Y., 1965. (I)

15. *Focusing*. Eugene Gendlin, Ph.D., Bantam, N.Y., 1981. (FGV)

16. *Get Out of Your Own Way*. Mark Goulston, M.D., and Phillip Goldberg, Perigee, N.Y., 1996. (F, I, and A)

17. *Making the Connection*. Bob Greene and Oprah Winfrey, Hyperion, N.Y., 12997. (EX, F, and A)

18. *You Can Have What You Want*. Julia Hastings, Berkley, N.Y., 1996. (FGV, F, and A)

19. *Getting the Love You Want*. Harville Hendrix, Ph.D., HarperCollins, N.Y., 1990. (E, I, and EFJ)

20. *The Psychologist's Book of Self Tests*. Louis Janda, Ph.D., Perigee, N.Y., 1996. (I)

21. *Feel the Fear and Do It Anyway*. Susan Jeffers, Ph.D., Ballantine, N.Y., 1987. (F and A)

22. *Wherever You Go, There You Are*. Jon Kabat-Zinn, Ph.D., Hyperion, N.Y., 1995. (FFM and FGV)

23. *When Bad Things Happen to Good People*. Harold Kushner, Avon, N.Y., 1981. (F and I)

24. *The Dance of Anger*. Harriet Lerner, Ph.D., HarperCollins, N.Y., 1997. (F)

25. *The Daily Journal of Kindness*. Meladee McCarty and Hanock McCarty, Health Comm., Delray Beach, Fla. 1996. (E and EFJ)

26. *Aerobic Walking*. Mort Malkin, John Wiley & Sons, N.Y., 1995. (EX)

27. *Healing and the Mind*. Bill Moyers, Doubleday, N.Y., 1995. (FFM, FGV, F, and I)

28. *The Road Less Traveled*. Scott Peck, M.D., Touchstone, N.Y., 1978. (F, I, and E)

29. *At a Journal Workshop*. Ira Progoff, Ph.D., Putnam, N.Y., 1992. (EFJ and I)

30. *On Becoming a Person*. Carl Rogers, Ph.D., Houghton-Mifflin, N.Y., 1995. (E and I)

index

abandonment fears, 116–117
acceptance
  differentiated from Empathy, 75–76
  self-acceptance, 97–98
Action Exercises. *See* EFC Action Exercises.
addiction
  case histories, 60–61
  Insight's effect on, 112–113
  narcissistic entitlement and, 125
  and self-control, 60–62
adversarial stances in relationships, 34, 82–83
aerobic exercise, 249
  benefits, 48
  biking, 261–262
  cross-country skiing, 263–264
  dance and step classes, 260–261
  for different fitness levels, 255–257
  jogging, 258–259
  precautions, 259, 260, 262, 263, 264
  rope jumping, 263–264
  rowing, 263–264
  running, 258–259
  sports, 262–263
  stretching as part of, 265
  swimming, 259–260
  walking, 257–258
affect identification and tolerance. *See* Feelings. Identification and Tolerance
affirmations, 45, 181–182
  Basic Track schedule, 157–158
  Customized affirmations, 187
  goal achievement, 189–190
after-work EFC sessions, 146
aggressiveness differentiated from Assertiveness, 38, 119–121
aging and meditation, 173
anger
  Assertiveness to relieve, 130–131
  case histories, 213–218
  and Feelings Identification and Tolerance, 60–61, 64
  Insight to relieve, 98
  meditation to relieve, 135–136
  and physical health, 136
animals showing Empathy, 79
anxiety
  case histories, 239
  and Feelings Identification and Tolerance, 60–61
  journaling for relieving, 239
  meditation for relieving, 67

appointments for EFC Program activities, 145–147, 156
Assertiveness, 13, 38–41, 119–140
  aggressiveness differentiated from, 38, 119–121
  Assertiveness Training, 133–135
  case histories, 18–19, 38–39, 128–129, 130–131, 132–133
  childhood origins, 122–125
  and co-dependency, 38, 126–129
  definition, 119–121
  EFC Action Exercises, 121, 129, 140
  and the EFC Program, 144
  emotional foundations, 134–135
  entitlement, 120–121, 124–126
  genetics and, 122–123
  goal setting, 140, 167
  journal work, 138, 232–233, 237, 240
  meditation to develop, 135–136, 185–186
  personal boundaries, 38, 123–124, 126–129, 130–131
  physical exercise to develop, 139–140, 244, 249, 267
  and physical health, 136
  risk-taking, 131–133
  in romantic relationships, 127–131
  Self-Assessments, 39–40, 163–164
  therapeutic role, 133–135
  visualization to develop, 136–138, 210–212
  women's issues, 133–134, 139
Assertiveness Training, 133–135
athletic performance enhanced by the EFC Program, 275
attitudes to change (EFC Action Exercise), 142–143

Basic Breathing Meditation, 177–180
  instruction checklist, 180
Basic Track, 49–50, 155–160
  Fitness Focused Meditation, 157–158, 181–183
  Fitness Guided Visualization, 158–159, 201–202
  journaling, 159, 229–230
  physical exercise, 159–160, 251
behavior changes from insights, 112–113
benefits
  of Emotional Fitness Conditioning, 24–26, 269–281
  of Fitness Focused Meditation, 171
  of Fitness Guided Visualization, 67–69, 195

of journaling, 46–47, 221–224
of meditation, 44–45, 66–67, 135–136, 171, 173–176
of physical exercise, 47–48, 159, 243–248
of visualization, 46, 67–68
Benson, Herbert, meditation studies, 174–176
bicycling, 261–262
biological origins of Feelings Identification and Tolerance, 52–54
body image enhancement through EFC, 270–271
bodybuilding, strength training differentiated from, 250
boundaries. *See* personal boundaries.
brain, left and right hemisphere activities, 198
breath meditation, 177–180
breathing techniques to manage emotions, 135–136
buddy system for the EFC Program, 151–152
business. *See* workplace.

careers. *See* workplace.
case histories
    addictive habits, 60–61
    anger, 213–218
    anxiety, 239
    Assertiveness, 18–19, 38–39, 128–129, 130–131, 132–133, 210–212, 232–233, 240
    Customized Track, 213–217
    depression, 217–218, 238
    eating disorders, 238–239
    Empathy, 20–21, 34, 80–83, 92–93, 206–207, 215–217, 231–232, 238–239
    Feelings Identification and Tolerance (FIT), 19–20, 30–31, 54–55, 60–61, 63, 68–69, 203–205, 213–215, 230–231
    friends and family, 92–93, 188–189, 232–233
    Insight, 21–22, 36–37, 101–102, 110–111, 208–209, 232
    marriages, 18–21, 82–85, 93–94, 116–117, 130–131, 203–205, 213–217, 231–232
    parenting, 30–31, 68–69, 87–88, 203–205, 213–217
    physical health, 21–22
    romantic relationships, 36–37, 54–55, 80–81, 110–111, 128–129, 210–212, 217–218, 238
    social phobias, 240
    visualization, 68–69
    workplace, 38–39, 101–102, 132–133, 136–138, 188–189, 206–207, 208–209, 217–218, 230–231
challenges
    of Empathy, 75–76, 88–90
    responding to, 62–64
change
    of childhood emotional patterns, 54, 273
    as danger and opportunity, 132
    EFC Action Exercises, 142–143
    from the EFC Program, 269–281
    progress chart of, 278–279
    in relationships, 272–274
    repetition and rhythm as elements of, 41–43
    resistance to, 26, 142–145, 152–153, 273
charts, EFC progress chart, 157, 297

checklists
    Basic Breathing Meditation instructions, 180
    EFC Program, 155, 170
    Fitness Focused Meditation, 191
    Fitness Guided Visualization, 220
    journaling, 240–241
    physical exercise, 267–268
    See also instructions.
childhood emotional patterns
    Assertiveness development, 122–125
    changing, 54
    co-dependency and, 126–127
    Emotional Templates, 108–110
    Empathy development in children, 88–90
    Feelings Identification and Tolerance origins, 52–54
    Insight development, 103–107
    intergenerational continuity, 105–017
    metaphorical thinking, 104
    narcissistic entitlement, 124–126
    personal boundaries, 123–124
    personal mythology, 106–107
    separation of child from caregiver, 104
    shyness predisposition, 123
    See also Insight; parenting.
choosing physical exercise types, 249–250, 253–254, 266–267
chore-sharing in romantic relationships, 83–85
circulatory and cardiovascular systems and physical exercise, 244–245
classes for physical exercise, 257, 260–261
co-dependency, 38, 123–124, 126–129, 130–131
combining Training Techniques, 162, 188–189, 219, 251, 252, 258, 260, 261
commitment to EFC Program, 142, 155–156
communication
    Empathy's role in enhancing, 73–74, 83–85, 88
    journals for developing communication skills, 138
    in romantic relationships, 80–86
    visualization to enhance, 91–93
computer journals, 225–226
concentration
    in Fitness Guided Visualization, 200–201
    in meditation, 178–180
conditioning of the past, 36
conditioning (physical), 252, 254, 258, 259
control, self-control, 59–62
Core Component journaling technique, 228
Core Components of EFC, 12–13, 29–41, 143–145, 156
    athletic performance enhanced by, 275
    body image affected by, 271
    Customized Track, 160–165
    ego ideal affected by, 272
    exercise choices and, 266–267
    goal setting, 165–169
    and journaling, 47, 159, 228
    and meditation, 45, 158, 182–186
    and physical exercise, 48, 160, 243–244
    in relationships, 272–274
    self-image affected by, 270
    and visualization, 46, 158
    in the workplace, 276–277

Core Components of EFC *continued*
  yoga to activate, 266
  See also Assertiveness; Empathy; Feelings
    Identification and Tolerance; Insight.
counseling. *See* therapy.
criminality and lack of Empathy development, 89
criticism, damaging effects of, 33–34, 83
cross-country skiing, 263–264
Customized Track, 50, 160–165, 280–281
  case histories, 213–217
  Fitness Focused Meditation, 186–187
  Fitness Guided Visualization, 164–165,
    212–218
  journaling, 233–234
  physical exercise, 251–252
  schedule for EFC activities, 164–165
  selecting Core Component issues, 160–164

dance and step classes, 260–261
dating
  and Feelings Identification and Tolerance,
    54–55
  See also romantic relationships.
daydreams. *See* visualization.
delayed gratification, 29–30, 58–59
depression
  case histories, 217–218, 238
  and Feelings Identification and Tolerance,
    64–65
  journaling to relieve, 238
  physical exercise to relieve, 71
  precautions for Emotional Fitness Condi-
    tioning, 22–23, 148–149
  visualization to relieve, 217–218
depth explanations, 100–102
  EFC Action Exercise, 102–103
diagnostic labeling of mental illness, 24
drugs and medication, Emotional Fitness Conditioning precautions, 22–23, 148–149
Dual Viewpoint writing, 55, 93–94

early rising for EFC Appointments, 145–147
eating disorders, journaling to relieve,
  238–239
editing journals, 225–226
EFC Action Exercises
  Assertiveness goals, 140
  Assertiveness level identification, 121
  Assertiveness in relationships, 129
  attitudes to change, 142–143
  EFC eligibility questionnaire, 26–27
  Empathy cultivation, 78
  Empathy in family relationships, 85–86
  Empathy goals, 95
  Feelings Identification and Tolerance, 57
  Feelings Identification and Tolerance goals,
    72
  Feelings Identification and Tolerance and
    procrastination, 64
  Insight goals, 118
  Insight on personal mythology, 107
  Insight surface to depth explanations,
    102–103
  See also questionnaires.
EFC eligibility questionnaire, 26–27
EFC Journal. *See* journaling.
EFC Program, 48–50, 141–170, 269–281
  adapting, 280–281
    after-work sessions, 146
    Basic Track, 49–50, 155–160
    buddy system, 151–152
    checklists, 155, 170
    commitment to, 142, 155–156
    Customized Track, 50, 160–165, 280–281
    early morning sessions, 145–146
    EFC attitudes toward change exercise,
      142–143
    EFC Progress Chart, 157, 297
    EFC Reinforcement Loop, 43–44, 144–145
    empathy toward self during, 169
    evaluating (questionnaire), 26–27
    goal achievement, 168–169
    goal setting, 72, 95, 118, 140, 165–169,
      213–214
    impact of, 269–281
    independent programs, 152–153
    issues to address, 152–153
    lifelong emotional fitness, 279–281
    lunchtime sessions, 146
    overcoming obstacles to, 142–145
    physical health affected by, 275–276
    planning, 142–147, 157–170
    Pre-Program week, 154–155, 177–180, 251
    precautions, 22–23, 148–149
    progress rates, 278–279
    relationships affected by, 272–274
    scheduling time for, 145–147, 156–157, 169
    self-esteem affected by, 270–272
    sharing, 274
    starting, 142–157, 170, 281
    support systems for, 149–152
    workplace satisfaction and performance,
      276–278
    See also EFC Action Exercises; Training
      Techniques.
EFC Progress Chart, 157, 297
EFC Reinforcement Loop, 43–44, 144–145
EFC. *See* Emotional Fitness Conditioning.
ego ideal enhanced by EFC, 271–272
elderly people, EFC techniques for, 113
Ellis, Albert, on Assertiveness, 134
emotional benefits of physical exercise,
  245–248, 249
emotional expression. *See* expressing feelings.
emotional fitness, 11–13
  Core Components, 12–13, 29–41
  effect of words on, 181–182
  issues, 152–153
  lifelong, 279–281
  and physical exercise, 245–248, 249
  and physical illness, 275
  Training Techniques, 13–17
  See also Emotional Fitness Conditioning.
Emotional Fitness Conditioning (EFC),
  269–281
  benefits, 24–26, 269–281
  cautions, 22–23
  and challenges, 62–64
  development of, 11–17
  evaluating (questionnaire), 26–27
  performance enhanced by, 193–195, 275–278
  precautions, 22–23, 148–149
  as preventive health care, 23–24
  resistance to, 26
  See also case histories; Core Components of
    EFC; EFC Action Exercises; EFC Pro-
    gram; Training Techniques.

Emotional Fitness Conditioning Journal. *See* journaling.
Emotional Fitness Conditioning Program. *See* EFC Program.
Emotional Fitness Conditioning Progress Chart, 157
Emotional Fitness Journal. *See* journaling.
Emotional Fitness Reinforcement Loop, 43–44, 144–145, 252–253
emotional foundations of Assertiveness, 134–135
emotional health. *See* emotional fitness.
emotional illness
  journaling to relieve, 237–240
  meditation to relieve, 175–176
  precautions for Emotional Fitness Conditioning Program, 22–23, 148–149, 176–177
  visualization used for, 217–218
  See also physical illness.
emotional patterns of childhood. *See* childhood emotional patterns; Insight.
emotional risk-taking, 131–133
emotional skills. *See* Core Components.
  Emotional Templates, 36
  ego ideal modifications and, 271–272
  genetic role, 109
  Insight to reshape, 36, 97, 108–110
  origins, 108–109
  See also childhood emotional patterns.
Empathy, 13, 33–35, 40, 73–95
  and adversarial stances in relationships, 34, 82–83
  case histories, 20–21, 34, 80–83, 87–88, 92–94, 206–207, 215–217
  challenging aspects, 75–76, 88–90
  childhood development, 88–90
  communication enhanced by, 73–74, 83–85, 88
  definition, 73–74
  EFC Action Exercises, 78, 85–86, 95
  as EFC Program self-care, 169
  goal setting, 95, 166
  hypersensitivity, 89–90
  Insight's role in, 98
  journal work, 85–86, 92–95, 231–232, 235–236, 238–239
  meditation to enhance, 90–91, 184
  nonjudgemental qualities of, 74–76
  in parenting, 33–34, 86–88
  physical exercise to enhance, 94–95, 243, 250, 267
  popularity enhanced by, 79
  in romantic relationships, 80–86
  Self-Assessment, 35, 162–163
  societal role, 78–79
  therapeutic role, 76–77
  visualization to enhance, 91–93, 205–207
  in the workplace, 74–76
energy level and physical exercise, 245
enjoyment as a key factor in physical exercise, 253–254
entitlement, 120–121
  narcissistic entitlement, 124–126
evaluating EFC (questionnaire), 26–27
evolution of empathy, 88–90
exercise. *See* aerobic exercise; physical exercise
exercises
  journal exercises, 57, 234–238

  See also EFC Action Exercises.
  expectations for the EFC Program, 189–190
expressing feelings, 53–54
  depression relieved by, 64–65
  identification with feelings, 55–57
  in journals, 222–224
  self-control, 59–62
  tolerance, 57–58
  about work, 277–278

family. *See* childhood emotional patterns; marriage; parenting; relationships.
fantasies. *See* visualization.
fear of abandonment, 116–117
feelings. *See* Empathy; expressing feelings; Feelings Identification and Tolerance; unpleasant feelings.
Feelings Identification and Tolerance (FIT), 13, 29–32, 40, 51–72
  and addictions, 60–62
  and anger, 60–61, 64
  case histories, 19–20, 30–31, 54–55, 60–61, 63, 68–69, 203–205, 213–215
  and changing emotional patterns, 54, 273
  definition, 51–52
  delayed gratification, 29–30, 58–59
  and depression, 64–65
  EFC Action exercises, 57, 64, 72
  and the EFC Program, 143–144
  expressing feelings, 53–54
  goal setting, 72, 166
  identification with feelings, 55–57, 60–61
  journal work, 57, 64, 69–71, 72, 230–231, 234–235, 238
  meditation to enhance, 66–67, 183–184
  origins, 52–54
  physical exercise to develop, 71, 243, 266
  and physical illness, 65–66
  and procrastination, 62–64
  in romantic relationships, 54–55
  Self-Assessment, 31–32, 162
  self-control, 59–62
  and stress response, 65–66
  tolerance, 57–58
  and unpleasant feelings, 30–31, 62–64
  visualization for developing, 67–69, 202–205
  See also expressing feelings.
FIT. *See* Feelings Identification and Tolerance.
fitness, emotional, 11–13
Fitness Focused Meditation, 44–45, 91, 181–191
  affirmations, 181–182, 187
  and Assertiveness, 135–136, 185–186
  Basic Track schedule, 157–158, 182–183
  benefits, 171
  checklist, 191
  combining with other Training Techniques, 188–189, 219
  Customized Track, 164, 186, 187
  and Empathy, 90–91, 184
  and Feelings Identification and Tolerance, 66–67, 183–184
  goal achievement, 189–190
  and Insight, 114, 184–185
  precautions, 176–177
  preparing for, 177–178
  sensory involvement, 199
  See also meditation.

Fitness Guided Visualization, 45–46, 198–220
  Assertiveness visualizations, 210–212
  Basic Track, 158–159, 201–202
  benefits, 67–69, 195
  checklist, 220
  combining with other Training Techniques,
    188–189, 219
  concentration techniques, 200–201
  Customized Track, 164–165, 212–218
  emotional illness relieved by, 217–218
  Empathy visualizations, 91–93, 205–207,
    215–217
  Feelings Identification and Tolerance visual-
    izations, 202–205, 213–215
  Insight visualizations, 207–209
  instructions, 201–202
  key elements, 198–199
  precautions, 199–201
  preparing for, 198–201
  purpose definition, 198–199
  scripting, 199, 201, 203, 205–206, 207–208,
    210
  taped visualizations, 201
  See also visualization.
Fitness Level identification (physical),
  254–257
fitness, physical
  identifying level of, 254–257
  See also physical exercise; physical health.
Fitness Reinforcement Loop, 43–44, 144–145,
  252–253
flexibility and physical exercise, 245
focus
  in Fitness Guided Visualization, 200–201
  in meditation, 178–180
food and self-control, 61–62
forgiveness differentiated from Empathy,
  75–76
format choices for journaling, 224–225
Free Flow journaling, 227–228
Freudian approach to therapy, 98–99
friends and family
  case histories, 92–93, 188–189, 232–233
  as EFC support systems, 151–152

genetic role
  in Assertiveness, 122–123
  in Emotional Templates, 109
goals
  achieving, 168–169
  Assertiveness goals, 140, 167
  Core Component goals, 165–169
  Empathy goals, 95, 166
  Feelings Identification and Tolerance goals,
    72, 166
  goal-setting case histories, 213–214
  Insight goals, 118, 166
  journaling goals, 47
  physical exercise goals, 48
  therapeutic goals, 133–135
  visualization goals, 46
gratification, delayed, 29–30, 58–59
guided imagery. *See* visualization.
guided visualization, 15, 45–46

happiness, increasing, 24–26
health, emotional. *See* emotional fitness; emotional illness.

health, physical. *See* physical health; physical
  illness.
history of meditation, 172–173
hypersensitivity, 89–90

ideals (ego), 271–272
identification with feelings, 55–57
  addiction as a means of avoiding, 60
  See also Feelings Identification and
    Tolerance.
illness, emotional. *See* emotional illness.
illness, physical. *See* physical illness.
imagery. *See* visualization.
impact of Emotional Fitness Conditioning,
  269–281
impulse control, 59–62
inadequacy, visualization to relieve feelings
  of, 203–205
independent EFC Programs, 152–153
infancy, crucial tasks of, 52–53, 88, 103–104,
  122
Insight, 13, 35–38, 40, 97–118
  behavior changes resulting from, 97–98,
    112–113
  case histories, 21–22, 36–37, 101–102,
    110–111, 208–209, 232
  childhood origins, 103–107
  definition, 97–98
  depth explanations, 100–102
  EFC Action Exercises, 102–103, 107, 118
  Emotional Templates changed by, 36, 97,
    108–110
  Empathy enhanced by, 98
  goal setting, 118, 166
  journal work, 116–117, 118, 232, 236, 239
  meditation to enhance, 114, 184–185
  and personal mythology, 106–107
  physical exercise to enhance, 117–118, 244,
    250, 267
  physical illness understood through, 105
  and romantic relationships, 110–112
  Self-Assessment, 37–38, 163
  therapeutic role, 98–100
  visualization to enhance, 114–115, 207–209
instructions
  Basic Breathing meditation, 180
  Fitness Focused Meditation to attune to
    Core Components, 183–186
  Fitness Guided Visualization, 201–202
  See also checklists.
intelligence
  meditation's effect on, 173–174
  physical exercise to enhance, 246–247
intergenerational continuity, 105–017
intimate relationships. *See* parenting;
  romantic relationships; sexual
  relationships.
issues to address in the EFC Program,
  152–153

jobs
  job satisfaction and performance enhanced
    by EFC, 276–278
  See also workplace.
jogging, 258–259
journaling, 15–16, 46–47, 221–241
  Assertiveness journal work, 138, 232–233,
    237, 240

Basic Track, 159, 229–230
benefits, 46–47, 221–224
and change, 143
checklist, 240–241
combining with other Training Techniques, 188–189, 219
as communication skills development, 138
computer journals, 225–226
Core Component technique, 228
for Customized Track assessments, 161
Customized Track schedule, 165, 233–234
Dual Viewpoint writing, 55, 93–94
EFC Action Exercises, 26–27, 57, 72, 78, 85–86, 95, 107, 118
Empathy journal work, 85–86, 92–95, 231–232, 235–236, 238–239
examples, 230–233, 238–240
exercises, 57, 234–238
Feelings Identification and Tolerance journal work, 57, 64, 69–71, 72, 230–231, 234–235, 238
Free Flow technique, 227–228
Insight journal work, 116–117, 118, 232, 236, 239
and letter writing, 224
preparations, 224–227
privacy, 225
procrastination journal work, 288
resistance to, 226, 227
revising and editing, 225–226
schedules, 229–230
scheduling time for, 146, 227, 228
Self-Assessments, 31
spontaneity in, 228–229
tape recorded journals, 226–227
therapeutic uses, 222–224, 237–240
training goals, 47
writing by hand, 224–225
jumping rope, 263–264

Kohut, Heinz, on Empathy's role in therapy, 77

learning
    repetition and rhythm as elements of, 41–43
    ritual as an element of, 42–43
left-brain/right-brain theory, 198
letter writing as therapy, 224
life expectancy increase from physical exercise, 245
lifelong emotional fitness, 279–281
long-term emotional fitness, 279–281
longevity from physical exercise, 245
Low, Alexander, Recovery self-help movement, 58
lunchtime Training Technique sessions, 146

mantras, 175
marriage
    abandonment fears, 116–117
    case histories, 18–21, 82–85, 93–94, 116–117, 130–131, 203–205, 213–217, 231–232
    Empathy's role in, 82–86
    personal boundary issues, 130–131
    See also parenting; romantic relationships; sexual relationships.

medication, Emotional Fitness Conditioning precautions, 22–23, 148–149
meditation, 14–15, 44–45, 171–191
    and affirmations, 45
    aging affected by, 173
    anger relieved by, 135–136
    Assertiveness developed by, 135–136, 185–186
    Basic Breathing Meditation, 178–180
    Basic Track schedule, 157–158
    benefits, 44–45, 66–67, 135–136, 171, 173–176
    Customized Track schedule, 164
    emotional illness relieved by, 175–176
    Empathy enhanced by, 90–91, 184
    Feelings Identification and Tolerance enhanced by, 66–67, 183–184
    history of, 172–173
    Insight enhanced by, 114, 184–185
    mantras used during, 175
    mental capabilities affected by, 173–174
    physiological effects, 174–176
    precautions, 176–177
    preparing for, 177–178
    "relaxation response", 174–17
    scheduling time for, 145–147, 177–178
    scientific studies, 173–176
    stress reduced by, 173–176
    and systematic desensitization, 14
    TM, 173–174
    See also Fitness Focused Meditation.
mental capabilities
    meditation's effect on, 173–174
    physical exercise to enhance, 246–247
mental health, visualization to enhance, 195–197
mental illness
    precautions for Emotional Fitness Conditioning, 22–23, 148–149
    visualization used for, 195–197, 217–218
metaphorical thinking development, 104
motivation for physical exercise, 253–254
musculoskeletal system and physical exercise, 245
mythology, personal. *See* personal mythology.

narcissistic entitlement, 124–126
nonjudgemental qualities of Empathy, 74–76

obstacles to the EFC Program, overcoming, 142–145
origins
    of Assertivenss, 122–125
    of Emotional Templates, 108–109
    of Feelings Identification and Tolerance, 52–54
    of Insight, 103–107
    of personal boundaries, 123–124
oversleeping, 101–102

pain and Feelings Identification and Tolerance, 52–54
parenting
    case histories, 30–31, 68–69, 87–88, 203–205, 213–217
    Empathy in, 33–34, 86–88
    and Feelings Identification and Tolerance, 52–54

parenting *continued*
  and Insight development, 103–107
  intergenerational continuity, 105–017
  responsiveness, 122
  and scheduling EFC time, 147
  teenagers, 87
  visualization techniques for, 68–69,
    114–115
  See also childhood emotional patterns.
parents
  case histories, 188–189
  See also parenting.
partners for physical exercise, 257
past, conditioning of, 36
peer support groups for EFC, 150–151
performance
  athletic performance enhanced by EFC,
    275–276
  enhancing with visualization, 193–195
  work performance enhanced by EFC,
    276–278
personal boundaries
  Assertiveness and, 123–124, 130–131
  case histories, 130–131
  childhood origins, 123–124
  co-dependency and, 38, 123–124, 126–129,
    130–131
  in romantic relationships, 130–131
  See also self-esteem.
personal mythology, 106–107
  affirmations to transform, 181–182
  EFC Action Exercise, 107
  visualization to rewrite, 114–115
personal trainers, 257
physical examinations before the EFC Pro-
    gram, 154, 248
physical exercise, 16–17, 47–48, 243–268
  aerobic exercise, 249, 255–264
  Assertiveness developed by, 139–140, 244,
    267
  Basic Track, 159–160, 251
  benefits, 47–48, 71, 159, 243–249
  biking, 261–262
  body image enhancement, 270–271
  checklist, 267–268
  choosing exercise types, 249–250, 253–254,
    266–267
  combining with other Training Techniques,
    188–189, 219, 251, 252, 258, 260, 261
  conditioning, 252, 254–257, 258, 259
  and Core Component enhancement,
    266–267
  cross-country skiing, 263–264
  Customized Track schedule, 165, 252–252
  dance and step classes, 260–261
  depression relieved by, 71
  Empathy enhanced by, 94–95, 243, 267
  Feelings Identification and Tolerance in-
    creased by, 71, 243, 266
  Fitness Level identification, 254–257
  Fitness Reinforcement Loop, 252–253
  Insight developed by, 117–118, 244, 250, 267
  jogging, 258–259
  and longevity, 245
  and mental capabilities, 246–247
  motivation, 253–254
  physical examinations before starting the
    EFC Program, 154, 248

Pre-Program week, 251
  precautions, 248, 259, 260, 262, 263, 264
  preferred types, 249
  repetition and rhythm, 244
  rope jumping, 263–264
  rowing, 263–264
  running, 258–259
  safety tips, 259
  scheduling, 145–147, 251–253
  sports, 262–263
  strength training, 249–250, 264
  stress reduced by, 71
  stretching, 250, 265
  support systems, 150, 257
  swimming, 259–260
  therapeutic uses, 247–248
  training goals, 48
  walking, 257–258
  weight training, 249–250
  yoga, 265–266
physical fitness, identifying level of, 254–257
physical health
  Assertiveness for enhancing, 136
  EFC Program combined with physical
    health programs, 150
  EFC Program's impact on, 21–22, 275–276
  Empathy for enhancing, 77
  meditation for enhancing, 67, 174–176
  physical exercise to enhance, 244–245
  visualization to enhance, 195–198
physical illness
  anger's role in, 136
  and emotional fitness, 21–22, 275
  Empathy in healing, 77
  Feelings Identification and Tolerance in
    healing, 65–66
  Insight to understand causes, 105
physiological effects
  of meditation, 174–176
  of visualization, 197–198
planning EFC Programs, 142–147, 157–170
pleasure
  delayed gratification, 29–30, 58–59
  and Feelings Identification and Tolerance,
    52–54
PNI (psychoneuroimmunology) visualization
  studies, 196, 197
popularity
  and Empathy, 79
  of narcissists, 125–126
Pre-Program week, 154–155
  Basic Breathing Meditation, 177–180
  exercise schedule, 251
  journaling schedule, 229
precautions
  Emotional Fitness Conditioning, 22–23,
    148–149
  meditation, 176–177
  physical exercise, 248, 259, 260, 262, 263,
    264
  visualization, 199–201
preparations
  Fitness Guided Visualization, 198–201
  journaling, 224–227
  meditation, 177–178
preventive health care
  diagnostic labeling, 24
  Emotional Fitness Conditioning as, 23–24

privacy for journals, 225
procrastination, 62–64
    EFC Action Exercises, 64, 288
    roots of, 30
    in starting EFC Program, 143–145
Progoff, Ira, on journaling, 229
progress rates
    in the EFC Program, 278–279
    EFC progress chart, 157, 297
psychological mindedness. *See* Insight.
psychoneuroimmunology (PNI) visualization
    studies, 196, 197
psychotherapy. *See* therapy.
purpose definition for Fitness Guided Visual-
    ization, 198–199

questionnaires
    EFC evaluation, 26–27
    See also EFC Action Exercises; Self-
        Assessments.

rates of progress
    in the EFC Program, 278–279
    EFC progress chart, 157, 297
recording. *See* tape recording.
Recovery self-help movement, 58
reinforcement, Emotional Fitness Reinforce-
    ment Loop, 43–44, 144–145, 252–253
relationships
    adversarial stances in, 34
    Assertiveness issues, 38–39, 129
    change in, 272–274
    co-dependency, 126–127
    Core Components in, 272–274
    EFC Program's effect on, 272–274
    as EFC support systems, 151–152
    insight as a factor in, 36–37, 110–112
    visualization as an aid to, 68–69
    workplace, 276–278
    See also Empathy; friends and family; mar-
        riage; parenting; romantic relationships.
"relaxation response," 174–17
religions, Empathy practiced in, 78
repetition and rhythm
    as elements of change, 41–43
    in physical exercise, 244
repressed feelings. *See* expressing feelings.
resistance
    to change, 26, 142–145, 152–153, 273
    to writing, 226, 227
responsiveness to children's needs, 122
results of the EFC Program, 189–190,
    269–281
revising journals, 225–226
rhythm as an element of change, 41–43
right-brain/left-brain theory, 198
risk-taking, 131–133
ritual as an element of learning, 42–43
Rogers, Carl, on Empathy's role in therapy,
    76–77
romantic relationships
    Assertiveness issues, 127–131
    case histories, 36–37, 54–55, 80–81,
        110–111, 128–129, 210–212, 217–218,
        238
    and chore-sharing, 83–85
    co-dependency in, 127–129
    communication in, 80–86

EFC Action Exercises, 85–86
    and Empathy, 80–86
    and Feelings Identification and Tolerance,
        54–55
    See also marriage.
rope jumping, 263–264
rowing, 263–264
running, 258–259

scenarios for Fitness Guided Visualization,
    199, 201, 203, 205, 207–208, 210
schedules
    Basic Track, 157–159, 181–183, 201–202,
        229–230, 251–253
    Customized Track, 164–165, 186, 212–213,
        233–234, 251–253
    Fitness Focused Meditation, 157–158,
        181–183, 186
    Fitness Guided Visualization, 158–159,
        164–165, 201–202, 212–213
    journaling, 229–230, 233–234
    physical exercise, 251–253
    See also scheduling time for the EFC
        Program.
scheduling time for the EFC Program,
    145–147, 156–157, 169
    journaling, 146, 227, 228
    meditation, 145–147, 177–178
    parenting obligations, 147
    physical exercise, 145–147
    Training Techniques, 145–147
    visualization, 145–147
    See also schedules.
scientific studies
    on meditation, 173–176
    on visualization, 196–197
scripting Fitness Guided Visualization, 199,
    201, 203, 205, 207–208, 210
SD (systematic desensitization), similarity to
    meditation, 14
security for journals, 225
self-acceptance, Insight to enhance, 97–98,
    112–113
Self-Assessments
    Assertiveness, 39–40, 163–164
    for Customized Track, 161–164
    Empathy, 35, 162–163
    Feelings Identification and Tolerance,
        31–32, 162
    Insight, 37–38, 163
    journaling, 31
    for lifelong emotional fitness, 280–281
self-asssertion. *See* Assertiveness.
self-control, 59–62
self-esteem
    Emotional Fitness Conditioning effect on,
        270–272
    and the Emotional Fitness Training Loop,
        43–44
    Insight for building, 97–98
    narcissistic entitlement, 124–126
    personal mythology's role in, 106–107
    See also personal boundaries.
self-expression. *See* expressing feelings.
self-help movement and tolerance, 58
self-image enhancement through EFC, 270
selfishness, 124–126
senior citizens, EFC techniques for, 113

sensory involvement in Fitness Focused Meditation, 199
separation (of child from caregiver), 104
sexual relationships
    Assertiveness in, 128–129
    case histories, 128–129
    Empathy in, 81–83
    See also romantic relationships.
sharing the EFC Program, 274
shyness predisposition, 123
skiing, 263–264
skills, emotional. *See* Core Components.
sleep problems, oversleeping, 101–102
social phobias, case histories, 240
societal role of Empathy, 78–79
spontaneity in journaling, 228–229
sports, 262–263
starting the EFC Program, 142–157, 170
step classes, 260–261
strength training, 249–250, 264
    Assertiveness developed by, 249
    bodybuilding differentiated from, 250
stress
    meditation for reducing, 173–176
    physical exercise for reducing, 71
    stress response, 65–66
stretching, 250
substance abuse, 60–62
    See also addiction.
support systems
    for the EFC Program, 149–152
    for physical exercise, 257
surface explanations versus depth explanations, 100–102
    EFC Action Exercises, 102–103
swimming, 259–260
synergistic effect of four Core Components, 40–41, 156
systematic desensitization (SD), similarity to meditation, 14

tape recording
    journals, 226–227
    visualization exercises, 201
teenagers, Empathy in parenting, 87
therapy
    Assertiveness as a therapeutic goal, 133–135
    combined with the EFC Program, 149
    conditions requiring, 22–23, 148–149
    Empathy as a fundament of, 76–77
    Freudian approach, 98–99
    Insight's role in, 98–100
    journaling as part of, 222–224, 237–240
    letter writing, 224
    physical exercise as part of, 247–248
    visualization's role in, 195–197
    Wolberg on, 99
time planning for the EFC Program, 145–147, 156–157, 169, 177–178
TM, 173–174
tolerance, 57–58
trainers, 257
Training Techniques, 13–17, 43–50
    affirmations, 45
    for athletic performance, 275
    Basic Track, 49–50, 155–160
    combining, 188–189, 219, 251, 252, 258, 260, 261

Customized Track, 50, 164–165, 280–281
Emotional Fitness Reinforcement Loop, 43–44
for lifelong emotional fitness, 280–281
repetition and rhythm, 41–43
schedules, 145–147, 280–281
scheduling time for, 145–147
self-esteem affected by, 270–272
and the workplace, 277
See also EFC Program; journaling; meditation; physical exercise; visualization.
Transcendental Meditation, 173–174

uncomfortable feelings. *See* unpleasant feelings.
understanding. *See* Insight.
unpleasant feelings, 30–31
    anger and anxiety, 60–61, 64, 67
    and depression, 64–65
    meditation to relieve, 66–67
    and procrastination, 62–64
    and risk-taking, 131–133
    stress, 65–66
    from visualization, 199–200
    visualization to relieve, 203–205

visualization, 15, 45–46, 193–199
    Assertiveness developed by, 136–138, 210–212
    Basic Track schedule, 158–159
    benefits, 46, 67–68, 193–197
    case histories, 68–69, 91–92, 114–115, 136–138
    Customized Track schedule, 164–165
    Empathy enhanced by, 91–93
    Empathy to enhance, 91–93, 205–207
    guided visualization, 194–195
    Insight enhanced by, 114–115, 207–209
    performance enhanced by, 193–195
    physiological effects, 197–198
    scheduling time for, 145–147
    scientific studies, 196–197
    in therapy, 195–197
    training goals, 46
    See also Fitness Guided Visualization.

walking, 257–258
weight training, 249–250, 264
"wellness" emphasis, 24
Wolberg, Lawrence, on Insight in therapy, 99
women and Assertiveness, 133–134, 139
words, effect on emotions, 181–182
workplace
    Assertiveness development, 38–39
    case histories, 38–39, 101–102, 132–133, 136–138, 188–189, 206–207, 208–209, 217–218, 230–231
    EFC impact on job satisfaction and performance, 276–278
    emotional dynamics of, 276–278
    Empathy in, 74–76
    lunchtime EFC sessions, 146
writing
    by hand, 224–225
    resistance to, 226, 227
    See also journaling.

yoga, 150, 265–266

About the Authors

Dr. Ronald Bergman is a clinical and consulting psychologist with a private practice in South Florida. He was named one of the nation's best therapists in an article by Daniel Goleman in *Town and Country* magazine.

A charismatic speaker and program leader, Dr. Bergman conducts seminars on a number of topics. His media experience includes a year as a talk show psychologist on a daily radio show broadcast by WKAT in Miami.

Dr. Bergman was trained as both a clinician and a research psychologist, and has employed both of these skills in developing Emotional Fitness Conditioning. His training and clinical background include psychoanalytic, behavioral, and cognitive therapy, as well as research. Dr. Bergman holds a Ph.D. in Psychology from the University of Miami and is board certified in clinical psychology and a Fellow of the Academy of Clinical Psychology. He is licensed to practice in both Illinois and Florida.

Before establishing his private practice in 1978, he held positions at the Manteno State Hospital in Illinois and the Institute of Human Relations in Miami. He is a member of the American Psychological Association and a past president of the Dade County Chapter of the Florida Psychological Association.

During the past three years, Dr. Bergman has developed the theory and techniques of EFC and founded the Institute of Emotional Fitness in South Florida. EFC has been incorporated into his clinical practice and proven to enhance the lives of hundreds of patients.

Anita Weil Bell is a freelance writer and publicist who specializes in psychology, health, and fitness topics. She is the co-author of *Dr. Lynch's Holistic Self-Health Program: Three Months to Total Well-Being* (published by Dutton in hardcover in 1994 and paperback in 1995) and *Better Than Ever: The Workout Program for Women Over 40* (with Lisa Hoffman), published in 1997 by Contemporary Books.

Ms. Bell is also the co-author with Dr. Jan Stromfeld of *Free Yourself From Headaches* (published by NAL/Plume in 1989 and reissued by the Upledger Institute in 1995), Her first collaboration, *Shopaholics* (written with Janet Damon), was published in hardcover by Price Stern Sloan in 1988 and in paperback by Avon in 1990, and excerpted in *Cosmopolitan* magazine.

Anita Bell has published articles on fitness, natural health, and relationships in *Cosmopolitan*, *Woman*, *Female Bodybuilder*, *Downtown*, and many other publications.

As a public relations consultant, she has more than ten years of experience with clients that include health-care professionals, businesses, and institutions.